STUDIES IN THE DEAD SEA ᴜᴄʀᴏʟʟˢ ᴀⁿᴰ ᴧ... .E

Peter W. Flint, Martin G. Abegg Jr., and Florentino García Martínez,
General Editors

The Dead Sea Scrolls have been the object of intense interest in recent years, not least because of the release of previously unpublished texts from Qumran Cave 4 since the fall of 1991. With the wealth of new documents that have come to light, the field of Qumran studies has undergone a renaissance. Scholars have begun to question the established conclusions of the last generation; some widely held beliefs have withstood scrutiny, but others have required revision or even dismissal. New proposals and competing hypotheses, many of them of an uncritical and sensational nature, vie for attention. Idiosyncratic and misleading views of the Scrolls still abound, especially in the popular press, while the results of solid scholarship have yet to make their full impact. At the same time, the scholarly task of establishing reliable critical editions of the texts is nearing completion. The opportunity is ripe, therefore, for directing renewed attention to the task of analysis and interpretation.

STUDIES IN THE DEAD SEA SCROLLS AND RELATED LITERATURE is a series designed to address this need. In particular, the series aims to make the latest and best Dead Sea Scrolls scholarship accessible to scholars, students, and the thinking public. The volumes that are projected — both monographs and collected essays — will seek to clarify how the Scrolls revise and help shape our understanding of the formation of the Bible and the historical development of Judaism and Christianity. Various offerings in the series will explore the reciprocally illuminating relationships of several disciplines related to the Scrolls, including the canon and text of the Hebrew Bible, the richly varied forms of Second Temple Judaism, and the New Testament. While the Dead Sea Scrolls constitute the main focus, several of these studies will also include perspectives on the Old and New Testaments and other ancient writings — hence the title of the series. It is hoped that these volumes will contribute to a deeper appreciation of the world of early Judaism and Christianity and of their continuing legacy today.

PETER W. FLINT
MARTIN G. ABEGG JR.
FLORENTINO GARCÍA MARTÍNEZ

JOHN MARCO ALLEGRO

The Maverick of the Dead Sea Scrolls

JUDITH ANNE BROWN

WILLIAM B. EERDMANS PUBLISHING COMPANY
GRAND RAPIDS, MICHIGAN / CAMBRIDGE, U.K.

This book is for my mother
Joan Allegro,
with thanks for a lifetime of support,
and in memory of my father
John Marco Allegro,
who would have enjoyed arguing about everything all over again

Wm. B. Eerdmans Publishing Co.
2140 Oak Industrial Drive N.E., Grand Rapids, Michigan 49505 /
P.O. Box 163, Cambridge CB3 9PU U.K.

Printed in the United States of America

09 08 07 06 05   7 6 5 4 3 2 1

ISBN 978-0-8028-6333-1

www.eerdmans.com

Contents

Contents

Editors' Foreword

For scholars and the public alike, the modern history of the Dead Sea Scrolls is a compelling subject. By the term "modern history" we mean the discovery of the Scrolls in 1947 (or 1946?), the acquisition of these precious documents by Jordan and Israel, the appointment of the first editorial team, and the convoluted story of — or battle for — their publication. Among the original team of editors that was set up by Father Roland de Vaux was John Marco Allegro, one of the most interesting Dead Sea Scroll scholars — and certainly the most controversial of them all.

The present volume has been written — crafted is a better term — by Allegro's daughter, Judith Brown. In clear but elegant prose, the author shares with her readers biographical and historical details that were previously unknown, submits interesting explanations for facets of her father's life and work, and on several occasions offers brilliant insights of her own.

Anyone who is even slightly familiar with Allegro's work knows that he was a provocative and controversial writer, especially with respect to the relationship between the Scrolls and Jesus and the early church. It is fair to say that, since the publication of *The Sacred Mushroom and the Cross: A Study of the Nature and Origins of Christianity within the Fertility Cults of the Ancient Near East* (1970), most biblical scholars and believing Christians came to view John Allegro as a radical who was opposed to the Christian faith. This is understandable since, among other things, Allegro proposed that early Christianity was a fertility cult that was based on the use of hallucinogenic mushrooms.

But as with all simplistic assessments, there is another side to the story, one that reveals much more in Allegro's work and his contribution to understanding the Dead Sea Scrolls. After reading this book most readers, like us, will still harbor strong reservations on any number of John Allegro's views. But, again like us, many readers will appreciate the positive aspects of his contribution that are usually overlooked in the rush to judge him a crackpot. As Judith writes: "I am writing this book to restore the balance" (p. xii). And so she has.

Among the many rich and informative themes in the chapters that follow, we draw attention to four.

John Allegro's Family and Personal Life

A biography is often best written by a member of the featured person's family. With recourse to a simple but brilliant device, Judith Brown imparts intimacy by referring to her father not as Allegro, but as John. It soon becomes clear that she is drawing not only on her own information and childhood experiences, but also on the rich input of her mother, Mrs. Joan Allegro. And when an author is literarily gifted to boot, as Judith is, the volume that emerges constitutes a well-crafted and intimate portrayal, a work of art, perhaps even a landmark.

The reader stands fascinated, for example, at the account of how Allegro's ship was lost at sea during World War II, the details of his early but short-lived training for the ministry, and his evolution from zealous Methodist congregant to humanist scholar. And we feel privileged to learn much of his character through his own correspondence: letters plotting the courtship between John and his wife Joan, letters to his Scrolls colleagues, and letters to friends scattered around the world. Times that were painful for the family are also clearly evident, masterfully presented by the use of understatement rather than gushiness and recrimination.

Perceiving the Relevance of the Dead Sea Scrolls

John Allegro understood all too clearly that the Scrolls and the message they contain are significant for Judaism and Christianity. Most readers will accept some of his views and will strongly reject others as being radical or untenable — yet Allegro's insistence that these ancient documents *matter*, that they are important for understanding Jewish and Christian origins, will strike a chord for the many thousands of people who follow the Scrolls. Or more accurately: the hundreds of thousands, to judge by the multitude of books on the subject, the thousands of articles, the scores of TV documentaries and videos, and the myriads who have attended recent museum exhibits (e.g., Grand Rapids, 2003; Ottawa and Houston, 2004; Mobile, 2005).

Allegro also perceived the necessity, indeed the obligation, of publicizing the Dead Sea Scrolls. He both spoke on radio programs and undertook numerous publicity tours as a necessary part of his editorial work. Most scholars will readily acknowledge the importance of such enterprises in order to raise the necessary funds for publishing the Dead Sea Scrolls; today, of course, funding is more readily obtained through the Dead Sea Scrolls Foundation and the generosity of various donors around the world. But there is another aspect to publicizing — proclaiming the importance of the Scrolls to the public and scholars of related disciplines.

John Allegro flirted with fame in his native Britain, where he became perhaps the best-known Scrolls expert. For many modern readers, especially in North America, this outcome is understandable, even admirable. But to others, for reasons of respectability or reticence or even jealousy, Allegro's popularizing and publicizing may be disturbing, especially when accompanied by his radical theories with respect to Christian origins. This was certainly the case with his colleagues among the original team of researchers.

Contribution to Dead Sea Scrolls Publication and Research

It soon becomes clear that John Allegro was a pioneer in several ways.

First, he left us vital early photographic records. Some older scholars who have worked on the Dead Sea Scrolls now regret the fact that few photographs were taken to illustrate their own work. Of course, several series of photographs have been taken of the Scrolls themselves, as well as of the buildings at Qumran and the artifacts found there and at other locations. But there are relatively few pictures of the scholars themselves at work and the accompanying human story of early research on the Dead Sea Scrolls. John Allegro is one of the best sources for the photographs that do exist, a number of which are published for the first time in this book.

Second, Allegro called, early on, for attention to the preservation of the fragile Dead Sea Scrolls. He seems to have been the first to note that the early method of preservation — placing fragments between glass plates — may not have been proper: "I am by no means certain that binding them tightly between glass is correct — a great deal of scientific research on this problem is required . . ." (p. 165).

Third, Allegro has bequeathed to us, by way of his letters, important information on the modern history of the Dead Sea Scrolls. In the post-discovery era when the publication of any new scrap becomes the news of the day, we read with fascination of those numerous times when a scholar might try to dodge a box of new fragments (p. 33), which meant only more work. We are told of the expansion of the editorial team leading to the introduction of such notables as Patrick Skehan and John Strugnell. And we are held spellbound as the author details the intriguing story of the unrolling of the Copper Scroll in Manchester.

This book also offers new insights on the rift between Allegro and the other members of the editorial team, a conflict that seems to have arisen in part from misunderstanding and a lack of easy communication between Britain and Jerusalem. The Jerusalem editors' perception that Allegro had gone back on his promise not to speak on the Copper Scroll and their rejection of his interpretations of the Teacher of Righteousness's ministry are documented in a fascinating and very readable manner. Judith Brown coyly writes: "John Strugnell later called him the 'stone in the soup' of the editing team; actually, he was more like the pepper" (p. 277).

Finally, Allegro foresaw or even initiated the controversy surrounding the slow pace of the publication of the Dead Sea Scrolls. Most readers, familiar with the heated debate surrounding the lack of access to Scrolls that raged especially in the late 1980s and early 1990s, will be surprised to learn that John Allegro's voice was the first to express criticism at the approach adopted for publishing Scroll materials (pp. 99-100). He later became convinced that a conspiracy was at work among the Roman Catholic scholars who eventually monopolized the team, a view that, although continuing to find an ear among the popular press, is today held by virtually no scholar.

John Allegro and Christian Origins

The pieces that eventually made up *The Cross and the Sacred Mushroom* began to surface in the middle 1960s at the time Allegro most had the public ear, during the famous and enormously successful exhibition of the Scrolls in England. He began decoding the New Testament stories to reveal hidden references to Essene titles and self-descriptions. "In short," he said, "nothing in the Gospels and Acts is what it seems. The Scrolls have given us the key at last to unlock the real truth" (p. 184).

In a plot that seems to leap straight from the pages of George Eliot's *Middlemarch,* Allegro began crafting his magnum opus, the grand, unifying theory of religion. But instead of bringing critical acclaim, *The Sacred Mush-*

room and the Cross ruined his career. The book, which was intended to explain all, convinced almost no one — Allegro was understandably stunned by the lack of acceptance for his theories. But the idea that the New Testament was really a cover story for instruction in drug lore was wildly improbable, and his etymological reasoning, which seemed so incontrovertible to Allegro, was too full of gaps. What appeared to him a "unifying theory of religion" has to most appeared only as "a house of cards," or at worst an academic farce. Brown's book is a riveting tale of the path of this destruction.

John Allegro's ideas on Jesus and early Christianity were most fully articulated in his later book, *The Dead Sea Scrolls and the Christian Myth* (1979). Here he posited that the writers of the gospels, who did not understand Essene thought, took the symbolic narratives found in many Scrolls for literal truth, giving rise to traditional Christianity. Allegro also traced several key ideas and practices found in early Christianity and Gnosticism from texts found among the Dead Sea Scrolls. In the chapter provocatively entitled "Will the *Real* Jesus Christ Please Stand Up?" Allegro illustrated his views that Gnostic Christianity arose from the Essene movement. Indeed, there was no historical person named Jesus Christ in 1st-century Palestine; instead, the Jesus of the gospels was an adaptation of the Teacher of Righteousness found in the Dead Sea Scrolls. For Allegro, the New Testament writers John and Paul were not the founders of an apocalyptic form of Judaism, but instead only popularizers of the message of the Dead Sea Scrolls.

It would be tempting for us as editors of a series issued by a Christian scholarly publisher to insist that Judith Brown downplay her father's anti-Christian stance, to sanitize him for the many Jewish and Christian readers of this book who are in the main interested in Allegro's contribution to the study of the Dead Sea Scrolls. But to have done so would have been the final disservice to John. We have allowed his voice to ring out to the very end — to do otherwise would have been hypocritical. And John Allegro would not have appreciated that!

MARTIN G. ABEGG JR. and PETER W. FLINT
Langley, British Columbia
The Third Sunday of Advent, 2004

Acknowledgments

Many people have helped in the production of this book. I should especially like to thank:

Professors Peter Flint, George Brooke, and Philip Davies for their comments and suggestions;

Stan Procter, who grew up with John in South London;

Anna Partington for casting light on some aspects of philology;

David and Richard Brown for technical assistance;

and, most of all, Joan Allegro, for allowing me to use her letters, pictures, and other documents and for sharing her insights about John's life and work.

Introduction

I came to know my father when he was sixty-two. Of course, I had met him a long time before then, but in those days the world, his and mine, was mainly for fun. He would stride through the house declaiming, "Joan, listen to this!" or "O Dearly Beloved Professor," or "Penguins on the phone!"

If people asked my brother or me where our father worked, we might have said "in his study" or "at the university," but we were just as likely to tell them "in a cave." For that was where his life and work focused in the 1950s and '60s — the dusty caves in the Jordanian desert where the first of the Dead Sea Scrolls had been found. The shepherd boy who came across them in 1947 began an adventure, a quest for knowledge of the past, which was to shape many people's careers. John Allegro made his name through helping to decipher the scrolls and then writing and lecturing about them, and the expeditions he led to look for more were highlights of a lifetime for everyone who went on them. Through studying the scrolls, he also came to question the conventional Christian teaching that many people accepted in those days as the moral corsetry that kept society in shape.

In 1970 everything changed. John published a book that was meant to demolish what he saw as the false and hypocritical hegemony of the church over the minds of men and women. He felt that religion should be a spiritual journey, the way to commune with one's God, to reach the ultimate understanding of life. He saw it in practice as oppression: antiquated trappings of belief and bigotry that stopped people thinking for themselves. He wanted to set people free to build their own morality on compassion and common sense.

Instead, the book ruined his reputation. After it came out, very little he had said in the past or would say in the future was given any attention. Outcast and frustrated, he lost his sense of purpose, his optimism, and most of his money. Family life fell apart; he went off pursuing freedom and it turned out a mockery.

Only in his sixties did he give up being angry and wishing to get his youth back. He began to settle down again to philology, the first intellectual love of his life. Then he looked for friendship, and I took to visiting him at his Sandbach home to listen to and try to keep up with his new lines of research. They were leading him back to the very origins of language and thought, and it was one of the most exciting journeys I had heard of.

So I am writing this book partly to restore the balance. There is no way to make up for my father's wasted genius, but I would like his contribution to Dead Sea Scrolls scholarship to be recognized, and his mistakes understood if not condoned. Because most of his books are out of print, I have given the gist of them in what I hope is a fair and readable interpretation. I would like people to value the gifts he left: his visionary imagination that could light up the past; his fearless condemnation of hypocrisy, especially of the institutional sort; his conviction that all men and women can and must make up their own minds and take responsibility for what they do.

CHAPTER 1

Early Years

John Marco Allegro was born on February 17, 1923, at Balham in South London, to Mabel Jessie and John Marco Allegro Sr. He had a sensible elder sister Sybil and a surprising younger sister Cynthia, and they lived on an unremarkable row with a few dusty trees in front and a park behind railings on the corner.

John's first seventeen years were as normal as could be expected in the household of a bottled djinn like his father Marco. Marco Allegro was an artist and master printer of powerful and restless originality who never found the space or opportunity that could contain him. A man of few words but many wishes, he left his son two main legacies: a love of clean white paper, and the conviction that, since second-hand ideas were stale, he must make up his own mind about everything.

Marco had come to England in about 1908 at the age of twelve, after the death of his mother Amy. He never spoke of the past; the few references that Sybil uncovered many years after his death suggest an unsettled childhood. Amy was a Lincolnshire farmer's daughter, who went to work as English governess to an Armenian family in Constantinople. When turmoil overtook Constantinople, the family fled, leaving her to pack up the house. She applied for a job at the Berlitz School in Bordeaux. Into the picture came a French vice-consul, Monsieur Worville or Norville. Seduction, rape, promises made and broken . . . whatever the story, Amy was left with failing health and a sickly child, appealing to the gentleman for money. He sent her one hundred francs but declined to visit. The name Allegro, Italian for "lively," seems untraceable; Sybil and John decided it must have been some sad little wistfulness on their grandmother's part. Amy died of tuberculosis, aged thirty, in a convent on the way home.

1

Amy's relations brought Marco to England. He was a dutiful orphan, who kept himself to himself and preferred his own company to the street gangs. He had little schooling and no choice of trade: the local draper needed an assistant and there he went as soon as he was old enough to earn a few shillings.

When the World War broke out, Marco joined up. Cool, upright, and quick to learn, he won a commission in the British army despite his lack of formal education, his illegitimacy, and his foreign birth. For those few years of war he achieved recognition and authority, and they suited him well.

After the war, it was necessary to start again. With a loan from an army colleague, Marco bought a printing press and taught himself to use it. He took a terraced house in Nightingale Road, Carshalton, and a grocer's daughter, Mabel, to keep it for him. The press went in the garden shed, and Marco set about making his living as a printer.

At first, everything went well. In the 1920s, any man who reckoned he was anybody wanted a car. Fords chugged out of factories, car salesmen grew sleek, and Marco's best customers were garage owners wanting posters or flyers to advertise their services. He did such good trade that the shed became a workshop, and then a larger workshop that took up most of the garden. Two men and a girl came to work for him. Marco bought an old car himself, as well as a dinghy that he patched up and moored at Rochester. The boat became his haven; he used to take his sketchbook and watercolors, potter upriver, moor by the bank, and sink his wishes in painting for an afternoon.

Mabel bore his three children: Sybil, John Marco, and Cynthia. Home and children were all she wanted. She was not keen on boats and distrusted cars. She went dancing a few times with Marco, who loved it, but she did not think she was any good at it and really felt more comfortable at home. The abiding memory of Mabel, for friends and grandchildren, is of a small woman in an apron at the kitchen sink. She had very little gossip or chatter, but she was always kind to children and her hands were always busy, baking or dusting or mending.

Marco had his boat, his painting, and the business. He ran the local art club. He read the papers from cover to cover, so he could argue better. He went to concerts — classics, dance bands, Ginger and Fred — and bought a record player. Two or three nights a week there was dancing at the local hall. He could never have enough of this bright dream-life, but there was always too much else to do on the car or the house or the workshop.

Sybil, the eldest child, was quiet, sweet-natured, and the most willing to listen to her father. They sometimes went off for painting days together, and he taught her to sketch and crayon and look at things with an artist's eye.

John and Cynthia were the bubbly ones, forever in and out of the house

John Allegro, aged about 20
Photo courtesy of Stan Procter

John and Stan, aged about 12, messing about at the boatyard
Photo courtesy of Stan Procter

with friends. Always in a hurry and frequently late, they played cricket and tennis, went to the cinema, joined youth clubs, and attended Ruskin Road Methodist Sunday School for a spell because their friends did, too. In their teens, John took Cynthia to dances on the back of his motor bike.

John's best friend, Stan Procter, lived on the street parallel to Nightingale Road. A strip of allotments separated the houses, and their signal for meeting was to make owl-calls from the tree at the end of the Allegros' garden. In the allotments they had dens, tiger patrols, cowboys and Indians; there were patches of waste ground for knocking a ball around; there were orange-box go-karts and brakeless bicycles . . . school-boy pastimes that now belong in sepia tints but were commonplace in the 1930s.

John followed Stan to Wallington County Grammar School for Boys on a scholarship. He gained his "sound grammar-school education" without much difficulty and matriculated at sixteen in 1939.

That, for Marco, was as far as it went. There was no question of his son spending time or money on college. Sixteen was old enough to earn a living. Besides, war was brewing in Europe. Everyone's hopes or ambitions fell under its shadow. John went to work at an insurance office for one pound a week,

4

and if it had not been for the motor bike, the cinema, and the Saturday dances, life would have looked very gray. As it was, he and Stan took a particular passion for motor bikes and vaguer passions for various girls. On one occasion, they fell for the same Margaret, who turned up her nose at both of them. Sometimes they visited Marco's boat at Rochester, looked across the river to where the Short Sunderland flying boats were built, and thought of the places they would go if they were among the young men training to fly them. Stan particularly remembers the day his bike broke down at Rochester and John had to tow him home to tea.

Men who had been through one war were full of misgiving. Newspapers crackled with rumor. Factories geared up, and church halls turned into recruiting centers. Cars and vans were requisitioned and so was petrol. Many garages closed, and with them went much of Marco's trade. He had to send away his workers and pull dust-sheets over the machines. When he spoke, it was with bitterness. The family lowered their voices to bicker.

At seventeen, John volunteered for the Royal Navy, on the strength of having paddled about the Medway on his father's boat. Also, he had heard enough about the trenches to want to avoid being drafted into the army. And there would be challenge, travel, a sense of purpose, and a complete change from life in an insurance office that overlooked other offices, and life in a suburban terrace that overlooked another suburban terrace and was full of his father's disapproval.

In December 1941, John completed his basic training on HMS *Collingwood* and was sent to join HMS *Airedale* at Scapa Flow. He spoke of the North Atlantic to Stan, but to no one else then or since. The sailors fought seasickness and the sea; they fought the bitter gales and the unending steel-gray heave. They expected to die, not in a sudden flame of glory but by choking on cold oily water.

The *Airedale* got through three months of the North Atlantic run. German submarines had picked off many similar escort ships and the convoys they were protecting. Often it seemed there was nothing but providence, or luck, between a sailor and a torpedo. Maniacal storms, a maniacal enemy. . . . If ratings asked questions, the questions came black-edged in the intervals between being sick and crisis alert. Then action, or fatigue, drove the questions out of mind.

Stan had joined the army.[1] When their home leave coincided, John bounced round to his friend's house to wow his mother with the naval uni-

---

1. Stan Procter tells the story of his wartime experiences in his book *A Quiet Little Boy Goes to War,* 2nd ed. (Hampshire, U.K.: RiteTime Publishing, 2004).

form, clap him over the shoulders as "my fighting friend," and carry him off for a dance or a drink. In the early 1940s, girls seemed prettier, band music racier. When you were on shore leave, war and philosophy could wait.

HMS *Airedale* was refitted for the eastern Mediterranean: Malta convoy duty. John, still a clerical rating and "shaping well as a writer" according to his captain's report, reckoned that at least it would be warm.

Early in 1944, the *Airedale* was moored off Alexandria when John took some minor infection. A liability on board, he was deposited at the hospital and was still there when the ship left to meet another convoy. They found him a shore job at the admiralty office while he waited for his ship to return.

Alexandria intrigued him: sun-baked houses, geometric shadows, arguments in many tongues, smells of spices and sewers, animals and motor-oil. Beyond Alexandria there would be little worlds like this one waiting to be explored in every port and every land; there would be countless faces questioning, wanting shekels or attention. For a curious traveler, an infinite wealth of people and ideas must be waiting around innumerable corners.

Now John had time to think. He thought of the long hours typing figures and addressing envelopes for the admiralty, and further hours doing much the same for the insurance company. He explored the alleys and street markets and read anything he could find, from P. G. Wodehouse to a Turkish dictionary. Someone reprimanded him for wearing white socks with his uniform: Only officers wore white socks. He wanted to think for himself and beyond the immediate necessity of standing in lines, ticking boxes, or wearing the right buttons. As a first step, he filled in the forms for a commission.

In Alexandria John learned that his ship and all on board had been lost to a German missile.

He walked and walked. In his naval uniform he was both conspicuous and faceless — half worker, half tourist; an observer. Against the loss of the ship, everything seemed sharper: colors, sounds, smells, the sense of being alone. Along an alley one evening, he heard people singing hymns in a little Swiss Protestant church. They were English voices, familiar hymns. He looked inside and could have been back at Ruskin Road Methodist Chapel. The welcome he received gave him back his sense of purpose. He heard he had been accepted for officer training, and he went home in August 1944 to complete it. His new ship, HMS *Montclare,* was sent to Greenock on the Clyde for a re-fit, and John went too on a temporary commission, as sub-lieutenant and acting paymaster.

Many young sailors had a spell at Greenock while they trained or while their ship was in dock. Their naval chaplain, the Reverend J. Brazier-Green (JBG), was also the minister at St. John's Methodist Church in Glasgow and

Home leave from the Royal Navy, January 1945
(*Left to right* — Stan Procter, Stan's fiancée Audrey,
Stan's sisters Joan and Sylvia, Cynthia Allegro, and John Allegro)
Photo courtesy of Stan Procter

ran a youth club there. Ostensibly, it provided non-alcoholic entertainment and Christian instruction for visiting servicemen. Chiefly it was a way to meet local girls.

The Lawrences lived in Rutherglen, a leafy part of Glasgow, in a tall stone house with big rooms that were excellent for singing in and impossible to heat. Joan, the elder daughter, had recently graduated from Glasgow University in mathematics, with distinction, and was training as an accountant. Her sister Anne was at the Royal Scottish Academy of Music, planning to teach. The twins Bill and Charles were still at school. All four did occasional penance on hard pews at the Church of Scotland down the road, but they much preferred St. John's in the city center, where there were plenty of friends and plenty to do.

Anne, the short merry sister with curly brown hair, liked getting people to stand up and sing with her. Young men queued up to ask her out. Joan was the tall, thoughtful one, rather like John's sister Sybil. She was secretary to St. John's social club, taught Sunday School sometimes, and always considered things before she said them. John wanted to talk to her himself. He would have liked to sit next to her at services. Observing this, the Reverend Mr. Brazier-Green let John know that the young men flanking her were her brothers and were distractible. Soon Joan and John were going to the theater together, and concerts, and the park, and soon after that she took him home to Rutherglen for Sunday tea.

It was a disjointed courtship, much restricted by naval regulations and hours of training. Letters had to make up for curtailed meetings.

> It was good to see you last Sunday even though it was only for a few minutes, a few minutes of utter blankness on my part in which I couldn't remember a thing I'd wanted to say.
>
> . . . I love the country and at present detest the sea. I like cheerful company, but am a terrible mixer. I'm very selfish, and get inexplicably annoyed at having these moments of solitude disturbed.[2]

Shortly afterwards, HMS *Montclare* set sail. From March 1945 began a series of letters in tiny maritime mail envelopes, all stamped "FROM HM SHIP. PASSED BY CENSOR" — who was more often than not, as Leading Writer, John himself. Servicemen and women were not allowed to say where they were writing from, or where they were going — except that when they crossed the equator John treated himself to describing how King Neptune came aboard, bringing his queen and nymphs in drag to shave and duck people, as he was wont to do. Joan wrote back c/o GPO, London, and her letters were sent ahead to await the ship's arrival at whatever port it was heading for.

Letters from home were one of the main attractions of the ports they called at. Ashore after eleven days at sea, John wrote: "Thanks so much for your letters. You've no idea how much it means to receive them. . . . I am refraining from sending you one of the real ersatz souvenirs they make by the thousand round here. Maybe the sea isn't so bad after all — at least it's clean."[3]

John formed a Methodist group on board HMS *Montclare*. It proved popular: Within a month it had thirty members, and numbers increased as they went further from home. They held discussion groups and hymn-singing as well as simple services. John said the singing made up in volume what it lacked in harmony.

2. Letter from J. M. Allegro to Joan Lawrence, February 13, 1945.
3. JMA to Joan, March 28, 1945.

8

In this group, John found fellowship and stimulation. It gave him a chance to think and talk, to get to know others as deeply as they were willing to let him. He discovered that he liked leading and organizing people, and organizing his thoughts, too, by preparing discussions. It was an escape from the monotony of life at sea, where method was everything — interminable method, unalterable routine, necessary for running any big machine and especially a military one. There were drills, ship's bells, procedures for this and that, dance bands on the wireless, drinking and souvenir-hunting on shore. Some people thrived on the life; they wanted to know only when the war would be over, not what would become of the world afterwards. Mulling over — in student mode — the sense of alienation that came upon him in idle moments, John wrote long letters to Joan, musing on things like how to fit dead Germans and Japs into the same after-life as dead Allies. He quoted Rupert Brooke to her: "I have need to busy my heart with quietude."

He also mulled over the question of what to do next. By early summer of 1945, the war was unmistakably winding down. The first thing he was planning to do, after months of pacing the deck, was to walk in the English countryside:

> . . . the most wonderful walking holiday, touring all the most English parts of England and the Scottish parts of Scotland (*excluding* Greenock), armed with an history book. . . . I want to do so much walking, and perhaps here and there a little sketching. Through all this sweltering heat and desolation it's that thought of my proposed holiday, and mail, that keeps me going.[4]

But the question of a career was less certain:

> I had a letter from an ex-insurance confederate saying that our company is shortly moving back to Fenchurch Avenue and have acquired some premises overlooking the fish-market!! My giddy aunt. Is it possible for anyone to leave a couple of hundred thousand odd square miles of open sea to sit over a fish market?!! It has at least made up my mind for me in that direction, but what then?[5]

"What then" during the summer of 1945 was the church. Religion offered challenge: to intellect, feeling, and leadership. It posed questions of philosophy to sharpen his reasoning; it tested the depth of compassion; and it

---

4. JMA to Joan, July 5, 1945.
5. *Ibid.*

gave opportunities to lead and teach that came as a novelty to John as a young untried sub-lieutenant. The appalling war had shown him atrocities, calamities, the heights and depths of what people could do, and the interminably dull stretches in between. The church offered hope and challenge, and friends along the way. From the shuttered and isolated unit of a warship thousands of miles from home, visions of preaching and pastoral care fired him:

> Lately I have been thinking more and more that I should like to enter the Ministry on my return to civilian life. I can't account for this sudden desire, and I certainly didn't think of it seriously before I left on this trip. I often feel I want to get up and tell everybody what a wonderful, happy, and glorious thing this Christianity is. I want to shout down and confound all those dismal people who proclaim it all so darkly, with threats instead of promises, with sadness where there should only be joy. If the Church ever needed that message, it needs it now to give to its congregation. This is such a wonderful opportunity, yet we are surrounded by ministers who preach Salvation through sinister threats of hellfire. I should want to make my congregation laugh and sing for the news I bring, not weep for sins long past and long forgiven.[6]

However, there were practical difficulties.

> Since I wrote to you of my thoughts on entering the Ministry, I have heard that the normal college time required is four years and after the war probably five. This rather leaves me out, for I don't expect to be released until 1947, by which time I shall be twenty-four, and with no means of supporting myself during those years of study. I have of course no degree (in fact you little realise how honoured I feel in writing to one who has!) and have forgotten the little I knew at school.[7]

Recognizing his own compulsion to question everything, John wrote Joan eleven days later:

> I assure you I have never yet propounded any theories to anyone but myself. I'm a rotten audience anyway, and will persist in asking myself questions that I can't answer.

Meanwhile, HMS *Montclare* reached Sydney. By now the crew members were allowed to say where they had been, if not where they were going. Syd-

---

6. JMA to Joan, April 2, 1945.
7. JMA to Joan, July 5, 1945.

ney was "a wonderful place; at night an amazing spectacle with all its lights gleaming, rising from both banks of the harbor. And the lighted bridge stretching between the two." He adds artlessly, "If I went back there I should take my wife with me, that is, of course, if I could ever find a girl quite mad enough to marry me."[8]

In Brisbane and the Tembourine Mountains, there was time to explore. Amid the enchanting countryside he came across an elderly English lady who showed him cases full of lace that had been handed down to her through generations.

> You have never seen anything so precious and lovely in all your life. . . . Flemish in origin, it was all worked by hand and has the most fascinating designs running through it . . . it speaks of other worlds, of crinolines and gay velvets, of dainty minuets and sparkling waltzes — in fact, it tells so many stories just by looking at it. I have the most wonderful ideas of what I shall do about it. I shall keep it in a red Moroccan box, lined with velvet, and on the top will be a golden heart which breaks open to reveal a tiny golden key to unlock the case. Inside the two halves of the heart I shall have a verse engraved — I don't know which yet. The case will only be unlocked on very special occasions. And the lace used on *very* special dresses.[9]

He felt that Joan, working dutifully on business accounts, had been missing out on discoveries like this. He wanted her to share the excitement of travel, to be as open-eyed as he was about everything new, to perceive his acute sense of oneness with people and places.

> There is so much beyond Glasgow, Scotland, and England, so much I want you to see, and be there with you whilst you were seeing it. The sunset across the Bitter Lakes of Suez; the Cape of Good Hope rising out of the sea in the early morning; the expression on the sun-tanned face of a soldier just down from months in the desert; sleeping under the tropic stars; the phosphorescence of the bow wave at night; all these are more than things and places, they are the Spirit of Living.[10]

The Methodist group on board ship spoke more clearly than ever to his need for fellowship and purpose.

---

8. JMA to Joan, July 17, 1945.
9. JMA to Joan, July 30, 1945.
10. JMA to Joan, August 1, 1945.

I felt I really had to write to you this evening. Our little group had its first Holy Communion service, and it was really wonderful. A Baptist minister from a visiting ship joined in. Time allowed only for singing, two gospel readings, and the communion itself. Somehow, creeds and collects would have seemed strangely out of place in the utter simplicity of that service. For myself, I have never felt Christ so near as in our small chapel this evening. I wish you could have been there.[11]

Above all, when the group learned that the wife of one of their members had died in a Tyneside hospital, the intensity of their fellowship and the healing power of the mind became clear. It was the most meaningful part of his life so far, and for a young man seeking deep meanings it was a pointer to the future.

The service began with the 23rd Psalm, and I was afraid I was not going to be able to get through the short prayer. I have never before been so conscious of the force of unity of prayer, and never so convinced of its effectiveness. J. has recovered in such a way that I never thought possible. He talks and laughs as before, the only visible difference being his strengthened purpose with regard to religion and the Church, and the much closer bond of friendship between us. . . . For me it has also done something else. Soon after that episode, the Padre from a ship nearby asked me whether I had thought of entering the Ministry. I had thought about it a good deal but relinquished the idea on financial grounds. I explained how I felt, and he answered that by scholarships I could do it easily. He has forwarded my particulars with a recommendation for my acceptance as a candidate for the Methodist ministry, and I am more set on it now than ever before.[12]

John had been through four years of war. He had traveled halfway round the world and met with many of its faces, from the ravaging storms of the North Atlantic to the serenity of a South African sunrise. From a torpedo destroying a ship full of friends to exquisite Flemish lace, he had seen the most terrible and the most beautiful parts of Earth and the most terrible and beautiful things that people could do to it. Now the atom bomb had given people power to overturn the world, life, and civilization. How could you make sense of the years to come? How could you know there would be any years to come? To surviving servicemen on a ship thousands of miles from home, these campus perennials sounded sharp and clear. So did the solution:

11. JMA to Joan, July 24, 1945.
12. JMA to Joan, August 25, 1945.

Our choice of two roads has never been more clear-cut. Either we do learn to love one another, or the whole awful experiment of humanity will come to a sudden and disastrous end. The Church must take the lead, and now.[13]

Joan and John now exchanged letters at least twice a week. She sent him the *Methodist Recorder,* St. John's program of events, and the occasional photo. As an undercurrent running beneath all his observations and career plans, his thoughts towards her were moving one way.

Today I had your letter of the 12th, enclosing your photograph. It was what I had been waiting for, for a long time. Excuse two letters in three days, which are partly because we are on the move tomorrow, but mainly because I enjoy writing to you almost as much as receiving your letters. It's nice to be able to pour out one's troubles, thoughts, and ideals on sympathetic ears. I hope you don't get bored.[14]

It suddenly struck me the other day that we have now been writing to each other for six months. So far, whether by intent or simply lack of room in our written thoughts, we have avoided any reference to our personal relationship. . . . My rather vague thoughts of the future are inextricably linked with thoughts of you. . . . I do want you to know, Joan, that I would wish above all things that our friendship be continued not only now but in the time to come when I return home.[15]

Thank you for the sweet thought that prompted the inclusion of a sprig of heather. It still had its scent on arrival, and I could almost feel the springiness underfoot, and the freshness of high air around me. . . . Do you think Scottish morality allows of an unchaperoned couple chasing around the country on a walking tour?[16]

HMS *Montclare* was now on the way to Hong Kong. John looked impatiently for mail, which came by way of their escorting destroyer. Meanwhile, the Methodist group on board continued their discussions with growing urgency.

This evening's discussion will be on Jesus' commandment that you love one another. How far can this apply to post-war international relations? Perhaps 'loving' Germany and Japan should be more akin to a father's

---

13. *Ibid.*
14. JMA to Joan, August 28, 1945.
15. JMA to Joan, September 1, 1945.
16. JMA to Joan, September 10, 1945.

correcting rod than endless money to rebuild their war machine — but hate and malice must go.[17]

They expected to be in Hong Kong for some time to oversee the beginning of peacetime administration. John was to be posted to the Office of the Rear Admiralty, Fleet Train. There was the relief of victory, of course, but in its aftermath the oppressive heat of Hong Kong made it hard to raise enthusiasm for the massive challenge of reconstruction, especially as this postponed the prospect of going home. First, however, came the event they had been waiting for:

> The surrender ceremony took place yesterday and the BBC correspondent made his broadcast from *Montclare,* using her W/T [wireless telegraphy] facilities.[18]

John had written to the Reverend Mr. Brazier-Green about training for the Ministry, and the church authorities had sent him details. His choices were either to seek nomination immediately and take the combined local preacher and candidature examination in February, or to wait a year to seek nomination, then take the exams in stages ending in February 1947. The second choice would mean a long wait, but the first would mean cramming a great deal of study into a few months, which would be difficult in the sultry heat without books to hand. Also:

> You must be wondering by now, poor dear, what on earth this has got to do with you. . . . You must have realised by now that I have serious intentions of disturbing your placid life in the commercial world, and the decision I make on this may hasten or delay the time of my being able to do so. (Whether or not you want your placid existence troubled or not, you see, doesn't come into it; which merely shows the selfish, intolerable, egoistic brute I really am.)[19]

His forwardness apparently scared Joan off. In a reply to her he wrote:

> Your writing, mood, and sense changed so completely in the writing of your last paragraph, I can hardly believe it was your work. If the expression of my hopes for a more permanent friendship has met with such a stonewall attitude, I dread to think what my later letters will do. Surely

17. JMA to Joan, September 7, 1945.
18. JMA to Joan, September 17, 1945.
19. JMA to Joan, October 10, 1945.

you will be shocked to the core at my presumptuousness in proposing a holiday together, for instance.

As you must know by now, my hopes for the future did not stop at mere friendship, but these I knew were only dreams that had to wait until I returned to materialise. These hopes have now faded a long way into the distance as a result of a decision I made two days ago. I then made up my mind to take the second of the two courses open to me in my offer for the ministry.

This would mean six years of study.

During those six years I could not marry or even think of it, and I haven't the right to ask any girl, however much I loved her or she me, to wait six years for no better prospect than that of being the wife of an underpaid Methodist minister. There, I have been very frank, and you must believe me, very sincere. Let's always keep sincerity the keynote of all our dealings with each other, always.

. . . I hope this letter doesn't upset you much more than the first offer of friendship seems to have done, and please don't talk of such foolish things as your 'letting me down' through being as I always want you to be. If you really mean you are not sure of me, say so. I'll understand, and will always value your honesty and frankness.[20]

Four weeks later he looked back on this letter with apologies:

Let us leave our personal relationship at any rate for my part as this: that I believe quite sincerely that in some inexplicable way the future of ourselves and JBG are bound up together. Whether it will be purely friendship alone or something deeper, I don't know.[21]

John spent more and more time pondering metaphysical questions such as the nature of the soul and life after death. Untrained in philosophy and unguided by formal theology, he started from simple assumptions about a loving God and asked questions from there. The questioning became the important thing.

Surely one has to believe that there is something which sharply divides man off from beast. But then I suppose much depends on the individual conception of a soul. If it is regarded as something quite personal to the

20. JMA to Joan, October 18, 1945.
21. JMA to Joan, November 19, 1945.

Joan Lawrence in 1947

individual, one runs up against difficulties in understanding which appear insuperable. For instance, if this is so, this sphere we call heaven must be composed of billions of human souls in various stages of development, growing by the thousand as each earthly day sends more released spirits in that direction. Surely it's going to get rather overcrowded!

On the other hand, if the soul is regarded as that part of God brought into a man's mind by his own acceptance of the existence and force of God, and that on death it merely returns to the original stream of Purpose and Life from which it came, extended, enlarged, fulfilled by man's use and development of it during life; then, the question becomes simpler but also more difficult in that we have lost sight of individuality after death. Although I have reasoned this alternative out for myself, I cannot somehow accept it easily. The only explanation I can consider of the obvious ability of people to gain spiritual help by consideration upon their contact either via a spiritualistic medium or through God Himself with a loved one lately departed, is that what they eventually contact is that essence of the good in that person loved and known so well which is, in effect, Love, which is God.

. . . Or suddenly, the thought occurs to me as I write, there should be no soul, but merely the Spirit of God working in the mind of man direct. In this case there can be no individuality after death. . . . This is absurd, for how can I worship Christ if His spirit bears no individuality? Where is the Doctrine of the Trinity? No, there is a soul in man, a receiving set for the Spirit of God. . . . It is that soul which is indestructible, but I cannot yet envisualise its relationship to the Spirit after death, nor its place in the life-stream which I believe is God.

Yes, there is a soul, there must be — but I can't prove it, and until I prove that, I cannot prove life-indestructible-after-death. . . . I shall not become a minister until I can, if it takes my whole life.

I refuse to look upon the Bible and Christ's words as things which cannot be argued about or proved to oneself. . . . If I were to preach a religion I did not understand I would be a hypocrite.[22]

But meanwhile he was looking forward to training under the Reverend Mr. Brazier-Green — in the hope of being guided out of his questioning — and was inclined to see the workings of fate in the opportunities he found.

I had a wonderful letter from JBG, saying he would accept me as a member of St. John's if I had no other home church. Won't it be wonderful?

22. JMA to Joan, October 30, 1945.

Hearing JBG every Sunday in a real live church, knowing oneself to be a member of it.

Regarding the books I needed so urgently for my studies, the most amazing thing happened which I am inclined to regard as more than just chance. A stranger appeared, newly arrived from Sydney, where he had been studying theology. He wanted to lend three books to our group library, two of which were set books for the LP [local preacher] exams. . . . Looking back over my service career, it is more than ever evident to me that this task I have chosen for myself seemingly, has in reality been chosen for me. My whole past life has seemed to work to this point, especially these last four years.

It seems to have started in Alex. I left my ship to go into hospital with a quite minor complaint only two weeks before the destroyer sailed on her last Malta convoy and was sunk by Stukas. There followed the German advance on Alexandria, and the subsequent evacuation of that city by the Navy, leaving only a few of us behind. This came between me and another sea-draft, which meant I stayed in Alexandria and was one evening mysteriously guided to the little church where later I became a church member, and discovered many wonderful things quite suddenly.[23]

In November 1945, John left the *Montclare* for SS *Aurangi,* a converted liner. He was writing from the Office of Commodore Fleet Train, British Pacific Fleet. He expected to wait until December 1946 for demobilization, but his thoughts turned increasingly back to Glasgow.

Was it really a year ago that we first met? Yes, I do remember the service but had forgotten that we first spoke to each other there. I tried so hard to sit next to you at Communion Service, and some great thug came and got between us at the crucial moment. (As a matter of fact I think the great thug was your brother, but don't tell him I said so.)[24]

These are breathless moments for JMA. Tomorrow or the next day I am expecting a signal saying whether I may or may not go home.[25]

December 7, 1945: "Home January. Write Arbiter. John."

---

23. JMA to Joan, November 5, 1945.
24. JMA to Joan, November 27, 1945.
25. JMA to Joan, December 7, 1945.

CHAPTER 2

Introducing the Scrolls

In September 1946, John became a probationer to the Edinburgh (Leith and Tranent) Methodist Circuit. He preached, led hymns, led discussions, buried the dead, visited the sick, ran youth groups, and generally looped along between Sunday and Friday — on Fridays Joan came over to Tranent by train. They walked and talked, took tea with John's kindly and keen-eyed landlady, and sometimes Joan stayed — chastely — at the inn. The following year, John was sent to the Hartley Victoria Methodist Training College in Manchester. He said he left the parishioners of Tranent a good deal more confused than they used to be.

First he and Joan took a holiday on Exmoor. He came back no less committed to the Methodist ministry but even more committed to Joan. There were two obstacles to marriage. One was money. The other was that the church expected six years' service from a probationary minister before allowing him to marry.

Joan said she would wait. She recognized that a calling to God could lead a man anywhere and could take years to come to fruition. She saw herself as a helpmeet and a homemaker. Now a qualified accountant, she also recognized that she was likely to be the wage-earner for some time to come. They talked about where John might go after training. Missionary work was a possibility, specifically in South Africa, where the church did not insist on six years' celibacy.

John did not want to wait for anything, least of all for Joan. He began college with his mind more than half on this question. Soon a new interest took over the rest of it.

One of the options on the theological course involved looking at the Bi-

19

ble in its original languages. The students went across to the university for classes in Hebrew and Greek. Most had set their sights on evangelizing Deptford or darkest Africa, not on textual analysis, and dropped out. John, who had picked up some French, German, and Latin at grammar school but not much except naval slang since then, discovered he loved the studying. Languages opened up new worlds of ideas and linked him with thinkers across the centuries. Greek fell into place, and Hebrew intrigued him. He liked the rigor of learning, the patterns of syntax, the new sounds, and the new ideas. In the case of Hebrew, where the vowels are not written and one set of consonants can have more than one meaning, he discovered there might be many alternative new ideas, and questions began to swarm.

If a language is so fluid that the same set of phonemes can mean many different things, how do we choose? From the context, of course. But if we are not talking to the person who uttered the words, can we be sure of the context? If what we know of the context is based on traditions hundreds of years old, how do we know that the traditions have not warped to a greater or lesser degree? What if the first speaker had quite a different context in mind, and where did that come from? What did the scribes of the Bible really have in common with its originators? They assumed a body of oral tradition handed down in synagogue or schoolroom. But what if they were mistaken? What other meanings could there be? What ideas, what worldview, shaped the meanings?

Instead of charging into the Methodist ministry with conviction blazing, John came to a standstill. To preach something he was not sure about was impossible. He was well aware that most people thought that the broader message — the moral certainty of Christianity sweetened by appealing stories — was more important than the absolute accuracy of the text. But for him, the Bible was turning from a block of authority to a mass of question marks. Where he found doubts, he felt compelled to ask and answer. With ancient languages, questions led to more questions, rather than to answers.

Conviction faded and enthusiasm went with it. John could not think of trying to reassure people anxious or doubtful about their faith without being wholehearted about his own. He felt he would be propping up a moral edifice cracked at its foundations. And he did not like being told what to do, what to think, or when to marry by men in black frocks. By mutual agreement, he left off training for the Methodist ministry to study full-time at Manchester University for a degree in theology, which included Hebrew, Greek, and logic. On June 17, 1948, he married Joan Lawrence.

In practical terms, the university accepted John on the strength of his 1939 school matriculation. He applied for funding to the Government's Further Education and Training Scheme, which had been set up to assist young people whose studies had been interrupted by the war. Joan, earning a steady wage as a cost accountant, paid the rent and bills and ran the home, an arrangement that held good for a large part of their married life.

In January 1949, John transferred from the B.A. in theology to the honors course in Semitic studies, which included Arabic. He picked up the David Bles Hebrew Prize in 1950, and in June 1951 achieved first class honors in Oriental Studies. He was awarded a graduate research studentship but resigned it in favor of a seventy-pounds-a-year senior studentship of the Treasury Committee for the study of foreign languages and culture. In John's case, this included Semitic philology and ancient near eastern history under Professors H. H. Rowley and T. Fish. He published papers, and in 1951-52 took his M.A. degree with "A Linguistic Study of the Balaam Oracles in the Book of Numbers."

At Manchester John was the golden boy, the rising star of the Semitic studies department. An academic career seemed the obvious way ahead. A Leverhulme scholarship boosted his income; he planned a doctorate on "Traces of Dialects and Colloquialisms in Biblical Hebrew." That summer Joan and he moved out of their flat into a semi-detached house in suburban South Manchester. His thoughts turned to buying a car. She had other preoccupations, for their first baby was due in December.

The foremost British scholar in Semitic languages at that time was Professor Godfrey Driver at Oxford. When it was suggested to John that he transfer his Ph.D. study there, he seized the chance. Joan stayed in Manchester to carry on earning their living. They did try to sell the house but had no takers, at least not at a price that could have taken them to Oxford.

Discoveries by the Dead Sea

In 1947, a shepherd boy looking for his goat among the cliffs near the northern end of the Dead Sea had come across a cave. In the cave stood tall earthenware jars. Fearing demons, Muhammed fled. But he told his friend, and next day they came back. They hoisted themselves inside the cave and opened the jars.

Demons? Ghosts? Gold and silver? All they found were some rolls of parchment covered in cloth. They took them back to camp to show the old men. Unwrapped, the parchment stretched the length of the tent. It was very dusty, too crumbly for patching or stitching, too flimsy to be burned as fuel. It was covered in strange writing. Someone, they supposed, might think it a curio. They stowed it in their saddlebags to take into town next market day.

In Bethlehem the cobbler Khalil Iskander Shahin, known as Kando, watched well-padded westerners poking along the back streets for souvenirs. When Muhammed's kinsmen opened their sack in the back of his shop, he guessed the strange manuscripts looked odd enough to excite some collector. He had no idea what they were or what they were worth. He did know that trading in unauthorized archeological finds was illegal; this boosted their price. Through insight, foresight, or speculation, Kando bought the scrolls. Kando was an Assyrian Christian, and the most learned man he knew was Mar Samuel, the Metropolitan of the Syrian Convent of St. Mark in Jerusalem, so there he went to find out more about the manuscripts. The Syrian bishop seized the opportunity. Later he spirited four of the scrolls to the United States and eventually sold them for a quarter of a million dollars. Professor Sukenik of the Hebrew University also heard about the treasure and, through great daring and determination, secured three scrolls. Muhammed el-Dibh, the shepherd boy, earned sixty dollars for finding the first seven of the Dead Sea Scrolls.

Kando foresaw gold in the Judean hills. Stakes were high, and the Bedouin were not slow to pick up the message. Soon scroll-hunting became a profitable pastime, a welcome addition to incomes traditionally based on herding sheep, raising goats, and smuggling. Scuffling traders, wary tribesmen, made their way into the cobbler's shop with a packet here, a matchbox full of scraps there.

Until May 1948, Jerusalem was part of the British Mandate in Palestine. At that date the city was divided into East and West Jerusalem, and Jordan took over the eastern part, which included the Old City. Some of the administrators from the British Mandate in Palestine stayed in their posts, including the keeper of antiquities and acting curator of the Palestine Archaeological Museum (PAM), Gerald Lankester Harding, who was assisted by the museum secretary Joseph Sa'ad. Nearby was the American School of Oriental Research (ASOR) under its director Dr. Millar Burrows and his assistants John Trever and William Brownlee, and also the École Biblique et Archéologique Française under Father Roland de Vaux. Harding and Burrows got together some cash for scrolls. Secretly and at acute personal risk, Sa'ad made his way to Kando's shop and let it be known that there was business, good business, in dealing with the museum. Meanwhile Harding and de Vaux, with the help of the Arab Legion, discovered where the illegal excavations had been going on and realized how urgently they would have to take control of the site before eager treasure-hunters devastated it, and with it all hope of a systematic, scientific search.

Harding had the wisdom to know that enlisting the help of the Bedouin by winning their confidence would take him further than trying to enforce

The Palestine Archaeological Museum

The Qumran monastery ruins from the cliffs, looking northeast

the law against illegal excavation. Because he respected the tribespeople and was willing to take the time to build friendships with them, and thanks to the persistence and courage of Joseph Saʿad in searching out Kando, the task of bringing the scrolls to light made progress.

The museum and the École soon ran out of money to pay for scrolls, and so Harding appealed to the Jordanian government. Jordan was a new and small country, struggling to provide water, roads, health care, and basic education for its people. Nevertheless, it contributed fifteen thousand dollars and as much goodwill and practical help as it could muster. Its antiquities were, after all, a resource with the potential to attract tourists and foreign investment.

By 1952, scroll-hunting had become big business among the Bedouin. Following rather belatedly in their footsteps came the official archeologists under Father de Vaux of the École Biblique. The boxes of fragments in the PAM mounted, and so did the excitement of historians and theologians, for what the early finds contained were books of the Old Testament one thousand years older than any extant text. Some of them represented a version used by neither the Septuagint (the Greek translation said to have been commissioned by Ptolemy Philadelphus at Alexandria in the third century B.C.) nor the Masoretic text (a version made in the eleventh century A.D. of a canon set in the second century A.D.). Some of the Dead Sea manuscripts corroborated both to a large extent, proving each had a very ancient Hebrew lineage, but others showed certain variations in the text that pointed to sources different from either. Early attempts at radiocarbon dating placed the scrolls between 168 B.C. and A.D. 253. Archeological evidence from the caves and ruins of the Qumran area, mainly coins and other artifacts, narrowed the dating to the period between about 100 B.C. and A.D. 70. Subsequent paleographic and textual analysis supported this. So the scrolls appeared to be about two thousand years old, and the people who wrote them and bundled them into jars in secret places had done so at or around the time of Jesus.

The first seven manuscripts to be discovered comprised scrolls of Isaiah, sectarian writings, and biblical commentaries. Professor Sukenik bought a text of Isaiah, the *Hymns Scroll,* and the *War Scroll.* Mar Samuel found he had another copy of Isaiah, a *Commentary on Habakkuk,* the *Rule of the Community,* and the *Genesis Apocryphon.* Of these, the *Rule of the Community* (also known as the *Manual of Discipline*) described the life and discipline of the people who wrote or owned the scrolls. They belonged to a sect that called itself the covenant, assembly, congregation, or community. Many scholars identified this sect with the Essenes, who, according to the first century natural historian Pliny the Elder, had a settlement by the Dead Sea in the years leading up to the fall of the Temple in A.D. 70. Most, though by no means all, scholars still think the same way.

Other biblical texts and commentaries followed soon afterwards. The full count of manuscripts from Qumran now numbers almost nine hundred. Approximately 220 of these are biblical, with thirty-six copies of the Psalms, twenty-nine of Deuteronomy, twenty-one of Isaiah, seventeen of Exodus, fifteen of Genesis, and thirteen of Leviticus. There are also:

- targums — Aramaic translations of certain passages, which show how the Hebrew text was read at that time;
- pseudepigrapha, such as the *Book of Enoch, Jubilees,* and the *Aramaic Levi;*
- commentaries on biblical texts, such as Habakkuk;
- the *Florilegium,* speaking of a spiritual temple and a Davidic messiah;
- the *Testimonia,* on the theme of three future leaders: prophet, priest, and "star";
- legal texts — the *Damascus Document,* the *Manual of Discipline,* the *Temple Scroll* (a later find, published by Yigael Yadin in 1977), and a text on the aspects of the Torah that outlines the differences between the community and other Jews;

- writings for worship — the community's own calendar, hymns, and poems;
- eschatological works, in particular the *War Rule* and the *New Jerusalem* document;
- the Copper Scroll (in some ways the most enigmatic right from the start, not least because it proved impossible to unroll).

But in the early years, 1947-53, only a few of these were beginning to appear, a few intact, most in scraps; and people could only guess at the full extent of the treasure waiting to be uncovered. Archeologists had been largely unaware of the caves, let alone the ancient artifacts they contained. Bedouin scrambling among the rocks in their unauthorized treasure hunt disturbed dust and rubble, and this was what led the officials to the scene.

The first scrolls brought in from Cave 1 were fragile but nearly whole, so handling them was comparatively straightforward. Cave 4 produced thousands of tiny fragments, many no bigger than a fingernail. To help in sorting and deciphering the finds, de Vaux called together a team of scholars. In theory the team was to be international and undenominational.

The first members were already there: Fr. D. Barthélemy and Fr. Josef Milik were members of the École Biblique and had begun on the Cave 1 material. Barthélemy unfortunately had to return to France for health reasons. To help them deal with Cave 4, de Vaux invited Frank Cross from McCormick Theological Seminary in Chicago. De Vaux also wrote to the leading British scholar in the field, Professor Driver at Oxford. Driver recommended his young Ph.D. student, John Allegro, whose study of Hebrew dialects in the Old Testament sounded like an ideal background for deciphering ancient texts. (Later came the American Monsignor Patrick Skehan; two French priests, Fr. Jean Starcky and Fr. Maurice Baillet; John Strugnell from Oxford and Dr. Claus-Hunno Hunzinger from Frankfurt.)

John was elated. It was an opportunity to get involved with one of the most exciting archeological finds of the century.

At the Scrollery

John arrived in Jerusalem in October 1953.

I cannot start work on the fragments until Harding and De Vaux get together and decide what to apportion to me. But Mr Sa'ad, who is Inspector of Antiquities, in charge of the Museum, has given me a temporary

Cave 4 (4Q) at Qumran with figures on descent

pass and shown me where I should work and the sort of fragments they have. They have a well-equipped photographic studio downstairs, and I hope to get some help with my own developing. The Museum is a delightful place, with a good library, and in the centre a court with a pond and lavender bushes growing round it. Very cool — delightful.[1]

Realizing the possibilities of the photographic studio was a flash of foresight. Over the coming months John was to take thousands of photographs, mainly documenting the scroll fragments allotted to him. He had in mind that the task of collection, transcription, and editing was unlikely to be completed by the time he was due to leave, so that working off his own infra-red plates would be the only way to continue research at home. He assumed that the museum's official archive of the complete scroll collection was to be available to all as a full, clear, and unalterable record of the original documents, so that scholars everywhere would be able to study and interpret them in years to come. That this should be so seemed to John an obvious principle of scholarship. In 1953 he would never have believed that by the end of the 1980s the original archive would still be far from available to all. As it was, he was later

1. J. M. Allegro to Joan Allegro, October 19, 1953.

able to draw on the set of photographs that were unarguably his own for lectures, articles, and books as well as research.

John spent the first few days finding accommodation, getting to know the city, and making friends among the Americans at ASOR and the British residents who met at the cathedral.

> This morning we all went to St George's Cathedral for morning service, and afterwards to the Bishop's house for lemonade and biscuits. Met several English people. . . . Within [the city walls] of course, it's pretty primitive — the bazaars and streets of the Old City are ancient and smelly. Still, the people are friendly and one wouldn't need to be lost for long. Outside the walls, there is just barren red soil and rock. In the walls, the old buildings tumble over one another.[2]

Frank Cross had his wife and child with him in a rented flat. Missing Joan badly, John was full of schemes to bring out her and the baby to share the lease on a house with another American family. He got as far as looking up the flight numbers and trying to convince her how comfortable she would find a night on a BOAC Comet.

Joan could not face the idea. She had let the house in Manchester and taken the baby to stay with her parents, now retired in Dorset. Two hundred miles in a train had been more than enough; two-and-a-half thousand miles in a plane seemed beyond reckoning. The idea shocked her parents. In any case, she simply did not have the hundred pounds for the fare.

On October 21 John started work on the fragments. He faced a long, painstaking task: a jigsaw puzzle with thousands of pieces missing, the rest overlaid with dust and ready to crumble. For clues they had paleography (analysis of the various scribes' handwriting), the condition and smell of the parchment, and where legible, the content. Often the letters, obscured by dirt, had to be dabbed clean, and in many cases the writing showed up only under infra-red photography.

> I started work on the fragments Tuesday afternoon and continued yesterday, cleaning and pressing and sorting them. The main thing is brushing them very carefully to remove dust and trying to bring up the lettering. Then we shall try to put them together, photograph, and read them where possible. These pieces are very very small, with only a word or two on each.[3]

2. JMA to Joan, October 20, 1953.
3. JMA to Joan, October 23, 1953.

... I spent two and a half hours this morning trying to find the home of a piece having about three words, and in the end had to decide it was non-biblical. There is great rejoicing in heaven when one certain identification turns up, you may be sure. . . . But it's all necessary.[4]

Soon the work built up momentum:

Great excitement yesterday and this morning at the Museum. We three were trying to crack a cryptic script in some fragments. Yesterday was easy — we simply had to read the spelling back to front, and start from the left instead of the right. However, mixed in with the Hebrew were some letters in Phoenician script, and some Greek letters, and others we just don't know. Today we got out some more fragments in this cryptic script to try and decipher the whole, but so far no good.[5]

Money was a constant concern for John, and for Joan paying her keep at home. A Treasury grant topped up John's studentship, but it was counted in pennies and no way compared to the level of his colleagues' university salaries. And the Treasury Committee did not fully understand what he was doing in the Scrollery, or how it related either to John's thesis or to their aim of promoting international understanding through study of languages. At Driver's suggestion they proposed that John should spend five to six months helping Mr. Harding and learning colloquial Arabic in Trans-Jordan, then another five to six months really mastering it in Syria and Lebanon.

Of course I can't possibly leave Jerusalem so soon, now I am onto this job of preparing my group of MSS for publication. It would be madness. I have written to GRD [Driver] and the Treasury today pointing this out, and urging them to reconsider the matter. I explained that I am not Harding's handmaid, doing just anything he cares to pass over, but am working on this stuff which is internationally owned, for publication throughout the world. The academic work is in fact closely related to the PhD work. Really GRD is a chump; he knows all this or ought to.[6]

John suspected academic jealousy. "Behind all this lack of interest in pushing my case with the Treasury is GRD's reluctance to attribute an early date to the scrolls, or much importance."[7]

4. JMA to Joan, November 11, 1953.
5. JMA to Joan, November 27, 1953.
6. JMA to Joan, November 25, 1953.
7. JMA to Joan, December 5, 1953.

I saw Pere de Vaux this morning and showed him the letter from the Trea-sury. He was aghast, especially since at a meeting of the Museum commit-tee the other day our Ambassador in Amman (who is on the committee) said that the British government were anxious to help with these scrolls and he regarded my Treasury grant as an example of such help.

. . . I think I told you of our day's fun the other day, having a go at the cryptic script found on some of the fragments. The honours fell to Abbé Milik who got the gist of the code. In the morning, however, Frank and I had worked on a piece, in normal script (except for three or four words), which made sense only when the words were read back to front. This not very brilliant discovery fell to me, and as a result Milik suggested yester-day that I publish it, which is very decent of him indeed since he discov-ered the really difficult parts. Good clean fun.[8]

Though ten days later the fun was wearing thin:

I worked this morning on my piece of the cryptic script, and after puz-zling all morning decided that the script was the least cryptic thing about it. It doesn't make sense, and I think some bored Essene was amusing himself making life difficult for a later generation.[9]

Visiting the archeological sites made a break from working on the frag-ments. With Cross and Milik, John scrambled around the caves and ruins at Qumran and visited a tomb outside Jerusalem.

They held the ladder while I climbed inside with my camera. A family lived inside the tomb — the cold shivering children, poor and ragged, made my heart bleed.[10]

They also got to know Kando.

This chap Kando has a cobbler's shop, very small and poky, and before one gets down to business it's a matter of squatting on a stool in the front of his shop, drinking mint tea. . . . He is a good medium between the Gov-ernment and the Bedouin, and since the Government take care that they owe him quite a bit of money, he's relatively straight and trustworthy. He opened a grimy notebook, and there between the sheets lay three pieces of our precious fragments. We took and read them, but they're not for

8. JMA to Joan, December 2, 1953.
9. JMA to Joan, December 13, 1953.
10. JMA to Joan, December 4, 1953.

private sale, thank goodness, and eventually we shall get them by government purchase. Then, he no doubt having summed us up, we went along
the street with him to a lock-up, where he keeps junk from his shop.[11]

Surrounded by a wealth of archeological remains, each a window on the
past, they were tempted to buy for themselves. Milik was offered a set of arrowheads, John some Roman glass, "with a wonderful mother-of-pearl-like
sheen about it which reflects all the colours of the rainbow when the light
catches it — unfortunately too fragile to take home."[12]

Everything about Jordan in those days enthralled John. It caught at him
with its beauty and its needs, its risks and promises, its contrasts and contra-
dictions. The desert entranced him: the way it threw a searing, stark challenge
to anything alive there, and flushed green with hope after rain, and hid thousands of years of human struggle in the sand. The people fascinated him, sin-
gly or together. There were shrewd and daring traders. There were tribes
whose old men traveled the desert in the ageless rhythm of seasons but whose
young men worked for a shanty-town existence with motor-bikes and factory
clothes. Women watched with deep eyes from the shadows of the streets.
There were ragged children and refugees displaced by the Israeli war, with
nothing to do and nothing to understand but how to scour a living day to day
and wait and wait. Hussein, the young king of a young country, needed to
build for it an identity and a future while balancing the myriad contradic-
tions of Middle Eastern politics.

Meanwhile, John settled down in his bachelor flat in cosmopolitan Jerusalem. There were plenty of friends and plenty of social activities, all very
congenial, though without Joan he was not entirely at ease.

Last night we went to the local cinema, where they showed one Arab film
and one English. The Arab one was most exciting — *The Victory of Islam*
— featuring the Crusades, from the *other* side. How the locals roared and
shouted when their hero Saladin rushed to the rescue on his fiery steed!

Today being Sunday, I don't know whether to go to church or go
straight to the Museum and get on with my large fragment. Probably the
latter. . . . We now have electric fires in the Museum and life is much more
comfortable. Another little comfort we have arranged is a cup of Turkish
coffee in the mornings about 10am. It helps the morning on no end.[13]

11. JMA to Joan, December 8, 1953.
12. *Ibid.*
13. JMA to Joan, November 22, 1953.

At least in these early months, John seemed entirely happy with work in the team. He was the junior member, and very much aware of the honor of being chosen. For Milik in particular he had tremendous respect: "an awfully good chap, and most interesting to talk to. . . . Admirable company, and a good archaeological guide."[14] They discovered a mutual admiration for P. G. Wodehouse and clubbed together to buy second-hand paperbacks.

Scroll fragments kept appearing, too fast for the scholars to keep up with. De Vaux talked of enlarging the team, but the idea of further division of labor seemed complicated and distracting:

> Milik asked me today — had I seen the rest of the Isaiah commentary? No — where was it? So we get Saʿad to open another cabinet, and he pulls out a large box full of fragments, yet untouched. This, it appears, is a bunch not yet paid for. Where does the stream end? Milik now says he thinks that the mass of stuff we have been working on is only about one third of the whole!
>
> I don't think Milik is very keen on [a second Englishman] coming out. He argues that what we want is not more men, which will complicate matters when it comes to close co-operation for publication, but money to allow us already on the job to stay longer or come out again for shorter periods, or a number of periods. (I am coming home on 25th July, money or not!)[15]

Christmas was looming, and however busy they were in the Scrollery, it felt strange to be so far from the family. He wrote somberly, reflecting on the stresses and strains of 1953, so often apart. However, jollity was as obligatory in Jerusalem as in England and went so far as to cause him to dress up as Father Christmas for the party at ASOR.

> On the whole their get-togethers at the School are quite jolly, but by no means unrestrained abandon. Whether it is that beneath the mufti most of the males are parsons, or whether it is something American, I don't know, but there is always something that holds them back from being really easy with one another.[16]

Some of the team also attended midnight Mass at Bethlehem. "Mass turned out to be a grand spectacle of lifeless puppetry, clothing and un-

---

14. JMA to Joan, December 16, 1953.
15. JMA to Joan, December 17, 1953.
16. JMA to Joan, December 24, 1953.

clothing a cardinal; singing and plenty of special effects; no spiritual ones at all."[17]

By New Year's Day John was thoroughly homesick. He lived off Joan's letters and her descriptions of what the baby got up to:

> I drink in every word, and imagine you two playing hide and seek round the chairs, of her laughing and singing, and my heart aches to be with you both. However, it would ache a lot more if I didn't think I was doing a worthwhile job out here which will amply repay our pangs of separation.[18]

Besides, he had set his sights on a car, "the new Ford Popular, 10 hp, 2-door and under 400 pounds," and to supplement their savings he typed other people's letters for them at three shillings and six pence each. He also sent a short article to the *Manchester Guardian;* to his delight they accepted it and he immediately planned some more. "£17 10s from the *Manchester Guardian!* Not bad, eh? It's the first real money I have earned with my pen."

Fresh scroll pieces kept coming in fits and starts.

> This afternoon I was walking to ASOR when the colonel stopped his car to say he was just going down to the Museum because he'd been offered some more fragments. So I hopped in with him and we went to see Mr Harding. But we just missed him and saw Mr Saʿad instead who, when he saw the pieces, suggested going to Jericho to catch Harding. [The Bedu] want £25 for the pieces. Harding said that was far too much.[19]

> The new lot of pieces look good and we hope to find some joining up to the same scrolls as those we have already laid out on the tables. Milik's bad; there are several boxes of these things — a dozen at least — and some of them contain very tiny pieces, so he got them together and put them back guiltily into the cupboard, leaving them for those who follow us! Very wicked, most un-Christian.[20]

At this time, Starcky joined the team, "a tall, thin, ascetic-looking chap with a lovely nature, and a great scholar. He's so quiet and unassuming but is a recognised authority in his field of Palmyrian and Nabatean culture. It's a

17. JMA to Joan, December 26, 1953.
18. JMA to Joan, January 2, 1954.
19. JMA to Joan, January 16, 1954.
20. JMA to Joan, January 18, 1954.

real experience to work with these people. Milik has offered me the best of his arrowheads as a gift."[21]

> We decided today to form an ecclesiastical see of Qumran: Milik is the Cardinal, Starcky the Bishop, Frank the Protestant clergy, and I'm the laity over whose soul the ecclesiastics fight. Frank doubted whether it was worth fighting over.[22]

> De Vaux called me outside this morning and discussed my publishing a piece of my 'pesher' [commentary]. He thought it would be a good idea, and suggested taking a difficult piece since it would provoke a response from the academic world; and the suggestions thus gained could help in our final publication. This encouragement from the great man himself is very heartening, and makes me feel even more securely part of the team.[23]

It may be noted that at this stage there appeared no difference of opinion within the team over whether to publish or hold back from publishing their material.

Up till now, John had been sharing a house with two American families. Relationships had become strained — bickering over bills, various neuroses surfacing among the under-employed wives — and so he decided to move to the mission hostel at St. George's School, where everything was clean, simple, and more straightforward.

> The other tenants are, for the most part, a gawd-'elp-us bunch. Excrewshiating pseudo-Oxford accents on all sides, especially the refugee-uplifters. You can imagine the spinster-types they get. But they're really most kind.[24]

> We got out the remaining boxes of fragments this morning. Six in all, mostly small, and we three gathered round them and snarled. We decided unanimously to give Abbé Starcky two boxes, because he is the new boy (and the oldest) so that left one each and one over. We looked at one another and then decided to toss for the wretched thing. Milik lost and got it all to himself to clean. Frank and I were highly delighted until we realised that the blighter is off to the Qumran dig in a fortnight, so we shall get it anyway.[25]

21. JMA to Joan, January 24, 1954.
22. JMA to Joan, January 25, 1954.
23. JMA to Joan, January 30, 1954.
24. JMA to Joan, February 2, 1954.
25. *Ibid.*

Spring flowers at Wadi Qumran

The work was expanding every day. Clearly, Frank Cross and John would be struggling to finish their sections by the time they had to leave in July, and they would have to carry on at home using photographs instead of the real thing — not easy alongside their university commitments. Milik's section was by far the largest, but he would be able to stay in Jerusalem to tackle it.

De Vaux applied for help. With some misgiving, they learned that another priest, Monsignor Pat Skehan, would be coming from America, and a young graduate called John Strugnell from Oxford: "a long-haired, unshaven, roll-collar-pullover and flowing BA gown type, who would talk the hind leg off a donkey."[26] Meanwhile, "we really are an ideally suited team, and this makes life very pleasant. We miss Milik when he's away, being unable to pull his leg every other minute."[27]

One day, the team took a day off for a trip to Samaria.

When we went on to Ta'anach it was just lovely. All the fruit trees are in blossom, and lots of bright red anemones and purple cyclamen are growing wild by the roadsides and in the wadis. The grain crops are coming up and the grass is so green, it was like riding through English countryside in springtime. All the flocks of sheep and goats have their quota of young, and when one considers that in two or three months all these places will be scorched brown again by the sun and will remain like that till next December, you begin to realise what a miracle spring growth must have seemed to these people of old — hence the famous fertility myths, etc.[28]

John had fallen in love with Jordan.

And with the work. To act the detective: teasing out first the words, then the meaning, then the significance; poring for hours over dusty scraps until they yielded their message. To gently brush sand off the parchment, to trace the ink that had dried on it two thousand years ago, to hear the ghostly scribe intone his verses through sun-striped courtyards. To realize that the privilege of handling this material would put him, John, in a unique position to share it with others through teaching and writing and would allow him to take the lead in debates across the world.

I have made a start on my fragment and solved a tricky line this evening before dinner, which counteracted to some extent the depressing effect of

26. JMA to Joan, February 13, 1954.
27. JMA to Joan, February 21, 1954.
28. JMA to Joan, February 6, 1954.

A street of old Jerusalem

the rain. A later scribe had written in a line over another, in a semi-cursive writing. It gradually resolved itself into a line of the Hebrew text which this chappie imagined the older scribe had left out. Since the line is dubious in the Masoretic Text, and since anyway this man makes an important correction in it, it's really quite interesting. The commentary itself is of interest too, for it has to do with the 'Last Days,' the banishing of the wicked from the earth, etc. So it will be a good piece to publish and will bring attention from all sides.

I have an idea to 'popularise' a piece Frank has published on Samuel. The interesting thing about this is that the Hebrew follows the *Greek* text to a surprising degree, and must indicate a recension from which family the Greek Septuagint was translated. I think I could boil this down to first principles for a small article in the *Manchester Guardian,* and include a photo of the piece. Really this opportunity of getting material first hand is too good to lose! Besides which, I need to make a hundred quid in six months to buy our FP [Ford Popular] with enough to spare for the holiday, house, etc.[29]

"I'm just in the midst of formulating yet another theory on my fragments. The trouble with these theories on dating the events of the sect, they fit one set of evidence and not another." He took his camera to Qumran again: "I bear in mind popular lectures in the future on the scrolls, and pictures of these caves will be especially valuable."[30]

John photographed everything, and often twice: once in black and white with a camera borrowed from the PAM, and again in color on his own small Kodak. To supplement the official images, he photographed the fragments as they were laid out, aware that a slightly different angle might help with decipherment, especially when working off prints away from Jerusalem. He photographed the team and other people, and the archeological sites, mostly with his own future publications and lectures in mind. He did not tell Joan much about this activity, probably because she would worry about the expense, but steadily built up a huge stock of photographic records that were to prove a valuable resource both for him and for later scholars.

As the jigsaw grew larger, it became more and more exciting.

I'm starting to prepare our new pieces of fragments and have already found a large piece of my Psalm 37 commentary which fits the piece I prepared for publication. Also, I have a large slat to add to my 'back-to-front'

29. JMA to Joan, February 14, 1954.
30. JMA to Joan, March 2, 1954.

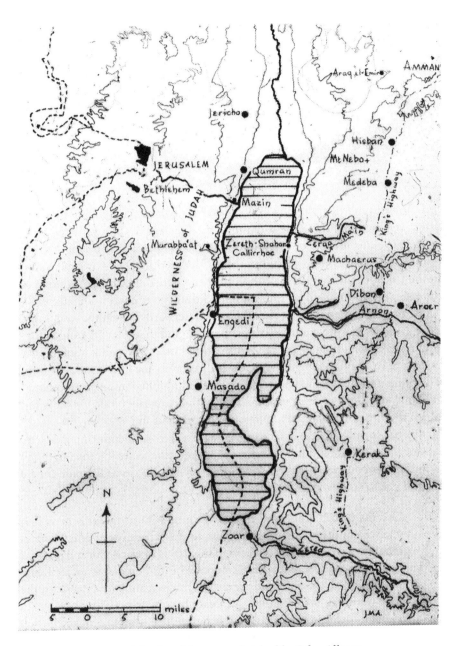

Map of the Dead Sea area, sketched by John Allegro

cryptic fragment, and most important of all, we've discovered a leather 'tag' containing what appears to be a list of names, some Hebrew normally, others in another language which is not Greek or Latin but may be Persian. All very exciting, for these are the first names to be found on the Qumran material. Very perplexing. Fun, though![31]

An interesting piece, or group of pieces — trying to put them together to make sense of them. It seems to be a discourse, illustrated with quotations from all parts of the Bible, on the Messiah and the 'last days'. I hope we get more, because it will be very important indeed.[32]

John found the religious import less immediately compelling than the detective process. "I think my soul must be quite dead. I was not stirred at all by the religious aspects of our pilgrimage [to Galilee], only by the natural beauty of the places and sometimes their historical interest" — even at a spot by the Lake of Galilee, a natural amphitheater where one of the party stood at the water's edge and read Matthew 5. John did still go to church sometimes — "quite boring, but a feeling of righteousness afterwards" — but he found that as he gained a sharper picture of Palestinian life and thought at the time of Jesus, he was losing hold of the religious concept of a god-man landing in the middle of it. "I am reading the gospels and certainly the Old Testament from a documentary angle, and when you do that, uninhibited by religious preconceptions, the story of the passion seems extraordinarily bloody. And is too much dwelling on it part of a religious person's sadism?"[33]

That spring they came face to face with a stark and enduring problem: lack of funds. The solution that John proposed came to set the tone of much of his subsequent work on the scrolls and to set him on a different course from the others for the rest of his life.

Milch (as we call him) came in this morning with the gloomy news that there's no more money in the chest to buy fragments with. There is probably one third as much again in the hands of the Bedu, and it seems Harding and de Vaux are losing hopes of ever being able to get them. Frank and I are shocked, and are sure that, given sufficient publicity, the funds would be forthcoming. . . . Possibly something like £10-15,000 is required — this is not an impossible figure. The trouble probably is that neither Harding nor de Vaux can spare time for a publicity tour, but I

31. JMA to Joan, April 12, 1954.
32. JMA to Joan, May 3, 1954.
33. JMA to Joan, April 7, 1954.

feel that this is just what is needed, complete with a short film, lots of slides, and samples from the fragments themselves. I wouldn't mind doing it myself![34]

"Fame is the spur," he had remarked on receiving his first check from the *Manchester Guardian*. In the scrolls he recognized messages for people everywhere who were interested in religion or willing to listen to the past. He knew he had the skill to help decipher the messages and set free the questions they would raise. He also felt he had the power to bring these messages and questions home to people by writing and talking in terms they would understand. And this mattered: People had the right to understand their heritage and ask their own questions. He guessed that many people would be interested enough to contribute money to enable the work to go on. He knew that the scrolls should be brought to a wider public and that he could be the one to begin the task.

It was a considerable challenge, especially in Britain:

Harding was in today. He needs more money to buy the remainder of the fragments from the dealers, or rather the Bedu who hold the stuff illegally. The $15,000 promised has not yet arrived, and is coming from McGill University in Canada. He tells me that he has sent a circular letter round the various bods in England (including HHR) [Professor Rowley] to get them cracking raising some funds. He says he is quite staggered by the lack of enthusiasm in the UK over these momentous discoveries. . . . It's being left to the Yanks and French to get in on them. I suppose it springs from the scepticism with which they were received in Oxford circles, and the country has followed suit — except HHR and a few others. There's lots of popular interest in them though, and I said I thought that the best thing from this point of view would be for the scientists in the States, now carrying out experiments, to report negatively on hopes of unrolling the copper scrolls now here in the Museum. Then the Jordan government would have to give permission for them to leave the country, to go to the UK for cutting in a first-class laboratory. We could make a lovely publicity splash with that. . . . An exhibition in the British Museum would soon raise quite a lot of interest. But the copper scrolls seem more intriguing to the popular mind, at least out here, than any of the rest, though they're probably the least important. Still, they are unique. They'd make the subject of a good TV programme![35]

34. JMA to Joan, February 3, 1954.
35. JMA to Joan, March 10, 1954.

Harding did in fact get a response from Rowley in Manchester.

HHR, characteristically, went hot-foot to the authorities of the University, and asked for £250. The Committee thought this was too little and are supplying £1,000 . . . a wonderful example of Manchester's liveliness, and HHR's in particular. He hopes I will keep an eye on their interests out here and see they get something valuable for their money.[36]

But there was no reaction at all from anywhere else. Driver wrote explaining that neither the Bodleian nor the British Museum would send any money until they could see the goods first. This enraged John: "The biggest museum in the world ought to be able to put money into the project of presenting these priceless things to the world without expecting to see bits and pieces like a bargain basement. If they financed research they wouldn't expect to see material things for their money."[37]

Making plans for the future was difficult at such distance. John was in line for an assistant lectureship at Manchester. Rowley had written encouraging him to apply in advance of his return; he knew he was fairly certain to get it and his home thoughts seemed unwontedly dutiful.

It's good for your soul that you went to church. I must say a philosophical or deeply religious thought starts looking around for a companion as soon as it enters my nut these days. At church I spend most of my time thinking of you, Judith, and our Ford Popular, and of all the things we're going to do when we get home. . . . I, as much as anyone, look forward to a nice long spell of rut-making quietly in Manchester. To have taken a big part in the publication of these exciting finds, however, will be worth half a dozen doctorates to me, and will be the big bump-up I need for a future chair.[38]

However, he would have liked to complete his Ph.D. as well and knew he would definitely want time off to return to the Scrollery. Despite what he said about rut-making, he felt tempted to abandon Manchester and return to Oxford for the doctorate, thinking the prestige of it might take him further in the long run. He tried this idea on Joan.

Her reaction was swift, unequivocal, and delivered in terms such as "impatient, impossible, impetuous, irresponsible."[39] John thereupon gave up

36. JMA to Joan, March 23, 1954.
37. JMA to Joan, May 15, 1954.
38. JMA to Joan, January 22, 1954.
39. Joan Allegro to J. M. Allegro, February 28, 1954.

dreaming of spires and settled his ambitions on home, family, and Manchester University.

Rut-making quietly, however, was not a likely prospect. For a start, serious rifts in outlook were apparent between John and his future professor even before he had secured his job. Rowley had supported, indeed encouraged, his application for the assistant lectureship, but took exception to the articles John was writing for the *Guardian*. One in particular was the re-working for a general readership of Frank Cross's paper on a text from Samuel, which he had earlier mentioned to Joan. Cross had already published the original paper, with full translation, in a learned journal, and had helped John with the presentation of the popular version. So when Rowley told the editor of the *Guardian* that it was a deception and a fraud, in fact cooked, John found it all

> a bit staggering. . . . There was no attempt at deception, a good deal had to be inserted, but sufficient was there to make plain that we had a Hebrew text which lay behind the Greek translation and was thus one of the greatest discoveries in the field of biblical criticism for literally centuries. Frank and I went carefully over the points yesterday afternoon. The readings were plain as a pikestaff; the reconstructions, where the text was broken, well founded. Then we began to look for another cause of this vituperation.[40]

They decided that it was a case of rivalry over theories about the Septuagint. John and Frank's work supported the idea that the Septuagint was a Greek translation of an earlier Hebrew version; others, including Rowley, held that no such Hebrew version had ever existed. In the teacup world of Semitics departments, this hurricane was enough to blast someone's reputation. For John it was merely a foretaste. He wound up his letter: "Next year is going to be one HELL of a year, believe me, keeping out of trouble," and he made up his own mind, as ever, about professors.

In the Scrollery the detective work went on, and the need for funds grew still sharper. The more they did, the more there was to do; it was nearly time to leave and frustrations were mounting.

> I was working on my Psalm 37 commentary yesterday once more, and managed one more join and to fit some more pieces into the jigsaw, or at least, suspend them in space where they ought to go. . . . I am certain there is more of this stuff still with the Bedu — one of the edges looks like a new tear.

40. JMA to Joan, May 13, 1954.

Above, some of the team at work in the Scrollery;
below, plate of mixed fragments, 1954

Above, John Marco Allegro studying pNahum, a scroll commentary on the book of Nahum; *below,* John Strugnell

Above, Claus-Hunno Hunzinger;
below, Patrick Skehan

Above, Josef Milik at
Cave 1;
left, Kando and
George Isaiah

> The most frustrating thing about our work on the fragments is that we are continually finding fresh pieces to fit on the plates when we had long thought we'd got everything available.[41]

Rowley was pestering for pieces. "Really I think HHR is losing his grip. . . . If the fragments were sent, how could we work on them?" A Cambridge college had declined to buy or donate, "since they thought it undesirable that the collection should be split up. Overlooking the patent fact that unless they're bought by somebody soon they'll go to the tourists!

"Poor old Harding; I wouldn't have his job for anything. And all this has only to do with the fragments from Cave 4. In Bedu hands are many, many fragments from Khirbet Mird . . . and other caves in the vicinity containing important early material. Money has somehow to be found to get in all this vast wealth of stuff. One day our museums will wake up — when it's too late."[42]

Frank Cross had to fly home because of ill health. His successor, Pat Skehan, arrived at the end of June, "a quiet-spoken chap, very nice indeed and, I believe, very clever. He took to scrollery like a duck to water and has got well into his slides."[43]

Another new collaborator that spring had been Dr. Claus-Hunno Hunzinger from Heidelberg, whom John immediately entitled Baron. A quiet, industrious Lutheran, he was allowed only a few months' leave of study in Jerusalem, but he struck up a steady and much valued friendship with John.

John Strugnell arrived from Oxford early in July. Social life at ASOR warmed up at once: "There was a carousal till 10pm — wine, liqueurs, and beer. Someone turned out to be an expert on the harmonica and with the aid of a songbook they had raked up we sang loud and long." A brilliant classicist before turning to oriental studies, Strugnell took to the scrolls with flair. At first John was dubious about his "Driver bias": "He is inclined to agree with GRD that the British Museum couldn't buy 'pigs in a poke' — until he realised what the real situation is. There is room for a lot of re-education back there quite obviously."[44]

John's own appointment at Manchester had been confirmed at last: an assistant lectureship at five hundred pounds a year. He had no intention of letting it tie him down. His plans encompassed a far more public role.

41. JMA to Joan, June 17, 1954.
42. JMA to Joan, June 18, 1954.
43. JMA to Joan, July 9, 1954.
44. JMA to Joan, July 10, 1954.

Harding was in yesterday afternoon and I asked him about taking back copies of the museum's photographs of Qumran and anything to do with the scrolls. He is agreeable himself and is going to see De Vaux today. I want to go through their collections and take anything I want for lecture purposes and popular talks to stimulate interest in these things. I also asked if he had any objection to my approaching the BBC and offering an illustrated talk using such pictures. He thought it a very good idea and I think it's worth trying, though the BBC may think it's too technical.[45]

De Vaux agreed, to his surprise.

We're going to put scrollery on the map in Britain! Harding says he's going to have another go to bring some fragments over to England for display next year. We've had a change of government here since the last one refused to let them out of the country at the last moment, so there's some hope. I would dearly like to bring some with me! . . . The trouble is that nothing of any consequence can be displayed before it has been published, and so little of our stuff has been published yet.[46]

Nine months in Jerusalem had given John a tremendous boost in skill, in confidence, and in ambition. How would he take to family life in a Manchester suburb? After waiting alone in the shadows for so long, Joan's eagerness to see him was edged with trepidation.

With two weeks to go, John wrote impatiently:

I just cannot imagine what you've been brooding about or what sort of 'tortured imaginings' have passed through your head. It can't be financial now. . . . I've got the job you wanted and the prospects look rosy. I'm sure you'll be much better when we're together again, but what worries me a little is that you seem to be longing for the sort of very settled and "one-rut" existence that I can never give you. I hope continually to be dashing around, though more often than of late with you and my family. But the impact of new acquaintances and experiences is all part of a stimulating life and keeps the grey matter from stagnation. I'm sure you'll feel like that when we are working together again. After all, we're young yet, and there's time enough for the old rocking chair when we get too old and impoverished to be able to move. I love you dearly and all will work out OK.[47]

45. JMA to Joan, July 7, 1954.
46. JMA to Joan, July 8, 1954.
47. JMA to Joan, July 12, 1954.

By mid-July, "my fragments are now at the stage of being laid out and pinned onto their glass plates, neatly labeled, for photographing." De Vaux seemed pleased with the progress the team had made on Cave 4; they had gotten through the major part of it and made the main identifications. But that was really only the beginning, for work on the scrolls in general and for John in particular.

> The more I think of it, the more I realise what wonderful prestige value this year is going to have. To be able to describe oneself as 'the British representative on a small international team of scholars whose task it is to prepare and edit this scroll material' really sounds awfully good![48]

48. JMA to Joan, July 8, 1954.

CHAPTER 3

The First Stirrings of Controversy

Writing *The Dead Sea Scrolls*

John took up his post at Manchester University in September 1954. He immediately began writing *The Dead Sea Scrolls,* the book that made his name. He stated the reasons for writing the book in his first proposal to Penguin:

> We have the remains of a very considerable library from the Essene settlement, of interest not only to specialist historians but to the intelligent public in general, for it is becoming clear that a study of the sectarian literature is going to play a large part in the understanding of Christian origins. . . . It has occurred to me that a Penguin prepared as we go along could be published almost simultaneously with the major publications [of the scrolls], and be first in the popular field by two or three years.[1]

The reaction was swift and favorable. In October John submitted the synopsis and began the lifelong habit of getting up before dawn for two or three hours of writing before the day job set in.

The Dead Sea Scrolls tells the story of the discovery of the scrolls; where they came from, what they contain, how they are studied, what they have to tell us about first-century Judea, and how they bear on the origins of Christianity. Founded on John's experience of studying the scrolls in Jordan, it was written very much for the general reader. It represents a fair summary of what the scholars so far knew about the scrolls and points to some of the most significant issues they raised. As John wrote to Penguin Books:

1. J. M. Allegro to Penguin Books, September 21, 1954.

If anything it may err on the 'popular' side, since to preserve a balance over the whole mass of material it is not possible to go into too much detail on any aspect of the literature — except for the last chapter, which will deal with the early Christian connections. Even so, the book will be entirely lacking in footnotes, thank the Lord, which will condemn it forever as a 'popular' book in accordance with current academic standards. But it will, I think, be readable, which is perhaps more important. It will make my academic friends tear their hair because I shall refer loosely to things which they won't see officially in print for another four or five years; but I am not writing for them. I have also got inside dope on the finding and purchase of the scrolls and fragments which has never before seen the light of day and which is at times quite exciting.[2]

The main sections cover the discovery and exploration, the daily life of the sect, their study and thought, the historical framework, and the role of the Teacher of Righteousness. The book goes on to explain the significance of the scrolls for Old Testament studies — that they prove the ancient Hebrew lineage of extant versions of the Old Testament but draw on a source still more ancient. It also brings together what scholars had so far gathered from their translations about the life and thought of the Essenes and their relevance to the beginnings of Christianity.

The opening chapters recast the spell of the scrolls. They describe how, out of the heat and the choking dust of the Dead Sea basin, were sifted the precious scraps of leather, many torn or nibbled or crumbled, holding messages from two thousand years past, maybe a hundred generations, recalling many more generations beyond that. The scrolls spoke of laws, traditions, and memories that reached towards the time of people's first writings. For John, the spell lay in the fragility of the past, the sense of consequence held in one's fingers: to handle material hidden by someone to whom its preservation mattered very much indeed — who had wanted to keep it secret and sacred when others threatened to destroy; who had even torn some of it to bits to hide its secrets. To handle what these frightened men had handled, to return to light their rules and messages, to hear their voices. And these voices could help people understand where their own religion came from.

The book describes how excavations at Qumran uncovered the Essene settlement where many of the scrolls were written and used before being hidden among the surrounding cliffs. John identified the Qumran community as Essene from the start and assumed that members of this community had

2. JMA to Penguin Books, August 2, 1955.

written at least some of the scrolls, mainly because the topography of the area, the archeological remains, and the textual evidence seemed to fit the references by the contemporary historian Josephus. Though some later scholars have been less convinced of the Essene connection, John had no doubts about it, so in this book his interpretation is followed.

To depict the daily life of the sect, John drew on two important scrolls: the *Damascus Document* and the *Rule of the Community*. To pursue the ideal of purity in communal life, sharing all they owned, depended on rigorous obedience to the rules. Stricter than the strictest Jerusalem sect, the community wished to wait in purest holiness for the messiah who would lead them out of the desert in a final cataclysmic battle against the forces of evil. Meanwhile some worked as healers, astrologers, scholars, and scribes; others tended the goats, tilled the soil around the nearby spring, prepared food, prepared parchment, and repaired the ducts and cisterns that led water from the wadi for ritual bathing and daily needs.

John outlines the sectarians' study and thought. They studied Scripture and interpreted it in the light of current events. Expecting the apocalypse, they took prophecies of its coming from their holy books and signs of its imminence from the strife in their homeland. But they were the chosen, the children of light; in the purity of their devotion they were to be saved. Rejecting the worldly compromises of the Temple, they followed their own rules and kept to a solar calendar with their own holy days. They studied the stars to know their influence on the human body and character, and they studied herbal lore to know the God-given essences of healing or harm. For they were *assayim,* healers; not in the modern sense of diagnosing infections or other physical conditions and then applying antidotes, but in the sense of searching out the evil spirits that took possession of a body. These they cast out by the power that came from knowledge of God and of angels and of the inmost nature of things. The men who had the power to discern bad spirits in an ill or troubled person also had the power to assess the qualities of those who applied to join the sect. These men were called physiognomists or scrutineers and were respected as leaders among the community.

The book summarizes the archeological evidence for placing the sect in a historical framework: from about 100 B.C. to the fall of Jerusalem in A.D. 70. It was a stormy time in Jerusalem, of dynastic rivalry, political and religious argument, shifting alliances, treachery, and opportunism. The leaders mostly hated and sometimes exploited the Romans; all factions killed and plotted in the name of God; priest-kings held sway in the Temple, marketplace, and barracks — though only till the next rebellion; piety stank.

The Essenes had their leader too, the Teacher of Righteousness, who, reenacting the exile of Moses, took them out of all this to preserve true holiness in the desert and to await the true coming, which amid the breakdown of all decency could surely not be far off. John thought they were in fact driven out by Alexander Jannaeus, a priest-king of the Hasmonean Dynasty, who ruled from 104 to 76 B.C.; some other scholars choose an earlier or later ruler. The high priesthood was seen as a divine office, spiritual and temporal, through which God governed his chosen people in every way. In the case of Jannaeus, he did it by fire and sword, and when other priests rebelled, they were hunted out by mercenaries. According to John's reading of the scroll commentaries on Nahum and Habakkuk, Jannaeus is the "Wicked Priest" and also the "Lion of Wrath" who persecuted the Teacher "in the house of his exile" (that is, Qumran) and executed him, probably by crucifixion, on the Day of Atonement. Since then the Teacher's followers had awaited his return as messiah in the Last Days. Then both he and the Lion of Wrath would be resurrected to judgment, and he, the Last Priest, would "stretch forth his hand to smite Ephraim," Ephraim being the pseudonym used elsewhere in the scrolls for the sect's enemies.

It must be said that not all translators agreed about the execution, still less about the crucifixion, and preferred to use the term "harassment" or "confusion" rather than "persecution." John's interpretation was to lead him into dispute with some of his colleagues on the team, a crack that widened into a rift when it crept into areas of religious sensitivity. Even if he had foreseen the trouble, however, he would have been unlikely to forbear from probing the crack.

What do the scrolls tell us about early Christianity?

John realized that these references to the messiah, crucifixion, and resurrection would lead his readers' thoughts one way. He shows how further parallels with Christian ideas ring through the language and doctrine of the scrolls. In the light of the scrolls, he realized that St. John's gospel, previously seen as written comparatively late and in the Greek tradition, could now be seen "to spring directly from a Jewish sectarianism rooted in Palestinian soil, and his material recognised as founded on the earliest layers of Gospel tradition."[3]

For example, a basic concept of the sectarians' world view is that of the two spirits — light and dark, good and evil. In the scrolls, the war between good and evil will culminate in an apocalyptic battle and is meanwhile reflected in the battle between righteousness and perversity inside every human being. People's behavior depends on which force is uppermost within them, in the proportions determined by the stars at their birth. By submission to God's law, by cleansing mind and body, people can prepare for salvation, but

3. J. M. Allegro, *The Dead Sea Scrolls* (London: Penguin Books, 1956), p. 128.

God must then redeem the soul. By studying the way of holiness, people gain knowledge of God: the spirit of truth lends understanding, "insight into the knowledge of the Most High." This spirit of truth comes "to enlighten the heart of man," for "from the fountain of his righteousness springs my justification, a light in my heart." Echoing these lines from the *Manual of Discipline,* the Prologue to the fourth gospel claims: "In him was life, and the life was the light of all people . . . the true light, which enlightens everyone, was coming into the world" (John 1:4-9).

Indeed, the terminology of Qumran is echoed time and again in the New Testament. For example, Covenanters are the children of light, the poor, the elect of God, those who choose the Way of God. Their sect is "an eternal planting, a holy house of Israel . . . the tried wall, the precious corner-stone, whose foundation shall not be shaken nor moved from its place." St. Peter addresses the early Christians: "Like living stones, let yourselves be built into a spiritual house, to be a holy priesthood. . . . See, I am laying in Zion a stone, a cornerstone chosen and precious; . . . you are a chosen race, a royal priesthood, a holy nation, God's own people" (1 Peter 2:5-9).[4]

In the scrolls as in the gospels, good will come out of suffering. For the sect, the savior of the world will come out of the suffering of the world, the messiah out of the suffering of the sect, as a woman suffers in birth.

The Covenanters voted through casting of lots, as did the disciples in Acts 1. They pooled their possessions when they joined the community. Every meal they shared was a rehearsal for the Messianic Banquet, when the priestly messiah would sit down with his Davidic counterpart and the Congregation of Israel under their elders and sages — as in the Last Supper of gospel tradition. This concept of two messiahs, priest and king, appeared in the gospels to become fused in Jesus.

So, as John saw it, the first Christians talked the language of the Essenes. They shared an eschatological outlook — always looking to the coming of the Kingdom of God — with a sense that doom was swiftly, surely, and disastrously about to overtake the world. For both sects, the chief enemies on earth were the people of hypocrisy, "seekers after smooth things." Both interpreted current events in the light of the Old Testament: Nearly everything Jesus is said to have done fulfills somebody's prophecy. Through word-play or annotation, the scroll commentaries exploit every biblical reference and are not above twisting words to fit the names in the Bible or the names to fit their interpretation.

The Dead Sea Scrolls outlines these similarities between the Essenes and

4. See Allegro, *The Dead Sea Scrolls,* p. 141.

the early Christians, but it also stresses the differences. At this stage John was a long way from identifying the two. As he makes clear, Jesus was not a priest or a monk, and he ministered to ordinary people, not to the chosen few. If he was influenced by Essene teaching and traditions and shared their healing skills, he was more likely to have learned them in the towns and villages, through another order of Essenes who, according to the first-century writer Philo, lived as part of ordinary communities and presumably traveled freely between the villages and their center at Qumran.

And the concept of a god-man was wholly foreign to the Covenanters. There was nothing supernatural about the Essenes' hero, the Teacher of Righteousness, and they were still waiting for his resurrection along with everyone else's. But for Saint Paul, and through him for the first Christians, "the whole of his faith hinged upon the historical resurrection of Jesus."[5] The biblical image of Jesus embodied age-old Jewish beliefs about sin, redemption, and the grace of God. By teaching that he was a real, live person as well as the embodiment of religious beliefs, Paul hoped to make these beliefs real and meaningful for ordinary Gentile people. He had to convince people that the magic powers ascribed to Jesus were emanations of the power of God. They did not simply flow from God through Jesus but were part of Jesus as Jesus was part of God. Hence his authority to lead the world, and hence the authority of the established church, through his nominated successor Peter.

In comparing the sectarian beliefs of Qumran with Christianity, John showed how the Jesus story fit into pre-existing messianic traditions. He readily acknowledged the differences between the church's conception of Jesus as a supernatural figure and the record of the scrolls about the sectarians' original leader, very holy but long dead. Still an occasional church-goer himself, John had not yet openly questioned the nature of Jesus — man, superman, or God — but in studying the way the scrolls were written, he began to study the gospels as literary creations too and to delve more deeply into the image in which the figure of Jesus had been drawn.

In this first book John did not attempt to examine wider questions about myth and religion. Later he was to look closely at other centuries-old myths and legends about resurrection, virgin birth, transubstantiation, and similar magic tricks or miracles of nature (as he saw them) and to ask why these should have been brought together and personified in, or appended to, one first-century Jewish healer. At this stage he simply began to open up the questions to public debate. The idea that some Christian concepts existed before Christ was neither new nor surprising, but at that time many people were

5. Allegro, *The Dead Sea Scrolls,* 1st ed., p. 162.

worried to think that the gospel story might not be wholly unique, and this was the focus of the debate.

The Dead Sea Scrolls was to come out eventually in August 1956. It sold out within a few weeks and went through five reprints in as many years. In the revised version, *The Dead Sea Scrolls: A Reappraisal,* which was written in 1960, issued in 1964, and is still read today, John gave more details of what the archeologists had found out about community life and the place of women at Qumran, and he speculated less hesitantly about Jesus and the sect. And he wrote to his publisher:

> I am more openly critical now of the original handling of the Scrolls af-
> fair by those responsible in Jordan, and some of the more recent develop-
> ments are most disturbing in view of the important and controversial
> stuff that is being shoved away out of sight for years and even 'lost' com-
> pletely. All this needs saying without further delay, in the hope that public
> reaction will result in a more open and scholarly attitude to the publica-
> tion of this material.[6]

But meanwhile the original book was translated into several languages and enabled the family to change the Ford Popular for an Austin Seven.

Jerusalem

Meanwhile, lecturing and translating continued. Teaching and preparing to teach, poring over infra-red prints of scroll fragments, typing and correcting and typing again in the spare room at home, John wanted very much to go back to the real thing. He wanted Jordan's red-gold spaces and sunny clut-tered towns and the comradeship of the Scrollery. As soon as Milik and Starcky invited him to join an expedition planned for spring 1955 to explore the Nabatean sites of Transjordan and Syria for inscriptions that would build up evidence of ancient language and culture, he was at the door of the univer-sity registrar with his application for two weeks' leave of absence. "These scholars, having in mind our happy co-operation in the work of editing the Dead Sea Scroll fragments, have done me the honour of asking me to join them in this expedition."[7]

So in March 1955, John returned to the Scrollery and "a good welcome from everybody, which was rather nice." He found the new members of the

6. JMA to Penguin Books, May 26, 1963.
7. J. M. Allegro to the Registrar of Manchester University, October 29, 1954.

team settling in well, "John Strugnell enjoying himself no end," and the German, Hunzinger, "young and very pleasant, speaking excellent English. He can only stay a year, with no hope of returning, so has asked for a limited section and one he can finish on time."[8]

A great deal more material had appeared, and the funding problem was more urgent than ever.

> This new Murabba'at scroll, in large lumps, is something the Bedu have only just parted with on promise — but no money seems forthcoming from the Government, who, it seems, are suggesting rooking the Bedu and just hanging on. Of course this would be fatal and we should lose all immediately — and probably to Israel.[9]

> Does the bloke who wrote for information on the scrolls sound wealthy? The German man who should be arriving on Sunday is bringing only about £4,000 and I fear this may not be enough. That would be a shame, for we do want to get *everything* in our hands now once and for all. Milik's section is now simply *vast*: heaven knows how he's going to edit it all, but he's here all the time. Strugnell's is big enough too, and even Skehan has a large lump now. They've really done wonders with the unidentified stuff and reduced it to insignificant proportions.[10]

The Nabatean trip itself was delayed for a few days. First the weather broke after a winter of drought. Jerusalem was cold and wet, but "one realizes out here what the rain means to these lands, and it makes the old fertility cults seem much more real and understandable."[11] Then he found that the Jeeps they had hired were appalling. No handbrakes, split tires, haphazard steering, faulty wiring (if any)... neither of John's unworldly colleagues had thought to check.

Once they got underway, with hired cars and drivers, it was a rewarding expedition. From cities such as Petra and Jerash, the Nabateans had commanded the trade routes north, south, east, and west since around the fourth century B.C. Through trading on their own account, and through providing protection and services for the camel trains, they grew wealthy and established a sophisticated and highly civilized community. Alexander and his successors plundered their wealth and left a legacy of Hellenistic ideas that intertwined with the Assyrian and Egyptian cultures. The Nabateans recorded

8. J. M. Allegro to Joan Allegro, March 11, 1955.
9. JMA to Joan, March 12, 1955.
10. JMA to Joan, March 15, 1955.
11. JMA to Joan, March 14, 1955.

their laws, transactions, religious ceremonies, and memorials in a vast store of inscriptions. Not all had been catalogued or translated, and these Milik and Starcky planned to investigate.

The tour was a rich experience for John. Leaving the tourist trails, they went searching for ruins and tablets in places uncharted by other archeologists. Once their car stuck fast in the mud of a wadi; the local doctor offered them shelter and soon the room filled with a thickening circle of villagers talking deep into the night.

Some friction developed between the two leaders: Starcky was "even less practical than Milik, and talks too much." John avoided crossing either. He and Milik planned a popular book on the Nabateans together, on a similar level to *The Dead Sea Scrolls,* in which Milik was to contribute the technical research but leave most of the writing to John. John had approached Penguin with the idea:

"My forthcoming expedition would give me first-hand experience of their sites . . . and perhaps the ability to transform lists of place-names, kings and dates into a living story of these remarkable Arabs who built a kingdom almost overnight."[12] Unfortunately other work crowded out this book and it never materialized.

They returned to Jerusalem to find yet more fragments arriving from Qumran. Most had been found by de Vaux's excavators on what was now an official dig. Kando was still a useful contact.

In the afternoon Milch and I went to see Kando, the Bethlehem dealer, who now is risen to respectability in a curio shop in the Old City. He's got a line on a tenth century Greek codex, two leaves of which I have in front of me now.[13]

A bit of good news yesterday to do with the fragments. There were several large pieces which clearly joined together and made the top of several consecutive columns, the biggest single slice we have. At first it was thought they were of a 'War Scroll', and Hunzinger, the German collaborator, was congratulating himself on his luck. Milch discovered it to be a *peser* on Nahum, part of which I already have. So in one fell swoop the biggest of the Cave Four fragments has fallen to me, and it is a very important piece, since it seems to have a historical commentary. It will rival the Habakkuk Commentary scroll recently bought by the Israelis.[14]

12. JMA to Penguin Books, December 13, 1954.
13. JMA to Joan, April 3, 1955.
14. JMA to Joan, April 9, 1955.

Yesterday, perhaps the biggest news on the scrolls since they were first discovered. That Nahum *peser* of mine turns out to have one complete and one broken *name* — historical, King of Yawan (Greece) — thus settling at last the historical background of the scrolls, right back in Seleucid times! This is really a world-shaker, and I'm going to ask permission to publish it in HHR's new journal. Or at least a bit of it, because we have the most of four columns in the biggest connected piece of all Cave Four. That it should have fallen in my section is really the most tremendous bit of luck for me — talk about the devil looking after his own. And if I do publish it separately it will be the most widely read article of any to do with the scrolls.[15]

Opening the Copper Scroll

Among the original finds from Cave Three, back in 1953, had been two rolls of inscribed metal: the two sections of the Copper Scroll. The brittle rolls of greenish copper lay in the museum, oxidized over the centuries, and there seemed no way to prize them open. Scholars in Jordan, Britain, and America had been discussing the problem since the initial discovery. John had mentioned in a letter to Joan the various proposals going around in the spring of 1954. Sensing that the Copper Scroll might arouse particular public interest and hence donations, he had added his own suggestion: to exhibit it in Britain and perhaps provoke British interest in taking on the challenge of opening the two rolls.

"I do wish I could have brought home the copper scrolls for exhibition. As I told you, they will probably now go to the States for this hardening process. All the same, I don't see why they shouldn't be put on show in the UK before they go to the States. I'll suggest it," he wrote.[16] At the time, nothing had come of this idea.

Scientists in America had discussed using chemicals or wax to open the rolls but had agreed on nothing. In particular, experts at Johns Hopkins University in Baltimore and at Harvard University had been researching the reconstitution of corroded metals in the hope of unrolling it, but they found the corrosion had gone too far.

No news yet of the copper scroll experiments in the USA. GLH [Gerald Harding] is very reluctant to let them go there anyway, and so is the Government. On the other hand, it was promised they should do so if a suitable

15. JMA to Joan, April 12, 1955.
16. JMA to Joan, July 8, 1954.

technique was devised. But after two years nothing much seems to have resulted, and I have put in a strong plea for Manchester's having a try.[17]

Harding asked him to look into it further. First John approached the Department of Metallurgy at the university, and also a Manchester engineering firm, the Carborundum Company, Ltd. Mr. Scoles at Carborundum replied regretfully that he lacked suitable equipment; Professor Thompson at the university was full of doubts. So John contacted the Principal of the Manchester College of Technology (which later became UMIST, the University of Manchester Institute of Science and Technology). Dr. Bowden was delighted with the idea.

Writing from Jerusalem, John told his professor what he had arranged.

By the middle of next week, one of the copper strips from the Third Cave should be in Manchester, bound for the College of Technology. Harding was up today with the news that the long-awaited permission from the Jordan Government has been granted, and he is bringing one with him when he leaves for the UK on Tuesday. The rest of the team, apart from Strugnell (whom I told) know nothing about it yet, and I await with apprehension the reaction of our American colleagues.

. . . Dr Bowden is being asked to maintain strict security on the strip during its sojourn in the laboratories, and only you and I will be allowed in, apart from his technicians. We have no idea how long the unrolling or cutting will take, but Harding is leaving England after a short stay, and the idea is that I shall then be able to keep a daily watch on the process when I am back in Manchester. If the reaction from Bowden and his colleagues seems favourable when they see the first strip, the second will follow.

My soundings on the attitude of Professor Thompson were unfavourable and I did not proceed any further in that direction, especially as Bowden's reaction was very enthusiastic.

I am very pleased that negotiations are coming to a fruitful conclusion in this business, and I think Manchester can feel proud once again to be taking a lead in the scrolls.[18]

Rowley bristled at the idea that the scroll should go to the Tech and not the university, but John had no doubts:

I am inclined to think that the more practical approach favoured by the School of Technology will prove of more use in the job of opening the

17. JMA to Joan, April 5, 1955.
18. J. M. Allegro to H. H. Rowley (HHR), May 30, 1955.

copper strips than the University's more theoretical approach, especially since the task is more mechanical than metallurgical. . . . There is, however, more to the business than mere professional competence. However good a team Thompson could have mustered, it would not compensate for his own very lukewarm attitude to the job — not so much pessimism as a decided unwillingness to spend very much time or energy over it.

He had even been unwilling to speak to John in person on the subject and had asked for no details.

Quite to the contrary was the reception at the School of Technology, where Dr Bowden was not only extraordinarily interested in the copper strips but went to some trouble there and then to call together his technicians to examine the problem. Their confidence in being able to tackle the job one way or another was impressive for the obvious determination to get down to the job and spare no pains until it is done. . . . I had therefore no hesitation in recommending the Jordan Department of Antiquities through Harding to send the strips to the School.

I can assure you that such a task as this requires more than just a willingness 'not to decline it', as you would apparently have expected from Thompson.[19]

What was Rowley afraid of? Not keeping up with this upstart assistant lecturer, who knew more than he did about the scrolls and the other people concerned with them? Letting a man fired by enthusiasm catch others in the blaze at the expense of scholarly caution and institutional prejudice? On scholarly caution, he had a point. But John felt that caution had tried and failed. None of the cautious scholars in America or Jerusalem had thought of a way of opening the two rolls of copper. In John's opinion, the opportunity was too good to miss. When some ancestor had gone to the trouble of inscribing a long message on expensive hammered-out metal and hiding it in a cave, was the message to crumble to dust after two thousand years? John wanted to know what it said. To fire his way through the layers of Jordanian bureaucracy, the possessiveness of de Vaux's team, and the infinitely cautious academic approach, he had to act with conviction.

In June 1955 the first part of the Copper Scroll arrived at the Manchester College of Technology, where Dr. Bowden's team began preparing to work on it. John was back in Jerusalem that summer and forging ahead with his work. As he wrote to his editor at Penguin Books:

19. JMA to HHR, July 11, 1955.

Get ready for a shock. I have been able whilst out here to make such progress on my *Dead Sea Scrolls* manuscript that I have every hope now of getting it to you before Christmas of this year. Working on the fragments of the scrolls in the morning and the book in the evening seems to have been a happy combination with the result that, with six weeks to go before I return to England, I am two thirds through the rough draft, and hope to finish that in a couple of weeks or so."[20]

He was asking about the timing of the publication in order to avoid clashing with forthcoming collections of essays by Cross and Milik. He also hoped, if possible, to coordinate publicity for Penguin with the opening of the Copper Scroll.

One of the enigmatic copper scrolls is now in Manchester, where it will (I hope fervently, since I arranged it) be opened out. It should be possible to give a press conference on its contents, and since I shall be superintending the unrolling and doing the reading, it might be possible to arrange the timing very nicely.[21]

Evidently he felt convinced not only of the value of the scrolls and their message, but also of his own role in bringing them to the public. Again and again, this was the perspective that directed his gaze: to communicate with the public; to let everyone know about their heritage; to stimulate talking and thinking in homes and classrooms and halls and meeting places everywhere; not to let important questions be hidden away on academic bookshelves or shared out in only the pre-masticated gobbets that those in authority decided upon. Apart from the articles in learned journals and the scroll translations in *Discoveries in the Judaean Desert of Jordan, Volume V (DJDJ V)*, John wrote all his books for ordinary people, the "thinking public."

On October 1, 1955, the first cut was made in the Copper Scroll. John immediately wrote to Harding:

Dear Gerald,

Professor Wright Baker has just been on the phone to say that he has made the first cut in the copper strip and has lifted the first section clear. The second cut will be made on Monday morning, when I shall go in and see it, advising on the spot. He was not able to go through the margin on the first cut since it would have taken the saw too far round, and made the section difficult to handle, but apparently he only had to go through two

20. JMA to Penguin Books, August 2, 1955.
21. *Ibid.*

letters, and since the cut is only two-hundredths of an inch thick, it will make no difference to the reading.

When I returned to this country I contacted Wright Baker and he showed me what he had prepared so far. I was quite staggered, for he had got his instrument makers on designing and building an apparatus to hold and cut the scrolls, so as to ensure a straight cut and the minimum pressure on the material. It consists of a bridge, carrying a high speed circular saw, about an inch and a half diameter, and a trolley which carries the scroll on a central spindle, the whole running on rails directly under the bridge. The blade is at the end of a spring-loaded arm, so that the degree of pressure on the scroll during cutting can be accurately controlled. Also on the arm is the nozzle of a small blower, coupled to a power-driven fan, to blow away the dust as it is formed. To clean the letters and face of the revealed surfaces, he has begged a dentist's electric drill with brushes to get in the corners. When the sections are removed, they are put into large boxes, and cradles made to fit each one out of plaster which is moulded to their shape. The plastic he uses needs to be baked for twelve hours, so he has rigged up an electric oven, and the whole apparatus is installed in a special room, equipped with more evacuating apparatus to rid the air of dust as it is brushed off. Quite incredible.

We are hoping that the scroll will have been opened a day or two before the 11th [when the Jordanian ambassador was due to visit], so that I shall have been able to read what is there and satisfy any curiosity on the part of the Ambassador. It would be very nice if you could have come, bringing the second one with you, so that we could start straight away on cutting that one too. Incidentally, Wright Baker asked me to tell you that the job has turned out to be less difficult than he imagined, and that the material of the scroll is quite hard. He has removed this first layer without a single piece breaking off or cracking.

If all goes well with the remainder of this scroll, and its legend is as exciting as we hope it may be, I am all for making the cutting and reading of the second a really good publicity 'do', Press, TV, and all the rest. It would not have done for the first one of course, since we could not be sure how it would go or what we should find. If you and your Government will agree to this, and the Ambassador here seems all keyed up about it, I could make all the preliminary arrangements, but should be more anxious than ever that you should be here to take the limelight. Who knows but we may stimulate some rich industrialist to give us the rest of the money for fragments.[22]

22. JMA to G. L. Harding (GLH), October 1, 1955.

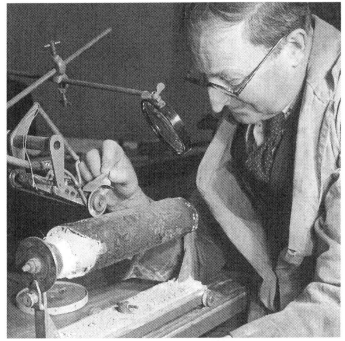

Professor Wright Baker of the Manchester College of Technology cutting the Copper Scroll

Wright Baker brushing the Copper Scroll

Above, John Marco Allegro looking at the unopened scrolls
Below, the Copper Scroll in segments after opening

Four days later the Copper Scroll lay in strips.

> Last night we made the last cuts in the scroll and it is now open. Next the sections have to be strengthened and cleaned for reading. The first section we mounted in plaster, which certainly strengthened it nicely for clean- ing, but made the whole affair rather cumbersome. So we took the plaster off and are going to coat several layers of Perspex on the back of each in addition to the Araldite already put on before cutting. This should give it strength enough for the considerable handling it requires for reading, for the thing has to be held to the light at the right angle to see clearly, rather like reading cuneiform. But the cutting of the letters in most places is re- markably sharp, though here and there I fancy the inner surface has gone leaving only indenting rather than the marks of the graving tool.
>
> These are, however, only preliminary observations. I have read one section, and I should say that it contains some sort of building instruc- tions, but the reading is difficult without more context, and I must wait until I have seen the other pieces before saying definitely.
>
> The writing is not so neat and regular as casual observation from the outside might have led one to expect. Clearly this man had not engraved copper strips often before, but it will, I think, prove palaeographically in- teresting, for he has had to make each 'pen' stroke very deliberately, and the way he forms his letters is interesting.
>
> The operation has been remarkably successful. Only in the case of one section was there any serious cracking, and that has been so well defined that putting the two or three pieces together has been very simple. There has been no shattering, largely due, I expect, to the Araldite bonding, but also the material is remarkably hard, and I think the metal is still there in some places. The great thing has been, however, the extreme delicacy with which Wright Baker, who has done all the work himself (aided only here and there in mechanical jobs by myself, though I have been present at all but the first cut), has handled the scroll. The machine he had built has cut without putting any real pressure on the scroll, and the cut is only a few thousandths of an inch thick.[23]

"Some sort of building instructions" turned out to be far more exciting:

> These copper scrolls are red hot. Somewhere in that pile down at Qumran there is, or was, 300 talents of gold buried, to say nothing of any number of deposits of silver.
>
> . . . So your three pots of silver coins [found under a floor in the ruins

23. JMA to GLH, October 5, 1955.

of the settlement] fall into place, and are merely three of dozens and doz-ens. I can hardly sleep at night. For goodness sake send or much better bring that other scroll; we can hardly wait till it arrives, and it will be cut within a week of its appearing.

. . . The rooms in the settlement are named — 'a house of meditation', 'a dormitory'. The watch-tower appears and seems to have been a favour-ite place for hiding treasure in or around.

. . . So much for the general idea, but all this is provisional. The reading is difficult, not because the writing is not clear — it is beautifully pre-served — but the language is late Hebrew and many technical terms ap-pear which are not in the dictionaries. Furthermore, all the letters are run together and division of doubtful words takes some time. However, it's coming along, and I am pretty certain of the gist. Each paragraph begins 'in the house' or 'compartment' or the like, describing its whereabouts, sometimes to the north or west, and then ending with the numerals and the metal, silver or gold. I have only deciphered two or three columns of this scroll so far; cleaning only finished today, and some words have to be cleaned still further as I progress.

Naturally, this increases enormously the need for absolute secrecy. One whisper that there is real treasure awaiting the digger at Qumran, and the Bedu would be down there in a flash and turn the whole joint upside down. Nothing will leak here, and I shall plaster the outside of this letter with 'personal' and whatnot. I respectfully suggest a very limited circula-tion of the news your end and cannot help feeling that the treasure hunt will have to be carried out without hired labour.

I am pressing on with the transcription and translation and will let you have them as soon as possible, but I would sooner give them to you personally than send them to Jordan, and ask you again if at all possible to bring the other Thing yourself just a.s.a.p. What shall I tell the Ambas-sador, who has had (mercifully) to postpone his visit to see them on ac-count of a Royal visit to England?[24]

And there was more.

You found three juglets of silver coins by the gate. You will be glad to know that these are, as we rather thought, the silver offerings of Atone-ment, but even gladder that those three are only part of a cache of *ten*, and with that lot there are, or should be, 300 talents of gold! You can re-tire in comfort, but I want half.[25]

24. JMA to GLH, October 14, 1955.
25. JMA to GLH, October 16, 1955.

However, even at this stage the amounts and measurements seemed impossible. John warned that the figures quoted in the scroll could not hold anything like their current value.

Harding shared his excitement. But he knew he had to be very cautious over what he said and to whom, and he urged the same on John. "Needless to say, this is not an official letter . . . in the words of somebody or other, 'You've told me too much: tell me more!' I can hardly wait."[26]

Line by line, the engraving released its message. But in the way of secret documents, at times it seemed as hard to prize out the meaning as to prize open the scroll. Writing almost daily to Harding, John kept him up to date on his findings and theories, but also on the questions rising on all sides.

> It is now becoming clear that this scroll is an inventory of all the possessions of the Community, not only their monetary wealth. Included are gold and silver vessels, which, since they are in the precincts of the Beth Shem (House of the Lord, and thus, a temple?!) would seem to imply something to do with a cult. . . . One very exciting and promising item, right at the end of the scroll, speaks of there being buried 'a copy of this writing', but directions are obscure.[27]

Unfortunately, Harding was unable to bring the second part of the scroll in person.

> There is much that I should have liked to talk over with you, for many of the readings depend on knowing what the places are supposed to represent, which requires the services of an archaeologist. . . . Several of the words are difficult to transliterate in any one way, since many of the letters could be read in more than one way, the choice depending on which is most likely from an archaeological point of view. However, in the full transcriptions I'll give alternatives as far as possible. I am pressing on as quickly as possible, but although I rush down to the Tech every spare moment, it is having to compete with a fairly heavy teaching programme, and the final version will not be away to you for a week or two. . . .
>
> I also would have liked to discuss the publicity angle with you more fully. I am giving three talks on the Home Service this winter on the scrolls, and whilst I was at the BBC in Manchester discussing things, a chappie asked me to let him have the first news of the cutting of the scroll for his Radio Newsreel. I said I would, and of course the Press have been

---

26. GLH to JMA, October 19, 1955.
27. JMA to GLH, October 21, 1955.

pestering poor old Wright Baker ever since. We shall have to let something go, but it is impossible simply to say that it's been successfully cut
without giving a fair idea of what it contains. . . . I really think a little publicity would do the whole project a power of good, so long as it comes at
the right moment. . . . I think I must hold back the Pelican until we can
see our way clear on these matters. It's no use sending it to the printers
when I know there's a bombshell in the background.[28]

John saw things from the point of view of the public at large. It was not
entirely the perspective of the other scholars. As noted before, he held that the
scrolls were part of everyone's heritage because of the light they shed on the origins of Christianity. Finding, buying, preserving, and studying them cost
money: public money. Raising money depended on arousing interest. Few universities had shown much interest, at least not to the extent of providing funds.
So it was logical to appeal to the public, who after all had a right to know and, he
felt, must surely want to know all about them. Everywhere he went — and he
was now in demand for lectures all over the country — he set people talking.
Questions flared like bush fires; supplying the answers looked likely to keep the
scroll scholars hard at work for years. And if they couldn't keep up, there would
still be the questions, the debates; questions would fire scholarship, everyone
would be talking and thinking, and he'd be in the middle of it.

It became more and more difficult to keep quiet about the Copper
Scroll. Understandably, the Jordanian government wanted to know what was
happening and sent their representative, Awni Dajani, to Manchester. Wright
Baker explained the cutting process as best he could: He "spent practically all
day with him, and bore it all with his customary cheerfulness and grace. He
demonstrated the machine and showed him a fragment of the scroll under
the microscope."[29]

Awni also wanted a translation. John convinced him — as was true —
that this was not ready yet and gave him a transcription instead:

Happily I had nearly completed a set of revised readings, which had not
got the translation side by side, so was able to show him those, and as I
suspected he was not able to read them for himself. . . . He, of course,
wondered why the Sect had gone to the trouble to write such nonsense on
copper strips. I let go the tidbit about the 'tomb of Zadok', in order to
make the thing more interesting. I avoided, however, saying anything
about the treasure, beyond saying that the list of rooms may have been

28. JMA to GLH, October 22, 1955.
29. JMA to GLH, November 18, 1955.

made to show where they used to keep certain objects. I gave him before leaving a very brief description of my findings — number of columns; written in Hebrew with Aramaisms in vocabulary and forms; a brief description of its contents — to do with the buildings, possibly throwing some light on the Sect's possessions, and the like. I only hope I have done the right thing. Since he was collecting information for the Government, I thought it best to be obscure.[30]

Obscuring the issue was not John's way at all, but both Harding and de Vaux exhorted secrecy. Of course, they were afraid that one hint of buried gold would mean that all the ancient sites would be turned upside down by treasure-seekers. John concurred in this, and changed his mind about broadcasting the exciting news too widely:

"If you find anything, the news will spread like wildfire, and no site in the vicinity will be safe to leave through another summer. I need hardly say that I should more than welcome the chance to come out again this spring and take part in the hunt. I could also bring back the strips of scroll with me, since you will want to refer to the originals to check my readings. But perhaps Gerald would sooner they were left here for the time being."[31] He planned at least to bring the transcriptions, translations, and photographs.

De Vaux was even keeping the rest of the team in the dark on the Copper Scroll. Strugnell wrote to John, after telling him about the latest influx of scroll fragments from Cave Four, "You deserve congratulations on the frustratingly vague pieces of information you gave us about the copper scroll — Frank also seems in agonies of ignorance."[32]

John felt just as awkward about not being able to talk openly with his colleagues.

I am the more grateful for your speedy passing on of the news [on the new finds], in view of the fact that I am having to be so reticent about 3Q [the Copper Scroll], and clearly you are taking it very decently. You will understand only too well when we are able to release the news why we are having to be so cagey: A rumour reaching the outside world could be disastrous.[33]

Less than wholehearted support from his own department in the university added to the awkwardness. Rowley had informed him he could not expect

---

30. *Ibid.*
31. J. M. Allegro to R. de Vaux, November 18, 1955.
32. John Strugnell (JS) to J. M. Allegro, December 13, 1955.
33. JMA to JS, December 20, 1955.

to have his fares to Jordan paid for work on the scrolls — "after all, I'm only an assistant lecturer," wrote John. The College of Technology staff were friendlier, and "far more interested in the scrolls than our department. Since the copper scroll came to them they have been agog with excitement. I have already given a background talk to their SCR [Senior Common Room] on the Scrollery, and they were very thrilled. Now they are laying on a large public lecture on the subject and are going to pay me quite handsomely to give it, I gather."[34]

In the text of the Copper Scroll, John found a few allusions that he thought backed up the historical references he had identified in the *Nahum Commentary*. The others had been cautiously interested in these. However, the identification was not completely obvious, and without solid agreement it was difficult to be sure about the Copper Scroll allusions. Indeed, it was difficult to convince anyone of anything from over two thousand miles away; they all would have felt on firmer ground, and would have been able to argue with more substance and less heat, if they had been together in the Scrollery. Writing from the United States, Frank Cross perceived the tantalizing possibilities of John's discovery and the frustration of not being there to confirm them:

"Needless to say I am beside myself with news coming in from you on the copper scrolls, and especially that everything is beginning to look towards a more or less consistent solution to the problems of the history of the damned sect." He was cautiously intrigued by John's historical references: "As for the *kepir haharon* and *Yaunay,* I think you are on the trail of something. As you know, I've been inclined to identify them . . . the historical connection is tantalizing and ought to crack open soon. Nuts! At long range all I can do is speculate."[35]

An air of friendly collaboration breezed through the correspondence during these weeks. De Vaux urged John to hurry up with his Copper Scroll transcriptions and translations, acknowledging that it would take a heroic effort not to tell about them. John sent what he had, and told him he had applied for leave to return to Jordan in the spring and how he hoped to avoid Rowley, who was also intending a spot of archeologizing there.

John dropped into the conversation a mention of something he found in his scroll fragments that was later to prove of volcanic consequence.

I have discovered a reading in one of my *pesers* which seems to give absolute proof that the MZ [Teacher of Righteousness] was expected to rise again at the end of time, and from other places that he was crucified at the

34. *Ibid.*
35. F. Cross (FC) to J. M. Allegro, November 3, 1955.

hands of *goyim* [Gentiles] and was expected to rise again as Messiah. We can now with confidence reckon the beginning of the sect to about 90 B.C., and see the main reason for persecution by Jannaeus as the usurpation by the Teacher of the duties of the High Priest — what else can the Temple of Qumran and the sacrificial paraphernalia hidden there indicate?[36]

Pieces of the story were coming together. He wrote to Harding: "This exciting new stuff about the Messiahs is all in my fragments, a bit here and a bit there, with deductions from the evidence which seem to me inescapable."[37] In the *Commentary on Nahum* he found references to the Teacher being dragged out while sacrificing to be hanged on a tree. The Copper Scroll list included "the sepulcher of the son of sleep, the hanged man," and in various places the Teacher was called the Messiah, expected to rise from the dead to return at the end of time.

A crucifixion and resurrection that foreshadowed Christianity? The implications disturbed de Vaux. He immediately begged John not to rush into print on it: There had already been more than enough speculation coming from careless leaks of information about the scrolls. On both the Copper Scroll and the *peser Nahum,* only wait, he urged. Come in the spring; talk it over and compare your interpretations with the team's. It was essential to be sure of the translation.

John was sure. His *peser Nahum* article was ready to send off to the *Journal of Biblical Literature,* and, as he told John Strugnell:

> I have completed the scripts of my three BBC Northern Home Service broadcasts, and I think we can look for fireworks. Pat may have told you that recent study of my fragments has convinced me that Dupont-Sommer is more right than he knew.[38]

André Dupont-Sommer of the Sorbonne had — bravely — suggested that the Teacher of Righteousness was a blueprint for Jesus Christ,[39] and he had been condemned on all sides for the suggestion. John was pursuing a similar line, with reservations, and anticipated a similar reception. What he did not expect was that the fireworks would come from his own colleagues. He did not commit himself so far as Dupont-Sommer — he more readily ac-

36. JMA to de Vaux, December 2, 1955.
37. JMA to GLH, February 3, 1956.
38. JMA to JS, December 20, 1955.
39. A. Dupont-Sommer, *Observations sur le Manuel de Discipline découvert près de la Mer Morte* (Paris: Maisonneuve, 1951).

Portrait of John in 1956

knowledged the differences between the Teacher and Christ — but he felt the similarities between the two figures were obvious, inescapably so.

John was naïve to assume that everyone else would find them equally inescapable. What was really inescapable was the effect the comparison was about to have on the church. Theologians had to ask again where the stories of Jesus came from: Were they, after all, less a unique revelation from God than a set of traditions grounded in the history and manner of thinking of first-century Jews?

Two free-thinking generations later, at least in Britain, the dichotomy seems not just simplistic but incredible. Why ever should a religion not be grounded in the thought and culture of its first followers? But in the 1950s it seemed that fewer people blinked at and more people basked in the sunshine of the state religion. To John, understanding meant enlightenment, and surely everyone wanted to be enlightened. It also meant discarding the irrational. He did not see that he was playing with the fears and hopes and whole worldview of people whose outlook depended on the received wisdom of Christianity. So he boasted lightly to Strugnell, who was then looking for a more permanent job: "I wouldn't worry about that theological job if I were you. By the time I've finished there won't be any church left for you to join."[40]

Strugnell replied in casual tones that he hoped John would be able to come out in the spring or summer:

> to pretend to work together again, and just natter about problems like we did last summer — we might at least find out what lies behind your sudden adhesion to Dupont-Sommerism. . . . Could you send, or get the BBC to send, a copy of your broadcasts out to us here? It would be interesting.[41]

John failed to notice the sheathed claws.

40. *Ibid.*
41. JS to JMA, January 3, 1956.

CHAPTER 4

A Rift Occurs

The Three Radio Talks

John's three fifteen-minute talks went out on the BBC Northern Home Service on January 16, 23, and 30, 1956. The first told the story of the discovery of the scrolls. The second outlined their content and placed the founding of the sect in its historical context. The third described the light the scrolls shed on Christian origins.

The first talk gave a vivid but straightforward account of the first discoveries, leading up to the formation of the international team and their work in the Jerusalem Scrollery. The second gave more details of the scrolls themselves: how they were made, the writings they contained, and the significance of these for biblical study. It also described the ruins of the settlement at Qumran and its historical background. As in his book *The Dead Sea Scrolls*, John assumed it to be a monastery and ascribed its foundation to a group of pious Jews under their leader the Teacher of Righteousness, driven into the desert by the "most hated of priest-kings," Alexander Jannaeus. John identified Jannaeus with the "Wicked Priest" and the "Lion of Wrath" whom the scrolls allege to have persecuted the Teacher and his sect.

The Teacher, he said, was a remarkable character who won the devotion of his followers and could well have written some of the hymns found in the scrolls and instituted the rules of the monastery. In this broadcast, John went on to say:

> But most remarkable of all is his manner of death, and the significance attributed by his disciples to its consequences.

Probably hardly a decade after they had established themselves in their simple buildings at Qumran, the terrible Jannaeus, the Wicked Priest as they called him, stormed down to their new home, dragged forth the Teacher, and as now seems probable, gave him into the hands of his Gentile troops to be crucified. Already in Jerusalem this Jewish tyrant had displayed his bestiality by inflicting the same awful death on eight hundred rebels, and a Qumran manuscript speaks in shocked tones of the enormity of this crime. For to a Jew, this death was the most accursed of all, since the body normally found no resting place but was left to moulder on the cross.

But when the Jewish king had left, and peace descended once more on Qumran, the scattered community returned and took down the broken body of their Master, to stand guard over it until the Judgement Day. For they believed that the terrible events of their time were surely heralding the Visitation of God Himself, when the enemies of Truth would be scattered and the Kingdom of Heaven come on earth. In that glorious day, they believed their Master would rise again, and lead his faithful flock, the people of the New Testament, as they called themselves, to a new and purified Jerusalem.[1]

Should John have foreseen the storm that the mention of crucifixion would spark? He does hedge the reference with "as now seems probable." He was certain of it himself, because the scrolls refer to "the hanged man" and "the tree" and speak with such horror of Jannaeus' crucifixion of eight hundred men as something "never before done in Israel" that it must have had particular significance for the writers. They do not speak explicitly of standing guard over a broken body, but once crucified the body would have been broken, and faithful disciples would have tended it. John thought he was retelling dramatic events with imagination and sympathy but no great shuffle of the evidence. Christian commentators saw it as a groundless takeover of the Jesus story, for nowhere is it stated explicitly that Jannaeus or anyone else crucified the Teacher of Righteousness. (Indeed, later scholars asserted that it was not the Teacher who was crucified, but another Jewish leader's opponents, who had been plotting in league with a Syrian Greek king.)[2]

The reaction took John by surprise. He told Strugnell: "A lot of stupid statements have lately been attributed to me, for which I am receiving unmerited blasts. On Tuesday the *New York Times* misreported at least one paragraph of my broadcast talks."[3]

1. J. M. Allegro, Broadcast Talk for BBC Northern Home Service, January 23, 1956.
2. *The Times* (London), December 27, 1991.
3. J. M. Allegro to J. Strugnell (JS), January 27, 1956.

What the newspaper did was to insert a few more imaginative details of its own: a reference to a sacrifice they said the Teacher was offering at the time Jannaeus dragged him out, a reference to his body being reverently buried in a tomb nearby, and the mention of "a recently discovered manuscript." The article stated:

> Eventually, Mr Allegro said, he [Jannaeus] descended on the Qumran community, "dragged forth the Teacher as he himself was offering sacrifice at the altar and, as now seems probable from a recently discovered manuscript, gave him into the hands of his Gentile mercenaries to be crucified." Mr Allegro ended by saying that when the tyrant left, "the scattered disciples returned and reverently buried the body of their Teacher in a tomb near by, where they settled down in the way of life he had ordained for them, to await his glorious return as Messiah of God."[4]

As the transcript shows, John's words were that the Wicked Priest Jannaeus "dragged forth the Teacher, and, as now seems probable, gave him into the hands of his Gentile troops to be crucified. . . . But when the Jewish king had left, and peace descended once more on Qumran, the scattered community returned, and took down the broken body of their Master to stand guard over it until the Judgement Day." He had not put in any reference to a sacrificial altar (though from archeological evidence — remains of pots containing bones — he did think it was likely), nor to a recently discovered manuscript, nor to a tomb nearby.

In the third talk, John drew the parallels more clearly: "Last week I said that the leader of this monastic community by the Dead Sea was persecuted and probably crucified by Gentiles at the instigation of a wicked priest of the Jews. For most of us, these events will associate themselves automatically with the betrayal and crucifixion of another Master, living nearly a century later." He went on to point out the many similarities in terms and ideas between the scrolls and certain New Testament writings, especially the fourth gospel and many of the ideas of St. Paul. Also, the scrolls included a collection of *testimonia,* "proof texts," a set of stock quotations from Old Testament prophecy — the same texts that early Christian writers would later use to support their messianic claims for Jesus whenever the occasion demanded. "It is, therefore, not impossible that the Church was able to take over such collections compiled long before its time by a similar religious community," John concluded.

Then there was the general air of messianic expectation: that a new age was fast approaching, with a tremendous battle imminent between the pow-

4. *New York Times,* January 24, 1956.

ers of good and evil, light and dark, a battle that echoed the struggle in the heart of every person between good and bad spirits. Jesus, like John the Baptist and the Qumran community, called people to overcome the spirit of darkness within by true repentance and obedience to God's law. And as Jesus carried to the cross the sins of the world, "the Qumran community also saw in the agonies of their Master and his followers an atonement for the world's iniquity." Penitence, atonement, exile in the wilderness in the time of trial (or "temptation"): all were to lead to a blessed release.

"Additional evidence," John continued, "now supports the idea that they expected the return of their priestly Master, glorified as the messianic High Priest of Israel. He would awaken from his tomb and lead the faithful from Qumran to the New Jerusalem, and there inaugurate an era of peace and plenty for a cleansed mankind, sharing its joys with the host of saints in Heaven."

Qumran and the church both expected their respective leader to return as messiah. Their views were not mutually exclusive. The scrolls refer to two messiahs: a priestly messiah (the Teacher of Righteousness), who would act as mediator between God and the people and govern all issues of faith; and the Davidic messiah, who would take an executive role in slaying the wicked and maintaining order. The priestly messiah took precedence, as is made clear in the rite of the Messianic Banquet, "already proposed by scholars to be the basic element of the Lord's Supper, or Holy Communion," John noted.

All these correspondences point at the very least to a common religious background for both the early Church and the Qumran sect. If, as has been suggested, they both have their roots in that rather ill-defined religious group called the Essenes, much is explained. We know from the ancient historians that there were cells of these pious folk living in the towns and villages of Palestine in Jesus' time, a kind of 'lay order' emulating as far as possible the irreproachable lives of their brethren in a monastic center by the Dead Sea whose geographical location would well suit Qumran.

It would not, then, be difficult to see how the disciples, and, indeed, Jesus himself, could have come in contact with Qumran doctrines and even documents. However that may be, there was nothing in the idea of a crucified Master, atoning for the world's sin in His suffering, and expected to rise again in glory as Messiah, which would have seemed out of place in the experience and most cherished hopes of our sect by the Dead Sea.[5]

5. JMA, Broadcast Talk for BBC Northern Home Service, January 30, 1956.

The *New York Times* trumpeted: "The origins of some Christian rituals and doctrines can be seen in the documents of an extremist Jewish sect that existed for more than 100 years before the birth of Jesus Christ." It went on to give a fair summary of John's talk but added, "He has also seen what he calls the 'dramatic contents' of one copper scroll now being examined in Manchester," and quoted the initial reaction of a Roman Catholic commentator: "'Any stick now seems big enough to use against Christianity' if it tends 'to dislodge belief in the uniqueness of Jesus.'"[6]

De Vaux took fundamental exception to broadcasting the idea of another crucifixion and resurrection. Harding assumed from the paper's invented reference to "a recently discovered manuscript" in the second talk and to "the dramatic contents" of the Copper Scroll in the third that John had been talking to the press about the Copper Scroll, betraying his promises to keep quiet on the subject. On February 11, 1956, de Vaux wrote in dismay to John, telling him that he had flouted the conventions that governed the work of the team. As soon as they had read the press articles, Strugnell, Milik, Skehan, and Starcky had gone to the museum in Jerusalem to look at the texts for themselves. He wrote to John, "There is *nothing* there that corresponds to your claims. Either you have made false readings, or you have interpreted the text arbitrarily. We are all compromised by your intervention."

De Vaux denied that this was a theological objection: They knew Jannaeus had already crucified eight hundred Pharisees, so one more hardly counted.

"It is not permissible that you should give out such conclusions without furnishing your proofs, i.e. the texts on which you base them," de Vaux continued. But since he had, and to a gullible public, it was now essential to provide with the utmost urgency the photographs and transcriptions of the evidence for the crucifixion of the Teacher of Righteousness at the hands of pagan mercenaries, his removal from the cross, and the guard of his body kept by his followers.[7]

John was puzzled by the fuss. On February 9 he had written to de Vaux:

I am accused of saying the most astounding things, some of which are true and are indeed astounding, others come from the bosom of eager reporters. I think Harding is under the impression that I held a press conference on 3Q [the Copper Scroll], or some other nonsense, which is of course quite untrue. I have written to him today, with details of what was

6. *New York Times,* February 5, 1956.
7. R. de Vaux to J. M. Allegro, February 11, 1956.

said and where. I think, also, that he believes that my broadcast talks contained references to items in 3Q. This, again, is quite untrue, and anything I said I can back with references to my leather fragments only. The trouble is that the little I said which was new, was taken out of its context and given (in an erroneous form) ridiculous weight.

The item which has caused most upset apparently is the mention of the Teacher being crucified. I said in the broadcast that this was possible: It is now *certain*. I have already sent Gerald a first translation of the first col. of 3Q. It contains the phrase: *bnps bn dmk hslysy,* 'in the sepulcher of the Son of Sleep, the Crucified (or Hanged)'. With this is to be read 4QpNah [*pesher* Nahum, a commentary on Nahum found in Cave 4 at Qumran]; speaking of the Lion of Wrath, Jannaeus, 'he used to hang men up alive [which was never] before [done] in Israel, for the man hung alive is called *sl[ysy]*. . . '.

Of course, the reading in pNah [*pesher* on Nahum] has become certain only since I read 3Q, and my original ground for believing that the Teacher shared this punishment was that immediately after describing this punishment, the writer says '*trph:* its interpretation concerns the Priest who. . . '.

. . . For the resurrection of the Teacher, my pPs127 [*pesher* on Psalm 127] . . . speaks of the Teacher and the 'end of time', and if you can make that refer to anything but his rising at the end of time I should like to hear it. Coupled with this is the calling of the Teacher 'The Last Priest' in a pHos [*pesher* on Hosea] . . . saying, in effect, that in the last days this Last Priest would get his revenge. Besides these references, of course, there is the mention of the coming of the Teacher of Righteousness in the last days in CD,[8] and the 'Interpreter of the Law' with the Davidic Messiah in my 4Q Florilegium.[9]

I hope I have written enough to convince you that I have not spoken without a good measure of documentary backing, even discounting 3Q, which, as I said, I have not used. Gerald implied that this was so, and I am very unhappy that you should think I should be so rash. I value your continued friendship too highly to let it rest there. In any case, *in their context* my remarks were not so staggering or new.

De Vaux was not convinced by this evidence. But before he had received it, and even before he had seen the text of the radio talks, he told John that, in

---

8. The Cairo Damascus document, found in fragments at Qumran and also as incomplete tenth- and twefth-century copies in a Cairo synagogue.

9. A text from Cave 4 about the "Last Days."

full accord with G. L. Harding, they would be sending a formal denial to the English and American press.[10]

After all the evidence that the team had been uncovering on the thought and philosophy of the sect, and previous interpretations by Dupont-Sommer and others, John had assumed that nothing in his radio talks would startle any fellow scholars. He expected fireworks, as he had told Strugnell, but not from academic circles. He thought his colleagues would be interested, naturally, but not so dazzled that they would turn as one person against him to deny his theories outright without any attempt at scholarly discussion. It seemed to him that they were responding in kind to a journalistic shower of sparks, a response he thought superficial in itself but of disproportionate effect.

They held that to say anything in public about the scrolls without discussing it with them and exposing it in a learned journal was rash and unscholarly. John was not minded to wait for a learned journal. He held that he was the scholar, and had more right than anyone to speak out on what he believed to be the truth. And everyone else had the right to hear it. And if he had not spoken out, no one would take any notice.

The Rift Made Public

In late February, John wrote letters to de Vaux and to Hunzinger about the media controversy.

20 February 1956

Dear Pere de Vaux

You will excuse me if I think that everyone in the world is going stark, raving mad. I am enclosing my broadcast talks, as you request, and if, after reading them, you are left wondering what all the fuss is about, you will be in precisely my own position. The journalistic riot which they appear to be having in the States is quite fantastic and mostly quite divorced from any point I have made. It is not without significance that such madness has been quite absent from the newspapers in this country where the broadcast was made. In fact, apart from enquiries from many calmly interested listeners, the things have passed off without undue comment. I respectfully suggest that a little more of this calm appraisal from other quarters would not come amiss. As for rushing into publication with scraps from my section of the scrolls, the answer is certainly not. My work on the fragments progresses normally the whole time, and when I am ready I shall,

10. R. de Vaux to J. M. Allegro, February 11, 1956

with your permission as editor-in-chief, publish the most important fragments. My *peser Nahum* is under way and will soon be ready for despatch. As a matter of fact, I had fully planned to have had it published before my broadcasts were made, but holding it back for 3Q has delayed it, and the talks could not, of course, be postponed at the last moment.

. . . As for the rest you are suddenly asking me to publish, you are asking too much. My information for these talks has been taken from all over my section. Are you seriously asking that pHos, pIsa, Testimonia, Florilegium, pPs 37, pPs 127 should all be published in the next BASOR? What I do think might be a good idea, and I was going to suggest it as a possible additional 15-minute paper at the International OT Soc. in August, if you agreed, is a fairly short article on 'Messianic Terminology in Qumran,' or the like.

I am rather amused by the idea of Strugnell and Milik preparing to demolish the dragon: I somehow feel that they will find themselves beating thin air! I am not waging any war against the Church, and if I were, you may rest assured I would not let any loopholes in a publication for John or Milch to jump in. I stand by everything I said in my three talks, but I am quite prepared to believe that there may be other interpretations of my readings and was more cautious than it served the purpose of certain newspapers to convey to their readers. You will find that caution reflected in any publication of scrollery that I make in learned journals — mine is not the habit of using such official publications as debating channels.

Tomorrow Yadin and I in Manchester are doing a trans-Atlantic broadcast discussion with two characters in New York. I shall take the opportunity of scotching some of the things which are being reported over there and putting the thing in perspective. That, together with a dignified silence (particularly where the press is concerned), is far more dampening to such nonsense than jumping into the fray with hasty and ill-formulated publications.

26 February 1956

Dear Baron [Claus-Hunno Hunzinger]

You may have heard a lot of fantastic rumours circulating by way of that hot-bed of hysteria, America, recently. These arose out of some very innocent radio talks I gave here recently, which were badly reported to the States and started off a witch-hunt. I am the great ecumenical movement of the history of the Church. A Roman priest, a Jew and a Presbyterian joined in one voice to condemn me to outer darkness. I have been blooded with letters from irate scholars over there, wanting to know what the hell, etc. . . . But here in England, hardly a whisper has been raised, apart from interested comments from listeners, for indeed there was very little in the talks of a revolutionary nature. And nothing from 3Q, despite fantastic rumours to the contrary.

. . . I think on consideration that the Teacher is expected to share in a general resurrection (after the Daniel 12.2 type), and that being the case, was expected to rise again as Messiah. I think it's quite possible that Jannaeus may have crucified the blighter, since such was his wont to do to political enemies, and I think the Teacher was one. For I am pretty certain that they had a temporary sanctuary down there, and that the Teacher was acting as High Priest, and thus deserving the death of a rebel. I believe I am quoted as saying that this makes him a pattern for Jesus and so on and so on — with the widest conclusions being drawn. This is, of course, sheer nonsense, though I do think (privately) that the manner of his death may have influenced Jesus to expect something similar, though I've not said so anywhere. The contacts between what the sect expected of the Davidic Messiah and what the Church quotes about Jesus are, however, most impressive, and I have no doubt that Jesus fitted *formally* into a pre-existent messianic pattern. This doesn't strike me as being particularly new, and in any case, in no way militates against the Church's position on the person of Jesus as far as I can see.

The formal messianic pattern was based on Old Testament prophecy and included elements such as the sojourn in the wilderness, the council of twelve, the messianic banquet, resurrection, and the battle of light against dark in the imminent apocalypse. In John Allegro's view, this was clearly distinct from the Christian idea that Jesus was a divine but historical figure. If he were, his followers could still make his story fit into the existing pattern of religious thought, and from the pattern it would have gained deeper significance and credibility in their eyes. Unlike scholars such as Teicher and Dupont-Sommer, John accepted that Jesus came of a different age and with a totally different message from the Teacher of Righteousness; nevertheless, his story as told (especially in the fourth gospel) draws on much of the language, imagery, and tradition of the scrolls.

John underestimated the flammability of Christian sensibility. Many people felt it heretical to question whether the gospel story was really whole, perfect, and unique, and they disregarded the obvious inconsistencies between the versions. And John overestimated people's ability to distinguish between historical narrative and underlying religious framework. People had painted so much fervor into their picture of Jesus Christ, their friend and savior, and had built such an edifice of morality and authority upon the idea that he was the one and only son of God, that a different perspective disturbed them deeply. So newspaper reports of a teacher who prefigured Jesus slurred the distinctions that John tried to draw and threatened to shake the assumptions of those who believed that Jesus was a unique divine being.

Frank Cross, writing from the States, urged John to defuse the row by publishing the *peser Nahum* and whatever other evidence he had as quickly as possible. Besieged by demands for information, Cross was having to explain to everyone that he personally had seen no proof for the "crucified messiah" theory, that he agreed that the Wicked Priest was probably Jannaeus, but that he remained to be convinced that the sectarians thought the Teacher of Righteousness a priestly messiah.[11] John wrote back gratefully with the facts he thought should convince him, enclosing the *peser Nahum* article and congratulating him on his promotion at Harvard — "not only because this Christianity business is played out (!), but because you can work more on research, and without the ties of denominational calls."[12]

The Second Part of the Copper Scroll

Meanwhile, the second copper roll had arrived in Manchester. John told Harding he had met the envoy and deposited the scroll at Wright Baker's bank: "How you must have breathed a sigh of relief to see it go; as much as I did to see Muhammed [Muhammed Salih, Harding's assistant] on London Road Station with a large box."[13]

A week later, the opening began.

> Just a line or two to let you know that at 5pm this afternoon the first slice was lifted off the cake. Very fragile it was too, and cut extremely quickly — something like three minutes. However, the Araldite held it together while Wright Baker manipulated it free, and it came away in one beautiful piece containing most of one column. We packed up immediately after, but a fine gentle brushing revealed the words 'and gold', so we're off again. Tomorrow we shall clean this piece, first giving it another coating with the dope on the outside, and whilst Muhammed and I do that, Baker will prepare for the second cut. If it all goes as well as today's, we should be finished with the cutting in ten days or so.
>
> Excitement runs high again.[14]

11. F. Cross (FC) to J. M. Allegro, February 27, 1956.
12. JMA to FC, March 6, 1956.
13. J. M. Allegro to G. L. Harding (GLH), January 3, 1956.
14. JMA to GLH, January 11, 1956.

John was planning to make a transcription and translation as before, ideally to take them back to Jerusalem with him at the end of term to discuss with Harding and the team. However, the university refused to pay his fare. But apart from that, his three talks went out on the air, the *New York Times* reported, or mis-reported, them, the Scrollery team picked up on the reports, and everything changed for John in Jerusalem.

Harding, as mentioned earlier, immediately thought that John had been talking to the press about the Copper Scroll. John hadn't, beyond mentioning that it was there. He had told Harding this. Having assured de Vaux of the same (in the letter of February 9), John assumed his denial was the end of the matter. Not realizing the depth of the rift, he went on writing to Harding on the question of publicity. He reiterated the fact that he had given away no secrets about the Copper Scroll, then went on to discuss what might actually be said about it, bearing in mind the interests of the other people involved — the British Council, the College of Technology, and members of the public who had paid for it to come:

11 February 1956

Dear Gerald

Viewing the subject of our recent correspondence rather more dispassionately now that a few days have passed, it seems to me that one or two points of interest might be raised at this juncture. However unfortunate the mention of the 3Q object might have proved to be, it did at any rate serve as a blind for the arrival of Muhammed with No. 2. I was at all times careful to avoid any reference to this event, and as far as I am aware nothing has been said here on the subject. At least, I was asked questions but adroitly put the questioners off. I also rang the British Council [BC] chap here, then Scott, the day after Salih arrived, and asked him not to make any statement to the Press on the matter, and he very decently agreed not to. But he did say then that he hoped very much that a statement could be made before too long and that the BC be given all credit due to them for the outlay of funds and time. Knowing something of the difficulties that admirable organisation has to face in getting funds, I felt for him in this matter. As he says, so often the subject of the work being done under their patronage gets the limelight and everybody forgets to mention the BC's part in it. I mention it now, because I do hope you will find it possible to release the news of No. 2's coming, and give the BC their share of the credit. Also, I do think it would be advisable to let Wright Baker make known very soon the manner of his work on them both. Not only will this scotch any silly ideas that may be knocking about concerning the process but will give the credit to the Tech, due to them, and would round off their generous work on the project very nicely, without necessarily giving anything away on the contents. I know that Baker is keen on doing this.

It could be done in a private lecture here. He actually thought of slipping it in at the end of one I am supposed to be giving on the Scrolls generally at the Tech by invitation of the governors. I would ask you to consider seriously another suggestion however. It is pretty clearly going to be impossible to arrange a public viewing of 3Q before it leaves this country. Whilst I, knowing the contents, can understand this, the general tax-paying public may well feel more than a little grieved when they are told that their money brought it here and took it away again and they were never given the chance even to catch a glimpse of it. This is not the way to keep public interest alive here, and by golly we need it if we are ever going to get that 'central fund' I am pleading for in my book. Actually, interest is mounting nicely here; not with sensational excerpts from my talks as in America, but sensibly. For instance, I was asked by the BBC this week to give a five-minute talk on 'Home and Abroad' (a Prime-Ministerish sort of programme, rather high class) on the recent Israeli release on the 'Lamech' scroll. I gave it last night and was able to put the thing into perspective with the whole of the Scrolls material, particularly our side of it. I also took pains to correct the report in several newspapers that this was the last of *all* the Scrolls to be opened and deciphered. (Incidentally, I did not mention even the *finding* of the 3Q thing, which probably caused more perplexity still, but orders is orders!) I mention this only as an example of how intelligent interest is growing here, although we are nine years behind the rest of the world, thanks to Driver and Co. What I suggest about the eventual release on the opening is a short TV (five-ten minutes) feature, using perhaps my film of the actual operation. This will give nothing away and make the public feel they are really in on the thing, and that their money has been used to good purpose. That is why I asked permission from you to bring in cameramen from the BBC for the purpose. You haven't replied, and it will be too late by the time you get this, for apparently Salih is planning to take the 3Q pieces down to London in less than a week (presumably whether the final readings are made or not — but that is your business). But with what we've got, plus some long views of the opened pieces, we could put together a nice little programme, which would be worth its weight literally in gold when we come begging again. Do think about it seriously, and after consultation with your Minister, let me know what you think.

The University have turned down my request for the fare to Jordan this Spring. I had been hoping to leave on the 10th of March, and bring with me complete transliterations and photographs of the Thing, and perhaps make myself useful to yourself and de Vaux, as well as going over the last received fragments. If you think that I could be of some service, I'll try any other source I can think of. Please accept my profuse apologies for any trouble I have unwittingly caused.

At this date, John would not have received de Vaux's letter of February 11 and was quite unaware of the reaction he had ignited in Jerusalem. Nor did he realize the absolute certainty (and panic) with which Harding decided he had betrayed his promise. The tone of John's letter is that of a scholar committed to working within the team on their mutual project, while bearing in mind the interests of the general public, who, after all, would be paying for the continuation of that project. It is not the tone of a self-seeker or renegade, which is apparently how some of his colleagues viewed him.

Harding did not reply. John found that he was neither welcome in Wright Baker's laboratory nor allowed to attend his lecture, in case he let slip any information on the content of the scroll to the crowds who wanted to question him about it. Bemused, he went on preparing the transcription and translation as best he could; within the week he had sent them off to Jerusalem. He wrote himself to Dr. Bowden, Principal of the College of Technology, on February 18, 1956:

> I expect that Mr. Harding will be writing to you shortly on behalf of the Jordan Government, but I should like to express my own personal gratitude for the enthusiasm with which you first welcomed this difficult task, and for your continued hospitality during the time I have been engaged on the reading.
>
> When the full story can be told, it will, I am sure, be evident to what extent the world of scholarship stands indebted to the generous facilities offered by yourself and the Board of Governors of the College, and to the skill shown by Professor Wright Baker in this difficult assignment.

But the full story was not told. John waited and waited. He put off the people who inquired every day; he held back the publication of his book; he watched time, interest, and money drain away from one of the most exciting adventures in modern Middle Eastern archeology.

With the team turning against him, John's attitude sharpened. He saw issues that needed discussing then and there; he was in no mood to prevaricate over the interpretation of scrolls. He believed in open argument, free thought, plain facts, and a clear-eyed view of the past and present, untrammeled by religious tradition or vested interests. He believed the Dead Sea Scrolls gave an insight into the life and thought of first-century Palestine and therefore a framework into which early Christianity must fit. He knew he was certainly not the first to question the perception of Christianity as a God-given apple that dropped into the lap of humanity, unique, ripe, and perfect, with the birth of baby Jesus. But if that perception prevailed, for the sake of twentieth-century honesty and clarity of thought John reckoned it was time to cut the apple.

Harding's suspicions over the Copper Scroll had by now turned to poison. Dismissing the references in the American press to its "dramatic contents," John had insisted he had not used the scroll in framing his theory about the Teacher's crucifixion. Yet he had told de Vaux that the reference in the Copper Scroll to "the sepulcher of the son of sleep, or the hanged man" had made him certain of his interpretation. He evidently meant that the evidence from the fragments was enough to prove the point, but that the reference in 3Q had confirmed his view in his own mind. He had certainly not quoted the phrase to anyone nor indicated what was in the Copper Scroll — all he had acknowledged in public was that the scroll was in Manchester and that he was working on it. But after the radio talks, or rather after hearing how the talks were received, Harding and de Vaux did not know whom to trust. Even when they read the scripts, they discounted the fact that John had called the crucifixion of the Teacher merely "probable" and had intended his account of the Teacher's story to be taken as an imaginative reconstruction: "We found in them *all* that had astonished us in the press reports . . . you cannot say that the press have distorted what you said."[15] So they were not minded to believe John when he denied giving out news on the Copper Scroll. They realized they had lost control of John. Instead, they did their best to control the response of all who came into contact with him.

Updating Frank Cross on progress with his articles, John wrote wearily:

> 3Q, with twelve columns of text, is away to Jordan, or at least the transcription and translation of it is. Muhammed Salih brought the second part over, but not for a month after we had cut the first, and by that time term was on us again, and it has been a mad rush doing everything at once. To make matters worse, Salih has made himself a blasted nuisance the whole time, spying on everything that was said in the Tech during the week, reporting back every word to Harding and the Ambassador, until in the end they all seemed to think we were trying to sell the thing to the Jews. Looking for a scapegoat, they settled on me, so that everything I have done on the job has been discredited, and every attempt made to belittle my contribution to all parts of the work. However, I have read it, and sent them a full translation (though provisional) and

---

15. De Vaux to JMA, March 4, 1956.

notes. But the affair has left a nasty taste, and I am heartily sick of all scrollery at the moment.[16]

The day before, John had written to Harding:

2 March 1956

Dear Gerald

I have received no acknowledgement of the safe arrival of the transcriptions and translations. However, this is hardly surprising in view of the treatment I have received at your and your minions' hands, and common courtesy has become a rarity from Jordan.

Your instructions have been carried out to the letter, probably even more. The release has been made of the cutting, my participation has been denied, and no credit has come to me for advising on every cut made, or reading and forwarding the transcriptions and translations. Wright Baker is apparently going round telling everybody, including my professors, that I have been definitely discredited by my colleagues in Jordan, and generally casting doubt on my personal and academic integrity. Salih is doing the same, only more so.

I presume this is all in accordance with your instructions, and I hope you are now satisfied.

On March 4, de Vaux notified John that the team in Jerusalem "will be sending a letter to the editor of *The Times* (of London) to say that in our opinion your claim about the crucifixion of the Teacher of Righteousness, his removal from the cross, and the guard by his disciples waiting for his resurrection cannot be found in any text properly read and interpreted."

7 March 1956

Dear Pere de Vaux

I have your letter of the 4th of March, and note with interest that you are sending a letter to the *London Times* with a rejection of my conclusions. This should be most interesting to the London public, who have never heard my broadcasts. I have already pointed out to you that these broadcasts were made on the local Northern station, as printed on the scripts, and the passages you take exception to were not extracted from their context by the press of this country, even in the North where they were heard. You and your friends are now apparently going to draw the attention of the gutter press of this country to these passages, of which

16. JMA to FC, March 3, 1956.

neither they nor the majority of their readers have heard, and start a witch-hunt over them. I congratulate you. What will certainly happen is that this press, scenting trouble, will descend like hawks on me and want to know what it is all about. They will then rush to the BBC, get copies of the scripts, and do in this country precisely what the American press has already done over there. Only this time they will have added fuel in what appears on the face of it to be a controversy developing between the ecclesiastics of the scroll team and the one unattached member. Having regard to what Wilson [the American critic Edmund Wilson, writing in 1955] has already said about the unwillingness of the Church to tackle these texts objectively, you can imagine what will be made out of this rumpus.

With all respect, I must point out to you that this nonsense of Wilson's has been taken seriously here. At every lecture on the scrolls I give, the same old question pops up: Is it true that the Church is scared of the scrolls, and can we be sure that *everything* will be published? That may sound silly to you and me, but it is a serious doubt in the minds of ordinary folk, particularly in this Protestant country. I need hardly add what effect the signatures of three Roman priests on the bottom of this proposed letter will have.

On Monday I am due to answer questions on the scrolls on the BBC Television service. If your letter has been published by then, a question on it will certainly be included. Tuesday morning will see the popular press full of the 'controversy', and then the fun will start. From being quietly left to die in the minds of a few thousand listeners in the North of England, these few phrases will suddenly have had a publicity before some nine million viewers, and again wrenched from their context.

Well, my dear Father de Vaux, I suppose you and your friends know what you are doing. I assure you I am not going to add fuel to the fire. But even my silence will imply to a sensationalist press that I am being gagged by my ecclesiastical colleagues. Whatever happens, I wash my hands of the whole business.

4QpNahum is away to Frank and then to Freedman for JBL [the *Journal of Biblical Literature,* edited by David Noel Freedman]. It includes a couple of passages from pPsalm 37 which I think pretty clearly point to a general resurrection after the fashion of Daniel 12.2 and the NT. I am now working on another article involving quotations from my Patriarchal Blessings, Florilegium, and pIsaiah, thus bringing together messianic material from my section. Might I suggest that before you rush again into print you see these articles, and you may possibly come to the conclusion that I have studied my material a good deal more thoroughly than anyone else in the scrollery is likely to have done?

. . . We can only hope for the best with this joint letter you are writing, or have written. I only hope for your sake that the editor of the *Times* is so completely mystified that he returns it to you. Otherwise, I fear that you are all going to look rather silly, if nothing worse. But don't say I didn't warn you about frantically beating thin air.

On March 16, 1956, the following letter appeared in the *Times:*

Dear Sir:

It has come to our attention that considerable controversy is being caused by certain broadcast statements of Mr John Allegro, of the University of Manchester, concerning the Dead Sea Scrolls. We refer particularly to such statements as imply that in these scrolls a close connection is to be found between a supposed crucifixion of the 'teacher of righteousness' of the Essene sect and the Crucifixion and the Resurrection of Jesus Christ. The announced opinions of Mr Allegro might seem to have special weight, since he is one of the group of scholars engaged in editing yet unpublished writings from Qumran.

In view of the broad repercussions of his statements, and the fact that the materials on which they are based are not yet available to the public, we, his colleagues, feel obliged to make the following statement. There are no unpublished texts at the disposal of Mr Allegro other than those of which the originals are at present in the Palestine Archaeological Museum where we are working. Upon the appearance in the Press of citations from Mr Allegro's broadcasts we have reviewed all the pertinent materials, published and unpublished. We are unable to see in the texts the 'findings' of Mr Allegro.

We find no crucifixion of the 'teacher', no deposition from the cross, and no 'broken body of their Master' to be stood guard over until Judgment Day. Therefore there is no 'well-defined Essenic pattern into which Jesus of Nazareth fits', as Mr Allegro is alleged in one report to have said. It is our conviction that either he has misread the texts or he has built up a chain of conjectures which the materials do not support.

Yours faithfully,
Roland de Vaux, O.P.
J. T. Milik
P. W. Skehan
Jean Starcky
John Strugnell

This attack on what they saw as unprofessional conjecture had the result that John had foreseen: publicity. In replying, John took the opportunity both to admit openly that his interpretations were conjectural and to establish why the conjecture was reasonable. In doing so he gave so much interesting information that readers could only be left wanting more:

20 March 1956

Sir

My attention has been drawn to a letter appearing in your columns of the 16th of March written by my colleagues of the 'Dead Sea Scrolls team' in Jerusalem. It appears they take exception to my reconstruction of the history of the Qumran sect and the death of its founder, the so-called 'Teacher of Righteousness', on the grounds that I have misread or misconstrued the evidence.

It should be appreciated by your readers, in the first place, that any such reconstruction must of necessity be based largely on inference, since nothing in the nature of a history book or 'Gospel' of the New Testament type has been or is likely to be forthcoming from Qumran. . . . We do have certain vague references in biblical commentaries from the sect's libraries, which have to be interpreted as best we can.

We know, for instance, that the teacher of righteousness was persecuted by a certain 'wicked priest', in the 'house of his exile', presumed to be Qumran. It was long ago suggested that this persecutor could be identified with Alexander Jannaeus, the Jewish priest-king of the second or first centuries BC, and this view has steadily gained ground among scholars. From Josephus we learn that Jannaeus practised the cruel punishment of crucifixion, and, indeed, on one occasion had 800 Pharisaic rebels executed in this way in Jerusalem, following an unsuccessful revolt. From this alone it would not have been an unreasonable inference that the teacher suffered the same fate, since he, too, had rebelled against the Jerusalem priesthood. But now, as my colleagues are well aware, a newly discovered biblical commentary from Qumran not only offers some support for the Jannaeus dating by certain historical allusions, but mentions this practice as crucifixion, or, as it says, 'hanging men up alive'.

Since the Qumran commentators do not refer to events unless they have some special importance for themselves or their times, we can reasonably assume that this form of execution had some particular relevance for their own history, although the commentary nowhere mentions their master. My publication of the column concerned has been unfortunately delayed for a number of reasons outside my control but should be available to scholars in the summer number of the Journal of Biblical Literature. Yet, important as this reference is, the theory remains no more than inference, claiming only probability, and I myself have never gone further than this in advancing it.

Similarly, an article on messianic allusions from various fragments was to be published shortly to substantiate the inferences on resurrection.

Yet, if indeed the covenanters did expect the resurrection of their teacher, as I am convinced they did, then they must have buried him with particular care and, if he had been crucified, taken his body down from the stake, instead of leaving it to moulder there, as was the custom with this form of execution.

I presume the real core of my colleagues' objections is in the inferences which have been drawn by others by a comparison of this hypothetic reconstruction of events with similar occurrences recorded in the Christian gospels. I, too, deplore such wide-sweeping generalisations about the historicity of the person of Jesus or the validity of the Church's claims from such points of detail . . . my talk made it clear that any further identification of the two masters was out of the question, since the one was a priest, expected to come again as a priestly Messiah, and the other was a layman, whose followers claimed for him the office of Davidic Messiah.

In the phraseology of the New Testament in this connection we find many points of resemblance to Qumran literature since the sect also were looking for the coming of a Davidic Messiah who would arise with the priest in the last days. It is in this sense that Jesus 'fits into a well-defined messianic (not 'Essenic' as I was wrongly quoted — the question of whether this sect were Essenes is still open) pattern'. There is nothing particularly new or striking in the idea. As far as I am aware, it has never been doubted that the messianic ideas and phraseology of the New Testament are taken over from Jewish sources. The importance of the scrolls is that for the first time we have contemporary documents bearing witness of this idea over the most crucial years before the Church's birth. The vast difference between the Greek Church's divine Saviour of the world and the Davidic Prince of Qumran is obvious enough. . . .

As to the question of whether I have misread my texts or not, the question can best be decided by the consensus of scholarly opinion when these texts have been published, but, in fact, it hardly affects the general inferences which I have drawn and which appear to be the subject of your correspondents' letter.

In John's terms, the scenes of the Teacher's crucifixion and burial were imaginative reconstructions and he saw nothing wrong with that. To bring history to life you need to imagine you were there. He explained why he thought the picture he painted was realistic. Since it was hypothetical, he thought it less significant than its context: the broader and undisputed correspondences in phraseology and eschatology between the scrolls and the New Testament. People's reaction had taken him by surprise: why the fuss over a hypothesis? But to church people any images of the tomb and deposition carried a deeply emotional burden. John should not really have been surprised that the sensation-seekers seized on them without paying attention to subtleties such as "probably" or "if."

However coolly John tried in public to put the argument in proportion, in private his anger was bitter:

16 March 1956

Dear Pere de Vaux and colleagues,

Your letter appeared in the *Times* today, and this evening within an hour or so of my getting home, the *Daily Express* and Reuters were on the telephone. There seems little doubt that all I foretold in my last letter will come to pass, and thanks to you, we may now expect the whole stupid business to become meat for those who are seeking to embarrass the Church.

In view of this trouble, I thought it best to reply to your letter and I enclose a copy.

In a few days I shall be sending you copies of my two articles, on pNah and the messianic material. When you have all read them, I shall expect to hear from you details of my 'misreadings' and the effect they have on the inferences I have drawn.

If you are not able to find these errors in my publications, I shall of course demand a public withdrawal, through the same channels as you have already seen fit to use, of your accusations of scholarly incompetence. You have made publicly very grievous charges and every word will have to be substantiated.

Thanks to you, and to Mr Harding, his subordinates, and Professor Wright Baker, who have circulated around the world accusations not only on my competence as a scholar but also on my personal integrity, my academic career is probably at an end. I hope this has satisfied your ecclesiastical honour.

He said more in a letter of the same date to de Vaux only:

... I am rather sorry that you saw fit to drag young Strugnell into the stupid business. I have told you in my last letter and I tell you again, that in this country not a word of these disputed passages had been given general publicity until your letter today. I hope my letter may do something to put the thing back in proportion.

However, in one respect your voluminous correspondence with scholars, including my own Professor, has had its presumably desired effect. My academic career is probably finished: I shall be lucky if I am allowed to finish my three-year contract with Manchester, and the chances of going elsewhere are nil. Harding's allegations, coupled with Wright Baker's, concerning betrayal of secrets (unspecified) have contributed. My God! When I think what I might have put into that book of mine but refrained from doing in case your release of 3Q had not been made before publication date. I even took out Sa'ad's Murabb'at story because Harding thought it might cause trouble with his employers.

Writing as calmly as though discussing a letter of the alphabet, instead of having just signed a letter blasting a colleague's reputation, Strugnell explained in his reply to John that after reading the scripts they thought his account of crucifixion and deposition unsubstantiated. "The passage that worried us was all there. Although you qualified your crucifixion with 'probably', you then elaborated your assumption with a deposition, i.e. a watch over the body, which is difficult because I cannot find nearly enough evidence for a crucifixion and none for the devotion to a crucified leader, which is such a feature of the New Testament. We wrote in *The Times* — you may have seen it — to say that we couldn't find in the texts enough to prove to our mind your theories." Strugnell went on to say that the known figure of Jesus influences ethics as well as the text of the New Testament, and "this thorough impregnation I can't find at Qumran."[17]

Strugnell had jumped to the same conclusion that the *New York Times* did: that John was saying the Teacher of Righteousness represented a direct parallel to Jesus, if not the blueprint for Jesus himself, in all sorts of ways including the ethical. For this, of course, Strugnell could find no evidence in the scrolls.

Publicity can work two ways. Having discovered the power of the press, John realized he was in a position to turn it to his advantage. The PAM team were a long way away; John was at home. He was suddenly in demand all over the country for lectures, broadcasts, and press statements, and what he said was listened to. He wrote again to de Vaux on April 13:

17. JS to JMA, March 9, 1956.

As I said in my previous letter, I shall be awaiting a clear statement of 'misinterpretations' and/or 'misreadings', and when I receive it I shall decide whether to raise the matter again in the daily press. I need hardly say that if you do not find them, or fail to reply, I shall certainly call your hand in this matter.

CHAPTER 5

Public Interest and Scholarly Reluctance

Bringing the Copper Scroll to Light

John needed to know when to expect an official press release on the Copper Scroll. People kept asking him about it and he hated having to dissemble over such momentous news. He wanted to include a brief reference to the Copper Scroll in his book *(The Dead Sea Scrolls)*, feeling it would otherwise be incomplete, so he had to ask Penguin Books to hold it back until the press release appeared. He was aware that he could not make any use of the full story until the official translation was out, but he was already looking ahead to a second edition and beginning to put together notes for a book on the Copper Scroll itself. With the letters to *The Times*, he had tasted the power of publicity and was quickly learning to wield it to his advantage. He wrote to de Vaux on April 13, 1956, asking for a date on the press release: "I have, of course, omitted all reference to the contents in my book but am planning to include the whole thing in its second edition, and I shall want to decide on its timing to follow your announcement. I should also be glad to know if I am allowed to take part in its publication."

De Vaux replied that Harding would be making his announcement "in a very few days," certainly in time for John's second edition. John's contribution over the Copper Scroll, according to the official statement, would be that he put the team in touch with the College of Technology, who did an admirable job in opening it. He had been made responsible for helping with the opening so that he could make transcriptions, which could have been used in case of emergency. But de Vaux did not think John's transcriptions and general interpretation sufficiently accurate, so he had asked Milik to take charge of editing it, using the scroll itself.[1]

Milik's takeover was not a problem. John expected it: He had always assumed that his would be a hasty, provisional translation, and that Milik's brilliant linguistic skill would predominate in the work — though he was sure that his own translation was not so flawed as de Vaux made out.

John pressed Harding again and again for a statement on the scroll. The passage he was planning to add to the Penguin was: "It is indeed an inventory of the sect's most treasured possessions, buried in various locations. Further information must wait on the release and publication of the whole text." He told Harding, "It seems to me you can hardly release less than that, and it is safe enough to ensure that the Bedu do not start digging the whole place up."[2]

But when the press release eventually came, at the end of May 1956, he could hardly take in what he was reading. Harding told him they had decided that the troves listed in the scroll had nothing at all to do with the Qumran sect. Harding told him, "It is a collection of traditions of buried treasure, such as we have many examples of in other languages, Arabic particularly. The quantities involved and the depth at which they are buried are obviously impossible."[3] The official release would consist of three short quotes; the full text must await final publication.

John could not believe he was serious and replied:

> I don't quite follow whether this 'traditions' gag you and your chums are putting out is for newspaper, government, Bedu, or my consumption. Or you may even believe it, bless you.
>
> I am quite ready to play ball if you let me know the party line, but please don't come this 'fairy-tale' business. . . . Incidentally, when I say I'll play ball this does not include perjury, which saying that I know no more than the official release would be.
>
> . . . Gerald, don't think me intrusive in matters much your concern and not mine, but don't you think a bit more ready information on these scroll matters might be a good idea? It's well known now that the copper scroll was completely open in January, and despite your attempts to squash it, it is also known that my transcriptions went to you immediately and that the scroll itself arrived back in April. I was asked only today why the news had not been given sooner. . . . A little general information on type of contents saves a good deal of rumour-mongering later, which

1. R. de Vaux to J. M. Allegro, April 20, 1956.
2. J. M. Allegro to G. L. Harding (GLH), May 23, 1956.
3. GLH to JMA, May 28, 1956.

has now taken on a somewhat sinister note. I warned my dear colleagues before they wrote the threatened letter to the *Times,* that if they did so on a subject on which most of Britain had no knowledge whatsoever, and America only such as their gutter press chose to give, the feeling would get around that the Roman Catholic brethren of the team, by far in the majority, were trying to hide things and setting up a 'man of straw' to knock him down again as part of a smear campaign against the one religiously-uncommitted member of the team.[4]

Apart from the question of the press release, John needed to know when Milik intended to publish the official translation of the Copper Scroll. His ideas for a book of his own on the Copper Scroll were breeding fast. He talked it over with David Noel Freedman, professor of Old Testament at the Western Theological Seminary in Pittsburgh and editor of the *Journal of Biblical Literature.* They planned *The Treasure of the Copper Scroll* as a popular pictorial guide to the scroll in its historical setting, including John's provisional translation. They agreed that publication should wait for Milik's definitive version, and Freedman convinced the publishers, Doubleday & Company, that it would be worth waiting for. Meanwhile, John put together a first draft and circulated it among his colleagues for comment.

By the early summer of 1956, some of the heat was going out of the dispute with the team. There was plenty of popular interest in the scrolls and much of it centered on John, so that he was often in demand for lectures or comment. Far from excluding him from the arena, the letter to *The Times* had stirred up interest in what he had to say; people were beginning to notice that the rest of the team by contrast said very little and published less. Then, despite his professor's disapproval, a lecture he gave to the College of Technology restored him to favor in Manchester, so for the time being he felt rather more secure in his job. That was some relief, as Joan had recently informed him a second baby was on the way.

John felt confident enough to write cheerily to Frank Cross, pressing for news of the recent excavations at Cave 11:

> Give, brother, give! What's all this 'fabulous' material from 11Q? And don't give me the stuff about not being studied yet, etc; you must know the sort of thing involved.
>
> What do you think of the Freedman-Allegro popular treasure book? I am hoping to see de Vaux shortly at Cardiff and get some sort of clearance. But the main point is: when is Milik intending to publish the official ver-

4. JMA to GLH, June 5, 1956.

sion? Can you find out for us; we don't want to jump the gate. At least, that's not strictly honest. I'd love to jump the gate, but think it wiser not to.

. . . Did you know I had been rehabilitated in Manchester? I gave a lecture at the College of Technology on the Scrollery, dished out a handout to the press afterwards, and had the Dean of Manchester second a hearty vote of thanks. They are accepting me into Holy Orders next week. (Rowley was not present, and boy! was he mad! Professor Fish [Akkadian] chaired the meeting, and is my champion in the lists, and hates Rowley's guts.)

Offprints of my *JBL* article on pNah will be in the post today for you all there. Will you ask Pat Skehan for a copy of his Exodus article, or am I too deep in hell-fire for correspondence from the Elect?

We are expecting Number Two in January. I hope to heaven by then we've managed to make some money.[5]

Frank Cross replied in similar vein, and pointed out how difficult it had become to work on 11Q or anything else in Jerusalem. The political situation that summer was so explosive that they might have to pack up the Scrollery any day, and it seemed doubtful whether scholars could ever enjoy a steady season's work there again. The scrolls were moved for safe-keeping out of the Palestine Archaeological Museum to the Ottoman Bank in Amman, and de Vaux had to re-negotiate access. Gerald Harding lost his job. The Copper Scroll remained unpublished; in fact, amid so much political turmoil the museum team were unwilling to let even Jordan's new Director of Antiquities know anything about it. The building atmosphere of resentment and secrecy put a block on normal progress.

John was disappointed that Cross fell in with the party line on the Copper Scroll:

You apparently acquiesce in a) the Jerusalem view of the relevance or irrelevance of the Copper Scroll; b) the advisability of keeping publication back for two years or so. On both points I am in hearty disagreement, and think the second is a very grave mistake which will go ill in many quarters. I am frankly glad at the moment that *The Times* letter has drawn a distinction between myself and those in Jerusalem of the team, because I hear growlings along the grapevine from world scholarship about the way this stuff is being handled, and I am not particularly keen to be caught up in the storm which is blowing up. I have a feeling that de Vaux, Milik and Co are in for a warm time at Strasbourg, and I am not sorry that I shall not be there. Happily my mass publication of the messianic material in the next

5. J. M. Allegro to F. Cross (FC), July 16, 1956.

JBL ought to put me in the right with the lads who are waiting impatiently for the stuff, and if you take my tip you'll get just as much stuff out as you can a.s.a.p. In lay quarters it is firmly believed that the Roman Church in de Vaux and Co are intent on suppressing this material. Nonsense we know, but this business of holding back important documents merely to boost a particular publication lends itself to such fantasies. Furthermore, the fact that it was lifted right out of my hands to be placed firmly in those of a Roman priest who already has enough on his plate for a decade has had its effect, despite my urging that in taking on the job of opening, I laid no claim to publication of the results.[6]

During the summer of 1956, John had an interesting exchange of views with Barthélemy, one of the very first scholars to work with de Vaux on the scrolls. Ill health had forced him to leave Jerusalem in the early stages of the work. John wrote:

On the matter of the copper scroll, I agree entirely with you, and apparently not with our colleagues in Jerusalem (not, you will gather, for the first time!). Your suggestion that we don't really understand the value of the talent seems to me very possible. We should also bear in mind that not all the amounts are anywhere near as great as those quoted by the press release. Indeed, one has a fraction of a talent appended, 20 mina I think, off-hand, which doesn't sound at all like a mythical body of ancient traditions. And similarly the depths given in the release are truly very great, but what has not been said is that many of the depths mentioned are much more reasonable, like 3 cubits, 6 cubits etc. . . . And other places mentioned are very much of interest to the sect.

In short, I find myself far more ready to believe that the people were not just wasting their time writing this twelve-column document on copper than de Vaux and Co. Just how far they really believe it quite irrelevant to the sect at Qumran, I am not at all sure. The whole of these scroll affairs are becoming so enshrouded in mystery and double-talk that I find it difficult to understand just what our colleagues really do believe.

. . . The treasure is a *Temple* treasure, explicitly so.[7]

De Vaux defused the smolderings within the team to some extent by discussing matters with John at a convention in Cardiff. As John told Frank Cross: "I must say I was glad to see de Vaux at Cardiff. We had, as I say, long

6. JMA to FC, August 5, 1956.
7. J. M. Allegro to D. Barthélemy, August 2, 1956.

talks and are good friends again. Indeed, he was at pains to point out that he was not the driving force behind *The Times* letter, but that it was 'the others'. I have since heard from another source who was out there at the time that in fact it was mainly Skehan, and, remembering his indignation at Wilson's article, I am not surprised. Catholicism in the States, I believe, is of a rather more ferocious kind than here."[8]

De Vaux offered to look over John's book for Penguin, *The Dead Sea Scrolls*. He came back with a detailed appraisal, and at last they were arguing again on a comradely footing. It was a friendly argument, but John soon realized he could not hope for a priest's assessment to be totally objective:

> From this point in your letter, your religious background comes to the fore, and you are on the defensive immediately from the word 'go'. . . . It's a pity you and your friends cannot conceive of anyone writing about Christianity without trying to grind some ecclesiastical or non-ecclesiastical axe. I really don't care, either way!
>
> How worried you all still are with the 'crucifixion' theory! . . . I had made nothing of it, and you all knew, as I did, that crucifixion was nothing uncommon and proved nothing about the historicity of Jesus.
>
> Again, how worried you all are on the resurrection of the Teacher, and the lengths you will go to disprove it to yourselves! There's nothing particularly extraordinary about a famous man in the past expected to be resurrected at the End Time, and I have no doubt from all the evidence that the Sect expected it of their Teacher. Why it's 'contradictory' to speak at the same time of a general resurrection (as evidenced by the Psalm commentary) I do not see. Surely the Christians believed in both? Anyway Matthew did and thought it had all happened, or so they tell us.
>
> . . . As for their thinking of Jesus as a 'son of God' and 'Messiah' — I don't dispute it for a moment; we now know from Qumran that their own Davidic Messiah was reckoned a 'son of God', 'begotten of God' — but that doesn't prove the Church's fantastic claim for Jesus that he was God himself. There's no 'contrast' in their terminology at all — the contrast is in its interpretation.[9]

In other words, John was saying, the Qumran community believed their hero would return as messiah at the end of time, and called him a son of God, though not God himself. The early Christians similarly expected their hero Jesus to return as messiah at the end of time. Obviously, he fit the existing

8. JMA to FC, August 5, 1956.
9. JMA to de Vaux, September 16, 1956.

messianic pattern. What made him unique was being called not just a son of God but God himself.

On the Copper Scroll, John added:

I don't really think you have the right to lay down ex cathedra opinions on the validity of the copper scroll inventory. You may be right, but you have yourself expressed your perplexity (or was it Harding) on why the sectarians should have bothered to inscribe such 'fairy tales' on expensive metal at such a time. Other scholars, even those having to rely on your meagre press release, have very different ideas, as I have, and I should have thought that the proper thing would have been to have published the text as soon as possible and let others decide for themselves . . . although you may be perfectly right, there are arguments on all sides, and the sooner the material is published for general comment, the better.

. . . My respect for you as a scholar is second to none, and if I am hesitant in accepting all you say without reserve, it is only that your religious convictions seem to me to warp your judgement slightly on any matter remotely connected with Christianity. This I can understand fully and expect nothing else.[10]

Leather Technology and the Scrolls

This is what the other scrolls were like to handle: "Fragment No. 2. This was light yellow in colour and resembled a leather in that it had a soft handle and a full substance. The sample as received was separable into three layers; the grain layer was brittle and cracky and showed a slight grain pattern similar to goat skin. The grain surface also showed a few yellowish brown stains but there were no indications of ruled lines or script. The middle layer was soft to the touch and showed little tendency to crack. The flesh layer, however, was slightly more brittle and like the grain layer was also stained by dark brown patches." This extract is from the first report on "The Material of the Skin-Type Dead Sea Scrolls," sent to John in June 1956 from the Department of Leather Industries at the University of Leeds.

While working on his fragments during 1954, John had wondered whether chemical analysis might disclose any more clues about where and when the scrolls were made. Early radio-carbon tests on the flaxen coverings of the complete scrolls had suggested a date between 168 B.C. and A.D. 233. At

10. *Ibid.*

the suggestion of Dr. Bowden, Principal of the Manchester College of Science and Technology where the Copper Scroll had been opened, he talked it over with Donald Burton, Professor of Leather Industries at Leeds. The Director of Antiquities in Amman agreed to supply samples, and when these arrived in January 1955, John sent them straight to Leeds.

Professor Burton and his team — Dr. Ronald Reed and a recently qualified postgraduate assistant, Dr. M. J. Wood — took a keen interest. Burton wrote, "You will see that our preliminary work shows the possibilities of obtaining information regarding the mode of manufacture, the place of origin, and the age of the scroll fragments. We think that work along these new lines could usefully extend existing archaeological knowledge and might lead to further exciting developments."[11]

The tests showed that the samples had been made of parchment — animal skins stretched to dry — rather than treated with tannin as is usual for leather. Most were of goat or sheep skin. The water that had been used in processing them showed no trace of magnesium, and therefore had come from a well or spring rather than the Dead Sea, which is rich in magnesium chloride. The scientists suggested that if they could analyze samples of water from Qumran and elsewhere in the region, they might be able to pinpoint where the scroll parchment was made. Forwarding their report to Harding in Jordan, John pressed him to follow this up.

Professor Burton foresaw two years' work on the scrolls, but needed money to do it, specifically five hundred to two thousand pounds to cover materials, apparatus, and Miss Wood's salary. With the Copper Scroll in the news, interest was catching on, and when the professor of physics at Imperial College read about the work at Manchester and Leeds, he offered to help. To Dr. Bowden in Manchester, Professor Blackett wrote:

9 January 1957

Dear Bowden,

I noticed in the *New Scientist* for the 3rd of January that it is stated that electron microscopic examination of the Scrolls is being held up through lack of financial resources available to Professor Burton of Leeds. Is this correct and is the work useful? If so, he can certainly apply to the DSIR [Department of Scientific and Industrial Research]. It would be fun to support such work.

Dr. Bowden passed on the message with a copy to John. As his note was in terms of "Dear Allegro. . . . Is there anything else I should do?" John was ev-

11. D. Burton to J. M. Allegro, June 4, 1956.

idently not on the blacklist in Manchester just then. He hoped that DSIR funding for research on the leather samples might add weight to his campaign for a general Dead Sea Scrolls research fund.

John urged Harding repeatedly not to let the professor down, but it proved rather difficult to get much cooperation over the water and leather samples, probably because hostility between Israel and Jordan made travel and forward planning difficult. Nevertheless, John's collaboration with Leeds was to continue into the 1960s, when he kept sending Dr. Reed (the new Head of the Department of Leather Technology at Leeds) samples of leather from the caves he explored on various expeditions. Even when they had little or nothing to do with scrolls, the samples were interesting from a historical angle; as Dr. Reed said, "They fill in the background of leather technology at that particular period of history." He added that analysis of samples from the Ain Feshka installation discovered by de Vaux "could find no evidence to support his view that it was a tannery, where animal skins were processed. Possibly Zeuner is nearer the mark in saying it was used for the storage or breeding of fish. Or simply, it could have been a water settling system."[12]

Shifting Relationships in the Team

In February 1957, John learned that his appointment at Manchester was not to be renewed, despite the previous summer's reprieve. He presumed that Rowley had blocked it on the grounds that he had been discredited by his former colleagues. Bitterness resurfaced. He wrote to Strugnell:

> You will be glad to know that your letter to *The Times* has at last borne fruit: My appointment at Manchester has not been renewed, to Rowley's joy and presumably yours also. At least, it has been renewed for one further year and finally, but I shall try and leave this summer if at all possible.
>
> I presume it was the job you were after, so I'll let you know immediately I know if I shall be able to find other means of support for my family this summer, and you can prepare your application.[13]

Strugnell denied that he was pleased John was leaving, or that he wanted his job, or that he was a friend of Rowley, and insisted the letter had been written because of the three BBC talks, not because of press reports or spite. This did not appease John, who replied to Strugnell:

12. R. Reed to J. M. Allegro, March 5, 1962.
13. J. M. Allegro to J. Strugnell (JS), February 6, 1957.

Since you persist — my dear boy, you speak as if you and your ecclesiastical pals were debating some little point of theology in a learned journal. You still do not seem to understand what you did in writing a letter to a newspaper in an attempt to smear the words of your own colleague. It was quite unheard of before, an unprecedented case of scholarly stabbing in the back. And, laddie, don't accuse me of over-dramatising the business. I was here in England, with my finger very much on the pulse, whilst you were shut away in Jerusalem surrounded with cheap Yankee magazines. Reuters' man that morning on the phone to me was classic: 'But I thought you scholars stuck together. . . .' And when it was realised that you were quoting things I never even said, the inference was plain. This letter was not in the interests of scholarly science at all, but to calm the fears of the Roman Catholics of America. And what it all boiled down to was that you guys did not agree with the interpretation I put on certain texts — where I have quite as much chance of being right as you. Rather than argue it out in the journals and scholarly works, you thought it easier to influence public opinion by a scurrilous letter to a newspaper.

You are quite right about de Vaux: a man of honour who has regretted that letter to *The Times* from the moment it was written — as his remarks to me last summer made clear. I rather gather too that even Skehan himself began to wonder afterwards whether it was worthwhile.[14] [John had perhaps overlooked the fact that he himself had first gone on the air with his views, rather than argue them out in a scholarly journal.]

John applied for and failed to get a fellowship at Cambridge. In Manchester, the press reported that he was being sacked for his views on Christianity. Whatever the truth of that — probably not much — his disagreement with Professor Rowley was well known.

John had been working steadily through the autumn and winter on infra-red photographs of his scroll fragments. Despite the uncertainty over his job and the political situation in Jordan, he badly wanted to go back there to complete as much as possible of his work on the scrolls themselves, and maybe for the chance to argue out differences of interpretation in person. As he told Strugnell in a letter of March 28, 1957, "lack of funds will not stop me coming, even if I have to pawn my wife." At the last moment — July 1957 — his post at Manchester was reprieved again, and he rejoined the team in Jerusalem, though at his own expense.

Everything seemed to go well, though relationships were a little more guarded. The Director of Antiquities, Awni Dajani, with whom John had al-

14. JMA to JS, March 8, 1957.

ready worked, gave permission for John to see and work on the Copper Scroll
— but only John. Distrust between the authorities and the rest of the team
made an awkward barrier.

In September, John returned to Manchester, only to be whisked back to
Jordan by the BBC to make a film on the Dead Sea Scrolls. They hit trouble,
which he described in a letter to Frank Cross.

31 October 1957

Dear Frank:

Thanks for your letter. Yes, the situation was that on our arrival in Jerusalem we went straight to see Awni, who took us round the next morning to get things moving with de Vaux. We foregathered in the École and
explained what we hoped to do, only to be met with a blank refusal by
de V to collaborate in any way. We stared open-mouthed for some time,
then Dajani and the producer started trying to find out what it was all
about. The whole thing was a complete knock-out because, as far as I was
aware, I had left my dear colleagues on the best of terms — or pretty
much so. Certainly no bitterness on my side about anything. But de Vaux
said he had called a meeting of his scholars and that they had agreed to
have nothing to do with anything I had anything to do with! My pal the
producer then took the old gent outside and explained in words of one
syllable that we were avoiding any controversial matter at all in the programme on the religious side, but he was quite adamant. He said that
whereas he could not stop us taking pictures of the monastery at
Qumran, he would not allow us in the scrollery or the Museum generally.

I was still completely at a loss to understand all this, but by now Awni
was beginning to get annoyed. For he saw this programme as a very defi-
nite boost for Jordan — antiquities and tourism — and certainly that is
how we intend it should look, and when we had left de Vaux, he gave us in
measured tones a lecture on who really runs the scrollery and what would
happen if its members did not collaborate with the government. Well, we
wanted no unpleasantness and set about collecting our material.

Needless to say, with Awni's full collaboration we were most successful,
and as soon as it became clear to my dear colleagues that even without
them the programme was going forward (it had cost the BBC about £800
already!) they started putting their cards on the table. It was not the programme they objected to, only Allegro. They did not, they said, want to be
monkeys in a cage to jump to Allegro's whip! They then called in a taxi at
our hotel and made the producer an offer — if he would drop Allegro
completely and have Strugnell as his scriptwriter, or Milik, they would

collaborate. Just how they thought either could write for a TV programme at a distance of some three thousand miles from the production staff they did not disclose. We laughed heartily and carried on. Then one day, after we had returned from Qumran, Awni phoned to say that he had got in to find a note (anonymous) waiting for him, offering £150 to him to stop us going to Amman and photographing in the Museum there. By this time we were beginning to wonder if we were not wasting good TV material on the scrolls themselves, and whether we wouldn't do better telling the story of the team's efforts at not being photographed.

Actually, of course, the only thing we wanted from them was to be seen pottering about the scrollery. We already had some film of de Vaux in the monastery from a previous BBC expedition, and he agreed to our using that!

They then tried to intimidate K. G. Kuhn, who was out there at the time. [In 1953, Kuhn had been the first to realize that the Copper Scroll was a list of treasure.] For naturally enough, we wanted him to tell us how he first deciphered the outside of the scroll. I may say that after Awni had had a few words with him, he was unintimidated and co-operated to the full.

Well, in the end we got everything, including the scrollery, for Awni pointed out gently to de V and Co that the government of that whole editing team and scrollery was not in his hands at all, but was guided by a committee, of which de V was only one member and the Mayor of Jerusalem the chairman. And that if there was any more non-cooperation with the government. . . .

So please yourself, my dear chap. If you'd like to come in, I'm hoping the second programme will have room for a short talk about the biblical texts. . . .

De Vaux seemed very anxious about the whole situation at the Scrollery. He may have been worrying over what wild theories John might come out with next, but he was more probably afraid of sparking off any political trouble, for almost any move might be misinterpreted by the Arabs or Israelis or both. John commented in a Christmas letter to a previous colleague from ASOR, Professor James Muilenburg:

I think it's mostly jealousy — in fact, at one stage the opposition sent a deputation offering to appear graciously in the film, provided I was removed from the thing entirely, and young Strugnell take over.

I think also that part of the trouble is fear of publicity in any form. De V is almost pathologically anxious to avoid further trouble with the authorities, having only narrowly escaped prison last year. The lengths to which he will go is evidenced by the fact that the Museum trustees were persuaded to spend £47,000 of trust funds to buy Cave 11 material, with the result that they do not know how to pay their staff. . . . I also learned that they have not yet given a copy of the translation of the copper scroll to the Dept of Antiquities.[15]

The People of the Dead Sea Scrolls

John's second book, *The People of the Dead Sea Scrolls,* came out in 1958 from Doubleday & Company in New York and in 1959 from Routledge & Kegan Paul in London. It tells the story of the Qumran community in words and pictures. The style was popular rather than academic: John aimed to keep the scrolls in the public eye and reward public interest. The Jordanian authorities were a little wary of public interest; political instability put them on the defensive. At first the Palestine Archaeological Museum was reluctant to let John borrow some of its photographs, though he pointed out that publicizing them might promote it as a national resource for education and tourism. John hoped that popular interest would lead to revenue, and revenue would give the authorities some self-confidence, or at least optimism, on the cultural scene. As he wrote to Joseph Sa'ad, curator of the PAM, "resultant publicity on the Museum's treasures will in some way recompense you for the loss of some secrecy, and redouble popular interest in your establishment and its work."[16] John had hopes of the scrolls as a tangible, though tenuous, link between people seeking peace, maybe even a bridge to reconciliation between the three religions of the area — Islam, Judaism, and Christianity.

Meanwhile, he strongly disagreed with the way de Vaux had persuaded the museum authorities to blow their whole budget on buying scrolls from the Bedouin: It seemed a short-sighted way for the museum to support future research or its own reputation. John held that the museum needed all the help it could get, including any publicity his book could bring it, to make up its losses. With the fee for the photographs, he enclosed a note to Sa'ad making his views clear: "As always, I am glad to be able to do anything to help the Museum in its work, and particularly in view of the appalling financial difficulties into which the Trustees seem now to have placed it. I hope that my recent book will do much to stimulate interest in the Museum and its treasures."[17]

15. J. M. Allegro to J. Muilenburg, December 24, 1957.
16. J. M. Allegro to J. Sa'ad, January 14, 1959.
17. JMA to Sa'ad, March 2, 1959.

John wrote *The People of the Dead Sea Scrolls* in association with Professor David Noel Freedman of Pittsburgh. They planned it as a companion volume to *The Treasure of the Copper Scroll*, which they were still holding back in anticipation of the official translation. Freedman helped decide the structure of the book and helped steer it through the publishers.

The People of the Dead Sea Scrolls outlines the events that led to the establishment of Qumran at the beginning of the second century B.C. and later to its overthrow during the Jewish Revolt of A.D. 68-70. It sets the Essenes' flight to the desert, under persecution by Jannaeus, in the framework of Old Testament tradition. In seeking the wilderness, the sect followed the prophetic tradition of Elijah, the same tradition that John the Baptist and Jesus later pursued. Through extreme asceticism, they sought utmost purity.

> There is something in the uncompromising harshness of the desert that brings a man face to face with spiritual realities. It is a life of extremes. . . . Moral issues are as sharply defined as the pattern of light and shade on the bare rocks: light and darkness, good and evil, God and Satan.[18]

The People of the Dead Sea Scrolls briefly describes the scrolls themselves and the insights they bring into the sectarians' philosophy. It shows how archeologists gain a picture of the life of the monastery: the cisterns for water supply and ritual bathing, the dining room for communal meals, the scriptorium where some of the scrolls were probably written, evidence of crop cultivation around the springs a couple of miles away at Ain Feshka. Although a good deal of the sect's home was destroyed and then overlaid by Roman occupation after A.D. 68, many of the buildings remained in outline, such as a smithy, grain-mill, and kilns where the cooking pots and scroll jars were made.

Also in association with Freedman during 1959, John planned another popular book, *Son of the Star*, about Simon Bar Kokhba (or Kosiba), leader of the Second Jewish Revolt in A.D. 132-135. The project began with a fragment found among the 4Q collection. John and Milik suspected this fragment came not from Qumran but Murabba'at, one of Simon's strongholds. A good deal of contemporary evidence had already been found there — biblical scrolls, private contracts, and letters written on papyrus by Simon himself. John's piece was a report from a messenger on the situation at some place apparently under siege from the Roman commander Rufus.

Simon Bar Kosiba (nicknamed Bar Kokhba, Son of the Star) led the Jew-

18. J. M. Allegro, *The People of the Dead Sea Scrolls* (London: Routledge & Kegan Paul, 1959), p. 24.

ish rebels against Rome through a guerilla campaign in the desert of Judea. It was essentially a religious movement, in which Simon claimed the office of kingly (Davidic) messiah, his colleague Eleazar that of priestly messiah. Their aim was to restore Jewish sovereignty and re-establish the Davidic dynasty in Jerusalem, which was then a pagan city. Simon gathered widespread support, though the Romans chased him into the desert and scattered his followers. After three cat-and-mouse years among the caves and hill fortresses, disaster at Bettir shattered Simon's hopes forever.

It was a stirring story, well documented with contemporary evidence. John got as far as negotiating terms with Freedman and seriously interesting Doubleday & Company. But he did not have the whole story, and the book was put on hold while he waited for it. He had to explain to Doubleday that the book was stalled, "pending publication not only of Milik's Semitic documents from Murabba'at, due any day, but publication of the new Bar Kokhba finds from Israel, without which any new documents on the Second Jewish Revolt would be hopelessly out of date." And in the end the book was simply crowded out by John's other concerns, and overtaken by a book on Bar Kokhba by Yigael Yadin.

CHAPTER 6

Seeking the Treasure

1960: *The Treasure of the Copper Scroll*

The Treasure of the Copper Scroll had been ready for the press in 1957. Again and again, John had written to his colleagues pressing for news of when Milik expected to publish his official translation. Again and again he held back his own, until the publishers all but lost interest.

Not only his own publication was at stake: Goodwill in Jordan and support from around the world were essential to Scrolls research and depended in part on a steady return of interesting results. The Jordanian government wanted to know what all the reticence was about and how much the Copper Scroll might be worth. John felt they had the right to know, and feared that de Vaux and his team at the Palestine Archaeological Museum would alienate the government by continuing to prevaricate. The Jordanians would have liked him to issue his own version, as he mentions in the foreword to the first edition of his book:

> I was invited in the summer of 1957 to publish the text by the then Director of Antiquities of the Hashemite Kingdom of Jordan, Dr Ghuraibi. This invitation has since been renewed by his successors, Mr Said Durra and Dr Awni Dajani.[1]

John also felt that further delay was unfair to scholars all over the world. He had warned de Vaux as early as September 16, 1956, "Whilst I appreciate

1. J. M. Allegro, *The Treasure of the Copper Scroll,* 1st ed. (New York: Doubleday, 1960), p. 6.

your feelings about holding it back, I cannot think they will commend themselves to scholars waiting to get hold of the text." De Vaux was afraid that to publish a list of buried treasure would start a gold rush that could endanger archeological sites; John felt that this fear, though reasonable, should not outweigh the need for openness in presenting the facts to public scrutiny.

Daily expecting an announcement from Milik, John urged both Strugnell and Cross to see whether they could discover his plans. But days became months. In the three years since the Copper Scroll was opened, nothing seemed to move. All the public had heard was a trifling and one-sided press release about the scroll as a work of fiction. Rumors about the suppression of truth were gathering force.

De Vaux decided he wanted everything published together in its finished form as *Discoveries in the Judaean Desert of Jordan (DJDJ)*, and in March 1959 declared that he was aiming to submit all the team's work to Oxford University Press in the following year, including that on the Copper Scroll from Cave 3. This further delay dismayed John. As he later described it, since 1956 de Vaux had been resisting

> all attempts to make an early publication of my views [on the Copper Scroll] until the authorities had published the full text. This, I thought, could not be long delayed. It was inconceivable that it should be held back until the definitive volume appeared, many years hence. However, when I pressed the need for an earlier publication, the answer was returned that since that particular volume of the series would otherwise be deficient in interesting material, the copper scroll must be held back to give the book added substance, a point of view hardly likely to commend itself to scholars whose researches were being seriously hampered for lack of authoritative information.[2]

In the end, the publishers Doubleday & Company arranged with John and his colleague David Noel Freedman to set a date for publication in autumn 1960, which they assumed would be far enough in the future to allow Milik to publish the official view first.

Milik's official version was not ready. However, he published a French translation of the text — without the Hebrew original — in *Revue Biblique* 66, July 1959, and also an English one in the *Annual of the Department of Antiquities in Jordan*, Volumes 4 and 5 (1960). John's book duly appeared in autumn 1960, as a hardback companion volume to *The People of the Dead Sea*

2. J. M. Allegro, *The Treasure of the Copper Scroll*, 2nd ed. (New York: Anchor Books, 1964), p. 35.

Scrolls. Reviewing both Milik's and John's versions in the *Guardian* of November 4, 1960, Yigael Yadin mentioned that by then Milik had also submitted his translation to the Clarendon Press for *Discoveries in the Judaean Desert,* though the volume was not yet ready for issue.

Later commentators, including some of the original editing team, have suggested that John pirated the Copper Scroll translation by publishing *The Treasure of the Copper Scroll* before the official version came out in *DJDJ*. But, as mentioned, Milik had published a preliminary translation in *Revue Biblique* in 1959. John did not describe his own translation as anything but "provisional" and held it back for over three years to let Milik issue his official version — hardly suggesting piratical intent. During December 1956 John and Milik were exchanging letters — calling each other "John Marco" and "Milch" respectively — over points of interpretation. On December 12, 1956, John wrote:

> Did you manage to solve all the riddles in the text? Including the Greek letters? . . . And of course I roared at your reference to the crucifixion motif. When are you going to write your next letter to *The Times*?

At least on John's part, there was difference of opinion between them, rather than competition, over the translation. After all, he planned the first edition of *The Treasure of the Copper Scroll* as a popular picture-book along the lines of *The People of the Dead Sea Scrolls* and did not try to present it as a definitive scholarly treatise. In the foreword to the first edition, he admits:

> The publication of a cryptic text of this nature presents many problems. So much depends upon individual readings that full explanations must accompany the translations offered, even though their technicalities must be of limited interest to the general reader. My notes have therefore been mainly attached to the translation alone, and even there, references to sources and other works have been kept to the barest minimum.[3]

In the chapter on decipherment he describes the problems of translating Hebrew technical terms that otherwise occur only rarely and with different meanings in the Old Testament: "It will be appreciated, therefore, that any translation of the copper scroll at this stage must be considered as provisional. There are often so many alternatives to the reading of a particular word, each dependent upon the true interpretation of another, itself perhaps resting on one or two other indeterminates, that, failing the discovery of new

---

3. Allegro, *The Treasure of the Copper Scroll,* 1st ed., p. 7.

evidence, the rendering can only be a succession of possibilities." What he presents is "my suggested, rather literal, translation of the text, together with a facsimile of the original and a transcription."[4]

John insisted how pleased he was that responsibility for official publication of the scroll was given to "my friend and colleague, Father Joseph Milik," whom he calls "the most brilliant of our little team of scroll editors" and "certainly the best fitted to carry the initial decipherment of the copper scroll a stage further."[5] John gives him credit for a more expert translation than his own in several places and admits, in the second edition, that he has revised his version in the light of Milik's:

> In the foregoing translation I have been able to utilize his work in revising my initial decipherment. We still differ in a number of points of detail, but in not a few instances I have felt that his choice of alternatives has the edge of probability, and specialists can see in most cases where I have followed his judgement. As always, his scholarship is impeccable and he has been able to bring to the linguistic and topographical problems of the scroll a breadth of knowledge that is remarkable in such a comparatively young man.[6]

Neither Milik's preliminary translation nor John's satisfied the critics, however, because they did not include facsimile photographs. John provided drawings and transcriptions of the text, but without photographs these could not be authenticated. Milik's, at this stage, did not even have transcriptions. The two translations differed markedly in several places and they began from two completely different assumptions. Milik's official line was that the treasure was fictional; John believed it was absolutely real. In his *Guardian* article of November 4, 1960, Yadin despaired of reviewing either version fairly without being able to see the Hebrew original.

The first edition of *The Treasure of the Copper Scroll* begins with the story of the discovery, opening, and decipherment of the scroll. It presents John's transcription and provisional translation, admitting that there are many questionable passages that await further study. It considers at some length the official interpretation — that the scroll was a fictional list of buried treasure and belonged with ancient legends of princely wealth and the riches of Solomon's Temple, legends that abounded in Middle Eastern literature.

John explains why he found this interpretation unconvincing. The Cop-

4. Allegro, *The Treasure of the Copper Scroll*, 1st ed., p. 31.
5. Allegro, *The Treasure of the Copper Scroll*, 2nd ed., pp. 32-33.
6. Allegro, *The Treasure of the Copper Scroll*, 2nd ed., p. 37.

per Scroll list took a much more prosaic style than the treasure-hoard stories. For example, item 9 according to John's first translation reads: "In the cistern which is nineteen cubits in front of the eastern gateway, in it are vessels, and in the hollow that is in it: ten talents."[7] It included holy but otherwise value-less items such as empty tithe vessels, "containing naught but the taint of sanctity," as he told Noel Freedman.[8] The weights and prices admittedly sounded enormous: "eighty talents of silver," "three hundred talents of gold," "vessels of silver and vessels of gold for tithe and money, the whole being six hundred talents," and so on. But as he had discussed with Barthélemy, "we have no certain knowledge what values were accorded the talent and its factors in Judaean common speech of the first century" and it seemed reasonable to downgrade the denominations from their modern values. Later scholars, such as Judah K. Lefkovits in *The Copper Scroll: A Re-evaluation,* have supported this and have produced a very much reduced list.[9]

And why go to the trouble of inscribing a fairy tale on expensive copper instead of parchment? The Copper Scroll was obviously designed to last. Most significantly, copper could be ritually purified, while parchment could not; therefore, copper would be more fitting for sacred uses. John was convinced that the list was Temple treasure, hidden in sacred places for protection and written on copper to prevent defilement.

What of the hiding places? The Copper Scroll mentions Secacah, which John identified as Qumran. He also thought he recognized the names of other locations in the Vale of Achor, Jericho, Hyrcania, and Jerusalem. Jerusalem itself was known to be riddled with underground passages, conduits, pits, and chambers linking palace quarters and the Temple itself — plenty of potential hiding places.

Who hid the treasure? Assuming it must be Temple treasure — given its quantities and sacred nature — John made a case for the Zealots, under John of Gischala. In messianic fervor they had deposed the High Priests and by A.D. 68 held Jerusalem. Josephus[10] had told how, preparing for a last pitch against the Romans, the Zealots fortified outlying posts such as Masada, overran Qumran, and even melted down Temple treasures to use in the holy war. What if they decided to rescue some of the treasure? Maybe they hid it, with an inventory inscribed on copper sheets. Meanwhile the Romans were being marshaled and drilled into an invincible war machine. In A.D. 68 they roared

7. Allegro, *The Treasure of the Copper Scroll,* 1st ed., p. 35.
8. J. M. Allegro to D. N. Freedman (DNF), January 12, 1959.
9. J. K. Lefkovits, *The Copper Scroll (3Q15): A Re-evaluation* (Leiden: Brill, 2000).
10. Josephus, *The Jewish War,* especially books 4.8.1, 5.13.6, and 5.1.5.

down upon Jericho, and two years later upon Jerusalem. In 73 they laid siege to Masada. They found it a ghost city.

> The dust of war settled slowly over that unhappy land; the Zealots were dead or scattered into exile; their scroll of sacred treasures lay undisturbed and unclaimed in a cave by the Dead Sea.[11]

John concluded his book by calling for a thorough archeological survey of all the sites mentioned in the scroll. He also proposed that an institute for Middle Eastern studies be set up in Jordan as an international center for research into the languages, thought, and civilizations of the whole area. The region had been the womb of three great religions; maybe an institute that brought them together to talk and write and share their research could engender a creative force for collaboration, friendship, reconciliation.

The kernel of this vision did not grow beyond the pages of the book. John had to watch his Arab and Jewish friends tear their country apart; the dust-clouds of war were continually stirred by disputes so complicated, deep-rooted, and noisy that it was difficult to keep sight of visions.

The 1960 Expedition

Convinced that the treasure of the scroll was treasure, not fiction, John set off in the early spring of 1960 in the hope of proving it. The expedition had two official purposes. The first was "corroboration of topographical references in the copper scroll" — to make preliminary investigations of possible sites and find out which of them looked most promising for further excavation. There was always the unspoken hope of finding more scrolls and even perhaps some of the treasure, but the chance seemed too remote to admit. The second aim was to raise funds to enable the Jordanian government to buy whatever scrolls or other artifacts were available and take the lead in the archeological search for more.

So far the Bedouin had done all the running: Scroll-hunting was a full-scale though illegal industry. Officially, anyone conducting an excavation had to have a license and could not legally take any archeological find out of the country. In practice, the Bedu swarmed through the cliffs and caves, ravaging the sites. It was said that any seekers with fifty thousand pounds to spend could be handed what they wanted within a few days of letting their request be known among the back streets of Bethlehem. Even thumb-nail fragments were

---

11. Allegro, *The Treasure of the Copper Scroll*, 1st ed., p. 129.

John at the Kidron Valley camp

fetching ten shillings per square centimeter. The Department of Antiquities could not compete — it had over-reached itself to the point of virtual bankruptcy in buying the latest cache of scrolls for de Vaux. And the amateur trafficking was doing the scrolls themselves no good at all: The fragments were far too fragile to be used as bargaining counters. Writing to *The Sunday Times* in August 1960, John described in frustration how the pieces crumbled under such handling and how the writing on them faded hopelessly with exposure.

At the same time, he was well aware that publishing the secret locations in his book could lead to more depredation. With the idea of getting in before the gold rush, and before his book came out, he talked over the expedition plans with Awni Dajani, Director of Antiquities, and also with King Hussein himself. The King was enthusiastic; he offered troops for protection and for transport. Sponsorship came from the *Daily Mail*, which also supplied a correspondent, Ralph Izzard, to send back daily dispatches. Many other people asked to come of their own initiative, hoping for adventure. The people John chose included Canon Robert de Langhe, Professor of Semitic Studies at Louvain University, who had conducted the first official excavation at Khirbet Mird in 1953; Howard Stutchbury, an architect and family friend currently teaching at Manchester University; Jock Wiatr, a Ministry of Aviation technician who was also an expert in crevasse detection; John Belshi, a geophysicist from Cambridge; and Stanley Jeeves from the Lake District, a climber, caver, and photographer.

John arrived in Jordan first to sort out permits and supplies. He also wanted to get some work done in the Scrollery. This proved a haven from time to time during the excavations. Will Oxtoby, a scholar from Princeton, was now in charge of the concordance; John found him capable and helpful. Matching some of the transcriptions he had made in Manchester from infrared prints against the original fragments in the museum was comparatively straightforward. Others needed updating:

> I'll collect the fragments together that I have, and have the lot re-photographed . . . new additions and joins have outdated my transcriptions. Largely assisted by John Strugnell, who could not have been more helpful.
>
> At the Scrollery they are quite friendly, I must say. I have done a deal with Milik for that strange Second Revolt tag, he having one of mine.[12]

Robert de Langhe came to Jordan as soon as his university term ended, "eager for the fray and to avoid meeting anyone from the École Biblique."[13] A

---

12. J. M. Allegro to Joan Allegro, March 30, 1960.
13. JMA to Joan, March 21, 1960.

Sunrise over the Dead Sea

couple of days later, the two expedition Land Rovers turned up. The *Mail* journalist Ralph Izzard came in one and seemed almost disappointed to have crossed Europe overland quite uneventfully, without so much as a flat tire.

Soon John found that the price of media sponsorship was media attention. He had foreseen having to negotiate for access to the Haram (where part of the Temple may have stood) and other archeological sites, since that was the way of officialdom, but he had not foreseen talking his way through a barricade of journalists to get to that point. As they stepped out of the hotel in Jerusalem, "a representative of the Arab news agency arrived and we had to have a long interview on the spot. . . . Where we had lunch, we ran into the BBC man. It was rather trying, avoiding telling him what we were about."[14]

For the press, the possibilities were so exciting that they proved impossible to hide.

> Last evening the hotel manager showed Ralph a long story in an Arabic newspaper from Beirut about me and the expedition. I read it through as best I could — it was mainly the harmless stuff I gave the man in Amman, *plus* a good deal more precise stuff supplied by the Inspector who was

14. *Ibid.*

also there and to whom I told something about Zadok and Gethsemane. So we are now looking in the Garden of Gethsemane for 200 tons of whatever, and more precisely 'between the trees' (from Milik's version?). Let's hope it is not taken up by the Beirut correspondent of a London paper. But I fancy the wires will be humming today.[15]

The expedition focused on three sites: the sepulchers of Zadok in Jerusalem; Khirbet Mird (Hyrcania) in the Vale of Achor; and Qumran. The Copper Scroll provided the clues. As John admitted, some of his early translations were tentative, and he revised many of them over the years, but most of the following quotations come from the list in the first edition of *The Treasure of the Copper Scroll*, since this was presumably the list he was using on the 1960 expedition.

According to John's translation, the tomb of Zadok held, or had held, holy things:

[Item 52] Below the portico's southern corner, in the tomb of Zadok, under the platform of the porch: tithe vessels.

[Item 53] In the exedra set in the cliff facing west, in front of the garden of Zadok, under the great sealing stone that is its floor: consecrated offerings.[16]

Zadok's was one of three ancient sepulchers that stood together outside the walls of Jerusalem, partly buried in earth that rain had washed down from the Mount of Olives. Scraping the soil away, the excavators found a low, hidden wall and a groove that could be an irrigation channel. Had there once been a garden there to irrigate? Zadok's garden or Jesus' Gethsemane? They dug all round the wall, hoping they might uncover a tomb complex behind the monument, but found nothing.

Mird looked more promising. It had once been Herod's palace at Hyrcania, and there was a *nephesh*, a funerary monument, that had never been investigated.

[Item 1] In the fortress which is in the Vale of Achor, forty cubits under the steps entering to the east, a money chest and its contents, of a weight of seventeen talents.

[Item 2] In the sepulchral monument, in the third course of stones: light bars of gold.[17]

15. JMA to Joan, March 23, 1960.
16. Allegro, *The Treasure of the Copper Scroll*, 1st ed., p. 53.
17. Allegro, *The Treasure of the Copper Scroll*, 1st ed., p. 33.

The *nephesh* at Khirbet Mird

Two thousand years of rockfall and desert wind had half buried the ruins in rubble and silt. What did they hide?

We have so far penetrated the outside wall to find an opening that has been closed by pieces of rock and stone, quite neatly, and apparently never disturbed. Roman pottery found in the clearing leaves no doubt of its age. The chances are that it is associated with the Herodian occupation. The trouble is that one's imagination can leap ahead too fast — dreams of Herod's own tomb, or that of his son who was murdered here. Herod was supposed to have been buried, with great pomp and loads of treasure, at Herodium (so Josephus). But no tomb has ever been found at the Herodium near Bethlehem. Could Hyrcania (Mird) have been renamed after Herod, Herodium, or was it just a mistake on the part of Josephus or his redactors? Even if it turns out to be a minor burial place (though this great cairn can hardly betoken anything minor), we should still have a *nephesh* — as per copper scroll. Of course, there is the possibility that it was just a lookout post.[18]

First they had to set up camp, and there the difficulties began. There were the problems of finding anywhere flat enough to pitch the tents and

18. JMA to Joan, April 4, 1960.

Investigating Mird

then securing them on peg-proof rock. Small but threatening rockfalls slid past now and then. The journalist was sure he saw scorpions in his tent.

Unpredictable weather did not help. Just after they had maneuvered the stores and water tanks into place, a storm hit the camp. It flattened four tents, wrecked the stores, and churned the ground around the water containers to mud. Around the ruins it left even more rubble to dig out than before. But when the storm had blown away and while they were still wondering where to start, the sound of an aircraft coming in low distracted them. It was a Royal Jordanian Air Force plane, tracking along the wadi and evidently looking for them. Soon afterwards, an Arab Legion car nosed over the brow of the hill, bringing reassurance and fresh water.

Water supply was the worst problem. Between rainstorms, the wadi was completely dry, with no spring within several miles. As a solution, they had been loaned two massive clay containers, which they lowered into pits dug in the sand and filled from jerry-cans. But they needed to refill the jerry-cans daily, a three-hour round trip by Land Rover to Jericho, and the supply was never enough. Izzard the reporter wanted more to drink than water; twice he took himself off and stayed out a day and a half. As he did not seem to take naturally to either archeology or camping, no one minded much, but they did miss the Land Rover he took with him, as it meant someone else had to stop work to go for water. John wrote:

> If the legion car had not been available they would have been mad with thirst by now. As it was we had to send our driver out during the day with our cans to Jericho to fill up with water, since Izzard had not taken them with him when he went the night before. Just as well in the circumstances, but quite inexcusable. This is the second time he has done this, and last time I made my feelings on the matter perfectly plain. I have half a mind to cable London asking for his replacement by some more responsible person. You cannot afford to take chances like this.[19]

The team uncovered a shaft where a flight of steps led into the rock: an ancient well. They lowered Jock Wiatr inside on a rope. He worked his metal detector all along the walls and floor — but disturbed only bats. Among the ruins were vaulted cisterns, which had once stored water, and the remains of splendid halls. Herodian pottery stuffed into interstices between columns suggested building or rebuilding work, and parts had been built over in Byzantine times. But vandals had wrecked the site. Marble pillars lay strewn down the hillside. A mosaic floor had been hacked to pieces. Mick Wright, the archeological surveyor, made drawings of what was left, but a full investigation would have to be left for a more thorough and professional excavation.

With disappointment, in the end they had to leave Mird's story unspoken. They had found Roman pottery nearby, and rubble-filled wells, cisterns, and passageways — but no skeletons and no treasure. The place was full of secret possibilities, but they remained secret. John continued,

> There was no way in, and it seems pretty certain that it was meant to be one solid block. I am pretty sure it was a monument of some kind, but no treasure so far, although it is by no means impossible that it was stowed behind one of the big stones in the courses or even hidden inside, though this is less likely.[20]

So they moved on to the Qumran area, six miles east of Khirbet Mird. Secacah is mentioned several times in the Copper Scroll and also in the book of Joshua as one of the six cities of Judah. From references in the scroll to its watch-tower, aqueduct, fissure and reservoir, and the nearby wadi and gorge, John identified Secacah with Qumran. He wrote:

19. JMA to Joan, April 5, 1960.
20. *Ibid.*

Howard Stutchbury examining the mosaic at Mird

Land Rovers at the Qumran camp

The party moves out of Mird today. Tomorrow JW and JB begin sounding Qumran with their instruments. Robert's men will begin work on a concealed cave high up near Ain Feshka, an impressive cave which had been largely closed up before. It could prove fruitful.[21]

Robert found bones and artifacts that showed people had lived in the cave from time to time since about 400 B.C. and probably up to the Second Jewish Revolt of A.D. 132. Among the ruins of the monastery, near to where de Vaux had found three juglets full of silver coins under a floor four years earlier, Jock Wiatr's metal detector produced some "promising pings." As the magnetic rock of the area was tending to distort the readings from the detector, they poked around the spot without much optimism but did in fact unearth some Roman pottery missed by previous investigators.

Item 58 in the Copper Scroll says, "In Mount Gerizim, under the entrance of the upper pit, one chest and its contents, and 60 talents of silver."[22] Today's Mount Gerizim, with its twin peak Ebal, dominates the plain near Nablus in Samaria, about thirty miles north of Jerusalem. It seemed unlikely that anyone

21. JMA to Joan, April 7, 1960.
22. Allegro, *The Treasure of the Copper Scroll,* 1st ed., p. 55.

from the Jerusalem Temple would take one item of Temple treasure so far away from the rest, and especially into the despised Samaria. However, John argued that Jewish tradition from the second century A.D., based on a reference in Deuteronomy 11:29-30, identifies Gerizim and Ebal with two fortified mounds built near the village of Cypros near Jericho. These mounds were part of a string of defenses erected by Herod — as were Hyrcania, Machaerus, Masada, and Docus. Docus is the Dok of Item 32: "In Dok, under the eastern corner of the guardhouse, buried at seven cubits: twenty-two talents."[23] (John did not identify this reference to Dok at the time of writing the first edition of *The Treasure of the Copper Scroll*; he realized its significance in planning the expedition and included it in the second edition.) All the fortresses in this defense system were set on steep hillocks, separated from the surrounding hillside by ditches; each could be used as a signaling station to one or more of the others; all had cisterns dug into the base of the mound to store water for the occupants.

John took his team to look at Cypros and Docus. Among the rubble were dismembered porticoes, lintels, steps into some lost chambers. At Cypros they uncovered a shaft leading into a vault, probably for water storage. Both sites, they decided, would repay full-scale excavation in the future. Whoever hid treasure in the forts had obviously been in possession of them, or an ally of the commander there. This gave a clue to their identity, for Josephus tells how rebels of the Jewish Revolt had seized Cypros from its Roman garrison and only surrendered it to Vespasian when he reached Jericho in June 68.[24]

John drove with Izzard to the Valley of the Shadows, six miles northeast of Jerusalem, looking for "the Ravine of the Deeps [or, in the revised edition, "irrigation channels"] that are fed from the Great Wadi" in item 46 of the scroll.[25] They were looking for a cistern where twelve talents had been hidden. This time they were turned back by Israeli soldiers — they had strayed too near the border.

Item 49, according to John, read: "Under the Monument of Absalom, on the western side, buried at twelve cubits: 80 talents."[26] There is a monument to Absalom among the tombs in the Kidron Valley, and a tantalizing story is attached to it. An old lady who had been a pupil at a nearby convent in 1900 told how the girls had been taken on a picnic outing to the spot. A friend, she said, had climbed through a hole and returned with her apron full of gold coins. The nuns had confiscated the lot, and no more coins had been

23. Allegro, *The Treasure of the Copper Scroll*, 2nd ed., p. 24.
24. Josephus, *The Jewish War* 2.8.6.
25. Allegro, *The Treasure of the Copper Scroll*, 1st ed., p. 51.
26. *Ibid.*

found or heard of ever since. The cistern that John pointed out behind the monument held only the echo of the rumor.

John divided his time among the various sites, the Scrollery, and ongoing administration: bills, accommodation, supplies, vehicle repairs, etc. He was still contending with the press:

> *The Daily Express* are still worrying their correspondent for pictures of me at work finding treasure. He tracked me down to Zechariah yesterday. He then pumped me for details about the tomb, which I gave very happily, and left him even more perplexed by the whole business.[27]

He also tried, day after day, to gain permission to work in Jerusalem, or rather under it. Under the Dome of the Rock was a labyrinth of passages, cisterns, and chambers, sealed since Crusader times. In the 1870s, Captain Charles Warren of the British Royal Engineers had undertaken a heroic survey of the underground systems of Old Jerusalem for the Palestine Exploration Fund. Crawling through sewers and rubbish-filled vaults and tunnels, he had most painstakingly mapped the outer areas, but he had failed to penetrate the thicket of bureaucratic and religious obduracy that sealed off the Haram. About two dozen of the hiding places mentioned in the scroll refer to the Temple area. Who knew what might still be sealed inside it? John wrote:

> Today Sami and I called on the chief of the Haram. A nice old boy; he had our licences but felt he could not give permission to work until he had a further letter from the Minister of Education in his capacity as Head of the Dome of the Rock, and supported by the Prime Minister.[28]

A few days later, John wrote:

> Yesterday Sami and I went to see the man in charge of the Haram again, with the message from the Minister of Education that his authority was sufficient. However he, though very interested, was still not happy, and we said we would go and see the Muhaffiz, the big cheese of Jerusalem. Which we did, and he said that all was OK, but first he would need to consult the military lest there be some objection on their part. He wanted to see a plan of where we intended to work. We had not got one, so rushed away to a bookshop and bought a couple of copies of a local tourist guide and on a map therein inscribed in red pencil the appropriate marks. What an expedition![29]

27. JMA to Joan, April 2, 1960.
28. *Ibid.*
29. JMA to Joan, April 10, 1960.

The Kidron tombs, viewed from the Haram, 1960

Three days later:

Today we duly met the Brigadier, and a whole procession of us went round the Haram. After this the soldiers went off, the Brigadier having a meeting with the Muhaffiz at 10am. We spent another hour or so wandering round, dispersed, and rang the Muhaffiz' office to see what the answer was, to be told to call again tomorrow at noon. Oh, the wonders of the mysterious east. This means that, Friday intervening, we cannot possibly start until Saturday, leaving at most only four days. This still could be enough, but I am more doubtful now whether, despite all the support from above, we shall get permission. No-one will actually refuse, you understand, but. . . .[30]

Next day at noon:

The Army, in the shape of the blasted Brigadier, opposed the idea of our work in the Haram. Why, nobody seems to know. The Governor said the only move I could make now was to get backing from the Army higher in

30. JMA to Joan, April 13, 1960.

130

the scale than this bloke. But I cannot see why it should have been put to him in the first place. It's not a military area, except insofar as Jerusalem is one. Anyway, time is now so short. Tomorrow is Friday and useless. . . . I fear we must forgo the pleasure. Nuisance when we had got so far. However, I'll keep trying.[31]

John guessed that the real reason for withdrawal of support was neither political, military, nor even bureaucratic. Some weeks later the journal of the École Biblique carried an article rejoicing at his failure to explore the secret places of the Temple; for, after all, the treasure was officially fictional.

The most they were allowed to visit were the Antonia cisterns under the Sisters of Zion Convent. John and Howard poked around the underground passageways and agreed gloomily that it was just the sort of place they were probably looking for, if only a large number of others had not already been there. They were escorted out feeling more frustrated than ever.

John also visited Kando, the cobbler-turned-scroll-trader in Bethlehem. Apparently, offers from the government and museum to buy his scrolls had turned out to be empty promises. He was exasperated beyond argument and ready to sell to anyone with real cash. It was a chance to renew friendship as much as to do business.

You will be sorry to know that Kando is suffering from his teeth. From this, together with the news that he is 51 (according to his reckoning) and that in Bethlehem these days he is constantly assailed by tourists requiring his photograph, and is thinking of extracting five piastres from each, you will gather that I saw him yesterday and he was in fine form. Effusively glad to see me, and to receive a copy of my book, with his four pictures. We went to Sami's house to talk. He has promised to get all the scrolls together that the Bedu have and bring them to show me within a week. If this happens, I shall be the first to have seen the whole group. I am then to list the contents of the cache as completely as possible, and armed with that information to try to get together the money required. I have a scheme which might do us all good if it comes off.[32]

Time was up for the expedition. The official report was able to claim, soberly if wearily, that it had achieved its primary aim, "corroboration of the topographical references in the copper scroll." They had found evidence of activity from Roman times around the sites, they had excavated and searched

31. JMA to Joan, April 14, 1960.
32. JMA to Joan, April 11, 1960.

Inside the Antonia cisterns

the tomb of Zadok and the *nephesh* at Mird, and they had found all sorts of possible places where treasure *might* have been stored. But as John sighed, "If only we had found one bit of treasure!" As it was, the strongest possibilities of all lay sealed below the Haram, "the last and most mysterious of the sites, still holding its treasure."[33]

The second edition of *The Treasure of the Copper Scroll*, published by Anchor in paperback in 1964, omits the facsimile drawings but tells much more about the decipherment of the text — and the disputes surrounding it — and about the historical and archeological background. Milik's official edition had by then been published, and John amended his version in several places in the light of this, giving due credit to Milik for a more convincing translation. But he was still absolutely sure that the treasure was real and not fictitious. Many later scholars agree with him, though they reach varying conclusions on who wrote the scroll and who hid the treasure.

For example, Yigael Yadin in translating the Temple Scroll (1969) casts some light on the relationship between the Qumran community and the Temple priests. He holds that the community were unlikely to have been Zealots or to have had much to do with them, because the Zealots were close to the Pharisees and the scroll condemned the Pharisees for their comparative leniency.

Judah K. Lefkovits[34] concludes that the scroll probably belonged to the Temple and was taken to Qumran — not necessarily by Zealots — to rescue it from the Romans or the Temple priests or both. He thinks it a genuine inventory of Temple treasure, mainly because the scribe went to the trouble of engraving it on copper, which was expensive but could be purified, rather than on parchment, which could not. It was probably made between A.D. 25 and 75 in the last phase of the revolt against Rome, and it was done with care, not haste. He agrees with John that one cannot ascribe today's values to the weights and measures quoted in the scroll, and on his own reading calculates a total of sixty tons rather than two hundred, seventeen percent of it in gold.

Further studies on the scroll are brought together in *Copper Scroll Studies*, edited by George J. Brooke and Philip R. Davies.[35]

Wherever it originally came from, twenty centuries of treasure-hunting do not seem to have unlocked the mystery of the Copper Scroll.

---

33. JMA to Joan, April 16, 1960.

34. Lefkovits, *The Copper Scroll*.

35. G. J. Brooke and P. R. Davies, eds., *Copper Scroll Studies* (London: Sheffield Academic Press, 2002).

CHAPTER 7

More Expeditions

Caves and Ruins

There was no more treasure, but there was plenty of interest. All sorts of groups and gatherings wanted John to lecture or debate or lead a discussion. One memorable lecture tour took the form of a Swan's Hellenic cruise in April 1961, when besides giving talks and slide shows on the ship he took a party ashore and led them around some of the archeological sites of Jordan. If he had known beforehand that this would involve negotiating bus tickets, booking taxis, coordinating museum visits with the times the Mandelbaum Gate was open into the Israeli side of Jerusalem, finding alternative hotels for splinter groups of the party, and so on, he might not have offered. On the other hand, the tour operator found it immensely valuable. And friends he made on this trip proved enthusiastic and generous supporters during the following years.

During the April 1960 expedition, Robert de Langhe and John had noticed an ancient and apparently unexplored ruin at Mazin. Set beside the Dead Sea a few miles south of Qumran and solidly built with massive stone portals, it could have been a trading base, perhaps linked with the monastery, or it could have been a military garrison or naval base — King Herod's boat-house, as they liked to call it. Or perhaps Bar Kokhba's rebels had used it during the Second Revolt. In December 1961, John gathered a few friends, including de Langhe and Howard Stutchbury, and set off to investigate Mazin.

The building stood right on the shore with cliffs at its back. The only access was by sea; military landing craft brought in the initial set of equipment and thereafter the expedition used an inflatable dinghy that had been do-

Land Rovers in the desert

Mazin from the south

Excavating Khirbet Mazin

nated by a well-wisher. John had tried it out at Poole Harbour during a wet and chilly family holiday, remembered mainly for standing on the shingle waiting for him to master the outboard engine, which would cough, roar, and die over and over again. On the Dead Sea it continued to do this, leaving the campers very dependent for practical assistance on the Jordanian army, or more particularly on King Hussein's British adviser Wing-Commander Erik Bennett. The weather also affected how much they could do, and several stormy days confined them to the rocky gorges near the campsite. Howard made detailed drawings of the "boat-house," and among the cliffs and caves overhanging the wadi they found signs of habitation — broken pots, animal bones, tool-heads. Who had lived there, and when, was uncertain.

When the weather allowed, they looked at more of the Qumran and Ain Feshka area. The springs at Ain Feshka had enabled it to be cultivated, generation after generation; there was thought to be a tannery and evidence of other agricultural business. At Qumran the cliffs still presented a honeycomb of tantalizing possibilities, for their caves could have sheltered hundreds of fugitives and witnessed countless stories of fear and flight, secrecy and endeavor. John had no time on that trip to make a thorough search, but he identified several places worth coming back to.

As they strolled through Bethlehem on Christmas Eve, in the last week

Howard Stutchbury and John in Cave 11Q

of their trip, an elderly Arab beckoned them into his house, calling "Something to show you, Mr Johnny." He brought out pieces of carved wood, some worm-eaten, some engraved or inlaid: a jewelry box, bowls, a tiny bottle, and a handful of coins that showed they came from the time of Bar Kokhba. "From a cave between here and the Dead Sea," said the old man. This could mean anywhere the length of the Kidron. But they went back to the gorge, and as they wandered along it wondering where to start, their Bedouin guide Salem pointed out an opening among rocks high in the cliffs, some way inland from previous explorations. It was quite a large cave, he said, big enough for a family.

Howard and John scrambled up to have a look. Headlamps fixed, they crawled inside. The cave went back a long way and led into other chambers. It became a tunnel, thickly silted with dust and bat-droppings. John, on a hunch, backed out to try the second chamber. Howard crawled on. Light and sound from outside were shut off; the air was thick with dust. The lamp went out. At the same moment, a mob of bats hurled themselves at his head.

John meanwhile, was feeling around the walls. His fingers closed on a hard, shaped object in the sand. He drew it out: a little pottery oil-lamp, late Roman. Nearby, Salem found a bone needle, an adze-shaft, pieces of leather thong from a sandal, and then a coin: Simon Bar Kokhba. So people had lived here once; what else might they have left? John wriggled backwards with his prizes and met a spluttering Howard in the sunshine.

Bats or no bats, Christmas Cave deserved full exploration. *Search in the Desert,*[1] written in 1964, tells the story of the major expedition that John mounted during the winter of 1962-63.

It was an exploration on three fronts: Mazin, Christmas Cave, and Ain Feshka. The aim was to look for artifacts, documents, signs of habitation — anything that might throw light on the history of the area between the first century B.C. and the end of the Second Jewish Revolt in A.D. 135. By filming and writing about the expedition, John also hoped to raise the profile of Scrolls research, and not only its profile but also funds for future research. To this end he established the Dead Sea Scrolls Fund in 1962 as a registered charity, and he publicized it wherever he lectured.

The lectures were hugely popular. In village halls and debating chambers up and down the country, from Townswomen's Guilds to professional institutes, at colleges, libraries, and literary luncheons, John showed his slides and talked, and his enthusiasm fired questions and applause. The ferment of ideas and suggestions and opinions that these lectures stirred up was what he loved. Among them were many offers: "Can I come on an expedition? Could you use a surveyor/mechanic/photographer/cook?"

From the most serious and persistent questioners he enrolled an expedition force. It turned out to be a mixture of experts and amateurs, professionals and students, from many walks of life. There was the archeologist John Gray, then Professor of Semitic Studies at Aberdeen University and once John's Hebrew tutor at Manchester. He brought with him a keen and skilled amateur archeologist, Douglas Miller. The two expedition doctors included the family's G.P., Dennis Broadbent. There were Dick and John Habershon, whose family business had recently been taken over, leaving them with plenty of time and a fund of skills as drivers, mechanics, photographers, and general handymen. There was a caver, David Roberts, and a climber (also the expedition comedian), Bob Trueman. The architects Howard Stutchbury and Keith Symonds brought skills in surveying and draughtsmanship. An Anglican vicar from Norfolk, the Reverend Hugh Edgell, came to learn about the land of Jesus' birth. He enjoyed debating and held the balance in the more-or-less friendly campfire arguments between the Roman Catholic Robert de Langhe and the Presbyterian John Gray.

Twelve student teachers from Alsager College came in a minibus with

---

1. J. M. Allegro, *Search in the Desert* (New York: Doubleday, 1964).

their tutors. Their enthusiasm overrode all John's warnings about stony campsites, desert weather, lack of toilets, and a diet based on dehydrated meals and soup mix. The college contingent contributed a good deal to the expedition in terms of laborious cave-searching, campsite housekeeping, and romantic interest — the latter not confined to the students. Finally two New Zealanders, Anne and Anna, traveling the world on a two-seater scooter, heard John lecture in London and talked themselves onto the expedition with cheerful determination — and as soon as they had arrived and taken over the cooking no one could have imagined coping without them.

As for supplies and equipment, many organizations offered all sorts of things, from adhesive bandages to mint cake. The gifts came out of each company's public relations budget, so of course they were not entirely altruistic, but some individuals were amazingly generous. For example, a company director whom John had met on the Hellenic cruise gave him one of the three Land Rovers, and a firm in Leicestershire provided two generators and an electric hammer on indefinite free loan. Throughout November 1962, crates piled up on the garden paths of John and his friends. "There was a general feeling in the neighbourhood that the sooner this expedition started off for the deserts of Jordan the better," wrote John.[2] Packing the Land Rovers took several attempts, and they began their journey across Europe grossly over-laden. John flew out ahead of them to organize paperwork in Amman and Jerusalem.

The quicksands were in the bureaucracy, not the desert. The excavation license was not ready, because, after keeping it on his desk for three or four weeks, the Minister of Education refused to sign it. He said foreigners ought not to be allowed to dig in Jordan. John was unimpressed. "I've been to Bethlehem and seen Ibrahim and laid on — hopefully — 16 men and camp boys for Thursday 9am at the naval base. Although we have no license I am carrying on regardless," he wrote to Joan.[3] It took a visit to the Palace next day to get things moving.

John's friendship with King Hussein began in the 1950s, when he had first met Wing-Commander Erik Bennett of the Royal Jordanian Air Force, a special adviser to the King. Erik took him go-carting and introduced the King, who was passionate about the sport. Erik's successor as special adviser was Tony Gardiner, and Tony's daughter Muna became Hussein's second wife. Their son Abdullah (now King) was still a toddler in 1962, "a wonderful lusty lad," wrote John, "adored by all, of course. His eyes are large and Arab-

2. Allegro, *Search in the Desert*, p. 43
3. J. M. Allegro to Joan Allegro, November 25, 1962.

shaped, but Muna's blue! He's taken his first steps and, like Mark, is not going to crawl."[4] (Mark was John and Joan's son, born in 1957.)

King Hussein took a keen interest in John's expeditions, and his help was most valuable, in fact essential, with each of them. On this occasion, after an hour's wait at the Palace, "with a large crowd of people who'd been there long before, I was called in and effusively greeted."[5] Through the army, the King laid on landing craft, a helicopter, dinghies, tents, blankets, and jerry-cans and promised to come and see the camp for himself. And with the Gardiners' help, John arranged for Joan to fly out at Christmas to join the camp for a week.

But by Wednesday November 28, the rest of the party had still not arrived. John wrote to Joan, "No more news of the landrovers. If they don't arrive today I shall have to stand off the operation — quite a business, and a bally nuisance. It would be easier if the telephone communication to the rest of the world were more than one weak line."

The King was less perturbed than John about where the students might be. "The monarch's face lit up when I mentioned them, especially the six girls! In fact, it rather looks, from the interest shown on all sides, that we shall be inundated with visitors. Could be a nuisance but good for PR."[6]

Everyone arrived together. The students burst out of their bus in Jerusalem to storm the filling station, cafés, youth hostel, and museums. The Land Rovers were checked, unloaded, reorganized, and reloaded. The New Zealanders arrived on their scooter. On December 1 the expedition set up three camps at Mazin, Ain Feshka, and Christmas Cave.

Getting there overland was not easy. The Land Rovers toiled up and down steep ravines and along the rock-strewn beds of the wadis. The heaviest things, such as the generators and water tanks, came by royal authority in an RJAF helicopter, much to the delight of the team, who all vied for a ride in it.

Pitching camp was not easy either, especially at Christmas Cave where they were trying to peg down their tents on rock in sand-charged gusts of wind. The Alsager students at Ain Feshka managed a neat row of tents, Boy-Scout fashion; the rest of the haphazard collection blew down from time to time. So did the canvas screen around the latrine; you had to pick quiet weather for a visit. Washing — self or clothes — took place in the nearby spring and offered good entertainment for passing shepherds and their goats.

The students' job was to search the lower cliffs behind the camp. They

4. *Ibid.*
5. *Ibid.*
6. JMA to Joan, November 28, 1962.

Joan and John at Cave 1Q

had occasional trips to other historical sites, but most of the time they worked patiently and uncomplainingly through the dust, washed as little as possible, and were thoroughly happy. Several paired off. One lad caused a major alarm by going off on his own during a visit to Mar Saba. His tutors waited up all night in mounting fear for his safety. But in the morning he walked into camp as calmly as if he had been down to the off-license, a shop selling alcoholic drinks. Some Bedouins had found him wandering, taken him to their own camp for the night, and showed him the way back after breakfast.

Everything seemed especially worthwhile in the evenings, when the desert sunset flared rose and gold. As it died, the thorn-and-dung campfires were lit, people ate and talked or sang, and sharing in friendship and adventure they wanted to be nowhere else on earth.

Joan arrived on December 23, leaving the children with their grandparents in a Dorset village blitzed by snow. In Jordan there were sand, rock, searing sun by day and deep cold at night, the bustle of the excavations, everyone freely talking and laughing and swearing just as they wanted to . . . it was a different world from a Britain grimly laboring through its industrial Christmas. It was clear why John came back to Jordan year after year.

A highlight of the whole expedition was King Hussein's visit on Christmas Day. Piloting his own helicopter, he called in on the camps at Ain Feshka

The Ain Feshka camp from the air

A bathing party at Ain Feshka

Above, H.M. King Hussein at Ain Feshka, Christmas Day, 1962;
below, the King drops in at Ain Feshka by helicopter

John at Ain Feshka

and Christmas Cave. He asked with great interest about everything they were doing, chatted over mugs of tea, and left crates of Christmas crackers to help them all feel festive.

The King continued to provide tremendous practical assistance. At the start he had got things moving by stopping the ministerial quibbling over licenses and by using RJAF resources to airlift equipment into camp. A week later, Anne (the New Zealand girl) injured her foot at Mazin, ignored it, and, when it became infected, needed hospital treatment urgently. John telephoned Tony Gardiner, and an RJAF helicopter whisked her to hospital in Amman at the King's expense. Anne protested all the way, but the hospital saved her leg.

Apart from Anne's injury, technical problems dogged the Mazin camp from the start. Getting fresh water was a nightmare, and there was never enough. The generator needed repair, and the dinghy's outboard motor did not work properly. They took to rowing instead, but after losing one oar and a pair of rowlocks during a squall, they rigged up a sail — picturesque, but of limited efficiency. They were finding archeological evidence in small amounts, but it seemed not enough to justify the trouble, and after ten days John pulled everyone out of Mazin to join the main camp at Ain Feshka.

Christmas Cave and the cliffs further along the Kidron were storehouses of history. The expedition confirmed that people had used the caves from Chalcolithic times up to the Crusades. Roman coins and artifacts showed that people were living or hiding there around the time of the First Jewish Revolt in A.D. 66-73 — tying in with the evidence from Qumran — and again during Bar Kokhba's rebellion of A.D. 132-35. But the main thing they learned, as ever, was how much there still remained to learn about the place. As had happened time and again, the day before they were due to leave they had news of fresh cave discoveries near Qumran. There was barely time to find the place, worm past the spill of soft sand blocking the entrance, and disturb some bats. Then it was time to go — reluctantly, with so much still to discover.

Shapira and the Mujib Expedition

In the late summer of 1883, an antiques dealer from Jerusalem called Moses Wilhelm Shapira had arrived at the British Museum with some documents he thought would interest them. Carefully he unwrapped fifteen frayed and faded strips of parchment inscribed in ancient Hebrew characters. He had spent much of the summer deciphering the text and found it to be part of the book of Deuteronomy, though with some divergence from the standard

Mist over Mujib

recension. Shapira said he had bought the strips from some Arabs, who had found them wrapped in cloth and hidden in a cave in the side of a rocky gorge of the Wadi Mujib, which runs into the eastern side of the Dead Sea. He wanted one million pounds for them.

The Museum commissioned a Bible scholar, David Ginsburg, to examine the manuscripts and judge their authenticity. Ginsburg was intrigued. He pored over the text for weeks and found it to be Deuteronomy mixed with other verses from the Pentateuch. The script was one of the most ancient he had ever seen, perhaps as early as the ninth century B.C., for it was similar to that found on a Moabite tablet recently discovered in Dibin, above the Arnon gorge. *The Times* caught onto what Ginsburg was doing and published his translation in installments under excited headlines. But some critics were skeptical about the scrolls' authenticity, and Ginsburg hesitated.

Then Clermont-Ganneau, a French scholar working in the same field, arrived in London. Clermont-Ganneau knew of Shapira: He had already come across some pottery that Shapira had presented as pre-Christian and had proved it spurious. Though denied access to the manuscripts, Clermont-Ganneau condemned them as forgeries because of the aberrant passages of text and because they had been written on strips cut from the lower margin of old law scrolls, themselves of unproven origin. And no parchment, he said, could survive two thousand years of the winter rains of Palestine. Ginsburg immediately agreed; the manuscripts and their owner were publicly vilified.

Throughout the next eighty years, various scholars had wanted to re-examine the case. Unfortunately, the strips themselves had disappeared. Photographs remained in the British Museum, and there had been a possible sighting in a London bookshop. But nothing had been seen of the manuscripts for certain since World War Two: They could have been destroyed in the Blitz or lost in the corner of an attic.

However, the discovery of the Dead Sea Scrolls undermined Clermont-Ganneau's arguments for dismissing Shapira's manuscript. The scribes who wrote the Scrolls had used similar techniques: patching together second-hand pieces of parchment, adopting a venerably antiquated Phoenician script, and using variant forms of biblical texts with many additions and omissions. And the caves of the rift valley had certainly preserved the Scrolls from the weather. J. L. Teicher made these points in *The Times Literary Supplement* of March 22, 1957, and now John took up the cause. For one thing, he felt it likely that even if Shapira's manuscripts never turned up again, others might yet be found in the same unexplored area of the east bank. And when he looked deeper into the case, he found Shapira himself an intriguing personality.

Dr. Moses Wilhelm Shapira was no ordinary antiques dealer. He supplied museums and libraries across Europe with ancient artifacts from the Holy Land. He was proud to entitle himself on his shop sign "agent to the British Museum." Day to day, he made his living selling curios and trinkets in Old Jerusalem. Shapira knew well how to titillate the tourists with incense and dim lamplight and part them from their jangling purses. But with certain visitors, who looked more keenly and asked deeper questions, he would talk for hours. He would show them the real treasures of his collection, unlock for them the myths and philosophies of the designs or words, speculate on where the pieces came from and who had owned them before. Shapira learned languages and studied philosophy. Born a Polish Jew, he converted to Christianity and married a German businessman's daughter. He spent his earnings on travel, always wanting to learn. At home, as his daughter Siona described in a BBC radio talk in 1957, he would now and then shut the shop and ride out of the cluttered city to seek space for his dreams on the windswept sands. Sometimes he met traders who, playing to his romantic streak, supplied quantities of authentic pulp for him to sell to tourists as curios.

But some of it was real. As he described in a letter to Professor Strack of Berlin University on May 9, 1883, "In July 1878 I met with several Bedouin. They told me that several years ago, some Arabs had occasion to hide themselves in caves high up in a rock facing the Mujib — the Biblical river Arnon flowing to the eastern shore of the Dead Sea. They discovered there several bundles of very old rags. Thinking they might contain gold, they peeled away a good deal of the cotton or linen, found only some black charms, and threw them away; but one Arab took them up, and since having the charms in his tent, he has had good fortune." Shapira asked to buy some, and piece by piece they brought him their scrolls.

Shapira believed absolutely that the Deuteronomy strips were as ancient as they appeared. He did not have enough formal training in archeology or paleography to prove it, but he staked his reputation and the livelihood of his wife and daughter on finding experts who could. He offered the manuscript to the scrutiny of both the Palestine Exploration Fund and the British Museum. The subject was laid before the public week after week in newspapers and journals.

When Ginsburg and Clermont-Ganneau found against him, Shapira could not bear his disgrace. On August 23, 1883, he wrote to Dr. Ginsburg:

> You have made a fool of me by publishing and exhibiting things you believe to be false. I do not think I shall be able to survive this shame. Although I am not yet convinced that the manuscript is a forgery — unless Monsieur Ganneau did it. I will leave London in a day or two for Berlin.
>   Yours truly, Moses Wilhelm Shapira

For some weeks he wandered inconsolate through the Low Countries, leaving a trail of discarded clothing and unposted letters. At last, in the Hotel of the Valley of Flowers in Rotterdam, he put a pistol to his head.

A scholar, a shopkeeper, a dreamer, a hunter of ideas — one can see why John was drawn to Moses Shapira. Believing his manuscripts were genuine, he was not afraid to stand out from the crowd and ask questions that went beyond conventional wisdom.

In the winter of 1963-64, John set out to explore the eastern side of the Dead Sea, to establish at least whether the conditions that had preserved the Dead Sea Scrolls on the western bank could also support Shapira's theory. With a team of eight he pitched camp on a patch of flattish land close to the eastern shore, where the Wadi Mujib runs into the sea. A small concrete hut belonging to the Water Board became the camp kitchen.

In early morning the air was still and clear, and at sunset the whole bowl of rock, sea, and sky flushed with flame. These were the most magical times. In-between, the valley held heat like an oven. The team worked along the seashore and the cliffs on either side of the wadi, looking for caves, ruins, or other signs of habitation. The rock was mainly sandstone, weather-carved

The Mujib in spate

John at the hot springs where Herod came to ease his sufferings

into weird and spectacular shapes. Imagination could people it with traders, travelers, anchorites, maybe King Herod seeking relief for his sores and itches in the warm salt water. But they all remained ghosts of the imagination, for they had left few material remains.

For several days the team worked peacefully at their charts and samples, visited only by an occasional curious shepherd. Then one day two Bedouin men arrived, talking fast and urgently. John interpreted: "They say the weather's about to break. Get the stores inside and secure the tents." The sky looked as calm and blue as ever, but the others obeyed with a shrug. In the middle of the night the storm struck, with a ferocity seldom seen in that area. It flattened the tents, overturned the jerry-cans, pounded the hut with all their belongings, and turned the wadi into a boiling brown torrent. Unable to leave or to work, they crowded into the biggest tent to wait. When at last the storm passed and the sun came pearling back through the mist, they bundled what was left of their equipment into the dinghies and headed back up the Dead Sea to the naval base. John admitted resignedly that on the eastern bank of the Dead Sea no manuscript, let alone Shapira's two-thousand-year-old parchment, could have survived without rotting under such a bombardment of rain, however irregularly it happened.

But they were not quite finished. They took a trip inland, heading east, to the upper reaches of the wadi. Here, as they crested a hill, they saw mile after mile of scrubby sand, rocky rises, white pock-marked cliffs. This was limestone country, scroll-cave country. It must be what Shapira had described in a letter to a German scholar eighty years earlier: caves high up in a rock facing the Mujib, and an old burial place. He had marveled at the dryness of the place, sheltered from rain by the north-south ridge, and had guessed that such a dry land might be able to preserve extremely old documents.

The Shapira question was still open. John wrote: "We should learn from the mistakes [of Shapira's detractors] and keep our minds open to possibilities and ideas that our present imperfect understanding cannot yet encompass. This is particularly so of the archaeological field, where almost every season brings fresh discoveries that demand a reassessment of outmoded theories."[7] His book *The Shapira Affair* was published by Doubleday and Company in 1965 and was generally well received, though not everyone was convinced that Clermont-Ganneau had been mistaken.

To reassess old ideas with a mind open to all possibilities: John's approach to Shapira was his approach to everything else, and he knew very well how it could lead to trouble in academic circles.

7. J. M. Allegro, *The Shapira Affair* (New York: Doubleday, 1965), p. 139.

CHAPTER 8

More Controversies

Scroll Publications and Delays

In Manchester, John worked steadily through his share of the Cave 4 fragments, using official photographs supplied from the Scrollery in Jerusalem and others he had taken himself, which were sometimes clearer and showed slightly different perspectives. Editing the fragments was painstaking work: grouping, regrouping, translating, and interpreting. To help with the translation he enlisted Arnold Anderson, a colleague at Manchester University. Together they were able to share insights or lay out arguments on a tricky word or phrase, and they made slow but steady progress. It seemed painfully slow at times, but theirs was a good deal brisker than that of other members of the team. *Discoveries in the Judaean Desert of Jordan V (DJDJ V)* had to wait for publication until 1968, though John reckoned much of it had been ready long before — he offered to submit it in 1960 — and had been held up while de Vaux tried to get the other editors' contributions in order.

Meanwhile, during the late 1950s, John published his sections one at a time in learned journals, mainly the *Journal of Biblical Literature, Journal of Semitic Studies,* and *Palestine Exploration Quarterly.* But the world went on waiting for *Discoveries in the Judaean Desert of Jordan.* The wait was to go on throughout the 1960s and beyond. In print and on air John deplored the delays in "the painfully slow release of scrolls texts." Replying to a letter in the *Sunday Times* in November 1965, criticizing him along with the rest of the team for holding back, he stated:

> As for my own contribution, the last I heard from our Editor-in-Chief on the subject was a letter dated June 5, 1963, urging me *not* to send my work,

long before completed, to Jerusalem. I still await further instructions, but in any case have already published the bulk of my section in preliminary form, as every specialist knows.[1]

Why the Delay?

John had suggested to de Vaux on September 16, 1956, on the question of publicizing the Copper Scroll, that in light of the conflicting theories about it, "I should have thought that the proper thing would have been to have published the text as soon as possible, and let others decide for themselves." Here he stated the principle he had worked on from the start: He made no claim to produce a definitive translation of any of the scrolls, but he did believe above all that all the manuscripts should be openly accessible for any scholar to work on and argue over. Only that way would people see their significance in a clear light and arrive at a true understanding of their heritage, undistorted by religious prejudice.

In this there seemed to be a fundamental difference — apart from the religious one — between John's outlook and the team's. John was all for publishing everything, ready or not, with open access and open discussion, so that scholars everywhere could share the debate over translation and interpretation, and people in general could know what was going on. Some later scholars criticized him for rushing flawed translations into print, and he was the first to give credit to Milik and others who improved on them. But as he wrote to Noel Freedman two years later, "I subscribe to the heresy that what scholars are wanting most is the text, and not clever remarks on same by the bloke editing it."[2]

The others were more cautious, more patient, and more painstaking. Perhaps they were also more concerned with the emotional sensibility of church people. No one could argue against scholarly caution: wanting to check and re-check a reading or translation. However, Skehan, who had instigated the letter to *The Times*, explained with rather tentative cordiality that his main concern was not to upset people:

> I presume you are still a lion of wrath, or something. . . . I trust you will eventually see that you were in fact disquieting a great many people for whom I would be bound to feel a direct and personal responsibility —

1. *The Sunday Times,* November 21, 1965.
2. J. M. Allegro to D. N. Freedman (DNF), November 19, 1958.

and that anything I've had to say about the Teacher of Righteousness business, jointly with others or separately, has been directly related to that.[3]

Disquieting people, in John's opinion, was no reason to forbear from open discussion.

John was a natural communicator: His talks and articles were entertaining, scholarly, provocative, or all of these at once. Being good at it, he saw no reason to hold back. In the early days, the other team members had encouraged him to go into print: "Milik suggested I publish one of my pieces, a commentary on a psalm";[4] "De Vaux called me outside this morning, and discussed my publishing of a piece of my *peser*."[5] Within a year or two, however, they were acting more cautiously, and seemed unwilling to publish much at all. Several reasons were put forward or assumed.

First, the work was difficult: There were thousands of fragments, many frayed or faded, some bearing a single letter or none, difficult to transcribe let alone interpret. Different scribes had produced variants on the same texts, with different handwriting and orthography, and paragraph divisions that were seldom obvious. All this gave more reason, in John's view, for sharing the challenge with others. By 1955-56 it had become obvious that Cave 4 was only the start, and an eight-person editing team could not hope to keep up with the supply of material. But de Vaux did not think to expand the team. Even when the discovery of Cave 11 brought in a rush of scroll fragments, it appeared to John that de Vaux was refusing to move on it. John complained impatiently to an earlier colleague, Professor Muilenburg:

> The rub comes with Cave 11. De Vaux stipulated that nothing should be done until Cave 4 was out of the way. There is of course not the slightest reason why a completely new set of scholars should not be brought in to deal with 11Q whilst we are clearing Cave 4. In fact, so vast are Milik's, Starcky's and Strugnell's lots of 4Q, I believe that they should be split up immediately and new scholars brought in to get the stuff out quickly.[6]

In the same letter John put forward a scheme for how to do this: "My plan, which I have suggested verbally to Awni, is that the committee issue invitations straight away to the academic institutions of the world inviting

---

3. P. Skehan to JMA, September 25, 1956.
4. J. M. Allegro to Joan Allegro, January 22, 1954.
5. JMA to Joan, January 30, 1954.
6. JMA to J. Muilenburg, December 24, 1957.

scholars who can spare six months or a year at least to come to Jerusalem and take their place in the team. The resident members would train them in the business of editing these fragments, and then divide the bigger collections among them." The plan was not taken up, but it showed how John was attempting to look beyond the original team structure.

Secondly, de Vaux was aiming at a definitive edition, presenting the whole text, translation and commentary complete and perfect. In the early days, while dealing with the Cave 1 material, this had seemed attainable, for the scrolls had been in much better shape and easier to manage. However, given the nature of the work and the nature of the material from Cave 4, it now seemed an unrealistic aim. In John's view, it was an attitude that impressed only those who held it, and went on so long that people began to suspect self-aggrandizement on the editors' part, and then to suspect suppression.

Thirdly, leaving aside suspicions, there was a basic division in method that reflected the difference in outlook. John published his translations first in learned journals, on the principle of getting them to the world outside as fast as possible and on the understanding that that was what they had agreed to do. He followed up these publications with *Discoveries in the Judaean Desert of Jordan V (DJDJ V)*, but he did not seem to think it just or necessary to fill the latter with his own commentary, which he felt would distract the reader from the text. As he stated in the Preface to *DJDJ V*:

> Most of these documents have already appeared in provisional editions in learned journals since that date [1953]. Both in these preliminary publications and here it has been my practice to offer no more than the basic essentials of photographs, transliteration, translation of non-Biblical passages where this might serve some useful interpretative purpose, and the minimum of textual notes. This should give the specialists at least the raw material for their work of elucidating the Qumran texts.[7]

Most of the team followed de Vaux's line: *Discoveries in the Judaean Desert* was to be final, official, definitive, and supported by comprehensive notes. Consequently, *DJDJ V* was a good deal thinner than the other volumes, and it has been left to later scholars to fill the gaps. Strugnell criticized John's edition for mistranslations, lack of commentary, little attention to line length, and no attempt to reconstruct the passages where words were missing.[8] Notes on paleography, orthography, line length, and paragraph division are indeed

---

7. J. M. Allegro and A. A. Anderson, *Discoveries in the Judaean Desert of Jordan V, Qumran Cave 4, I (4Q158-4Q186)* (Oxford: Clarendon Press, 1968).

8. J. Strugnell, "Notes en marge du volume V de 'DJDJ,'" *RevQ* 7 (1969-71): 168-76.

missing from John's version. However, a good proportion of his translations have been accepted in subsequent publications of the Scrolls. While working on them, he did in fact reconstruct complete passages of biblical text. Notes left with Arnold Anderson and later passed to George Brooke show pages of reconstruction.[9] However, John had crossed them through and included none in the published version. He may have thought he had no right to hypothesize about text that wasn't there, as this would have gone against his stated principle: to publish the text as soon as possible and "give the specialists at least the raw material for their work of elucidating the Qumran texts." Evidently he did not think of himself as a specialist in the rank of people like Milik.

Scholarly caution was root and branch to the team's approach, and it was flamboyantly missing from John's. His way was insight first, substantiation later. Conjecture was the way to original thought, and original thought was what he valued most of all, in himself and in other people. Substantiation counted most among academics, but conjecture was more fun. Frank Cross warned him, in a letter of October 2, 1959, that rushing into print was the way to "scholarly suicide"; the risk delighted John.

Another difficulty was that editing scrolls was a part-time occupation for most of the team. Only de Vaux, Milik, and Strugnell stayed in Jerusalem all the time, while the others had teaching commitments at home and had to use vacations or special leave to visit the museum. In John's case, Arnold Anderson's help as a foot-slogger with the translations enabled him to branch out. He was busy lecturing around the country, writing and organizing expeditions as well as teaching at the university and working with Arnold on the scroll prints. Closer cooperation with the team, on both sides, might have narrowed the divide between John and the others, so that they could have discussed with him where he might add more detail to his presentation and he might have persuaded them to offer the questionable parts more readily to public scrutiny.

Other suggestions that commentators have raised to account for the delay in publication included political instability — which certainly made de Vaux feel less secure in Jerusalem and probably less willing than ever to invite controversy — and sloth. Some have blamed professional jealousy or empire-building, which arose from the initial agreement that each team member would own the right to publish his section. Some members later appeared to extend the "right to publish" to the theses that their graduate students wrote about these sections.

---

9. G. J. Brooke, "4Q158: Reworked Pentateuch[a] or Reworked Pentateuch A?" *Dead Sea Discoveries 8,3* (Leiden: Brill, 2001).

A Catholic Monopoly?

Many, especially in the popular press, blamed religious fear and bias. At first John foresaw criticism on this front but dismissed the idea. He warned Frank Cross in a letter of August 5, 1956, that outsiders suspected suppression: "Nonsense we know, but this business of holding back important documents merely to boost a particular publication lends itself to such fantasies." But rumors of suppression or conspiracy were fuelled, not stifled, by the apparent secrecy surrounding the scrolls, and eventually John came to think there could be something in them. It seemed to him that de Vaux was building up "a Catholic monopoly on the Scrolls." As he described to Muilenburg:

> The affair is taking on more sinister aspects. From the way the publication of the fragments is being planned, the non-Catholic members of the team are being removed as quickly as possible. Milik's section now totals nearly 200 plates, Starcky's nearly a hundred. Strugnell has about the same and is becoming a perfect little yes-man, for his money depends on de V's good graces. . . . Meanwhile, the world waits for Milik to deal with the whole of the Murabba'at semitic stuff, having done Cave One, and the bulk of Cave Four, and any odd thing that comes within the reach of the École Biblique in the meantime (like the fraudulently named "Unknown Provenance" material). And there is no doubt in his own mind that he is going to deal with most of Cave Eleven.
>
> I learned this summer from Awni that in fact de V. has not the complete control of the Scrolls that one would think from his decrees. He is merely one member of a committee, headed by the mayor of Jerusalem, and containing representatives of the ASOR and the Dept. of Antiquities. I don't know whether this committee ever meets, but it has had little effect so far in breaking the Catholic monopoly on the Scrolls. But a dangerous situation is fast developing where the original idea of an international and interdenominational editing group is being bypassed. All fragments are brought first to de V or Milik, and, as with Cave Eleven, complete secrecy is kept over what they are till long after they have been studied by this group. Even the purchasing has been kept in this closed circle, to the extent of crippling the Museum finances. For if the purchasing was the result of a public appeal, I have no doubt that it would have to be done by a committee of more than the École Biblique gang. Something, sooner or later, will have to be done about this situation, but just what, I don't know.
>
> . . . I believe that a rule should be laid down that preliminary publica-

tions must be made *immediately* the document is collected as far as it seems possible, and that a steady stream of these publications should be made in one journal, so that they can easily be found by other scholars the world over without searching through every journal that is anywhere published. An idea might be to make the Jordan Department of Antiquities Annual a quarterly and use that, to the joy of the Department of Antiquities.

This business of holding up publication of fragments merely to avoid the 'deflowering' of the final volume seems to me most unscholarly. There was perhaps good reason for restricting the number of collaborators when we were in the first stages of collecting the pieces. But now that most of this work is done, anybody can work over a document and publish it in at least provisional form.[10]

John became increasingly convinced that de Vaux, and perhaps the religious order that subsidized the École, was deliberately suppressing or slowing down work on the scrolls and that a Roman Catholic clique had a stranglehold on the Scrollery. As he told Dajani on January 10, 1959, after the BBC film had failed for the fifth time to be screened when scheduled, "I am convinced that if something does turn up which affects the Roman Catholic dogma, the world will never see it."

The plea for openness was one that John went on making for thirty years, right up to his death. It was only to be achieved in 1991, and then largely through the efforts of other scholars who were bold enough to stand out against the establishment.

The Plan to Widen Access to the Scrolls

As the only member of the original team without an ecclesiastical interest, and known for his independent stance, John felt he had a special responsibility to the cause of objective scholarship. He had a plan to open up access to the Scrolls. He first intimated his ideas to Professor Muilenburg on October 31, 1957:

> I am starting a campaign, very quietly for the moment, to get the scrollery clique broken up and new blood injected, with the idea of getting some of that stuff Milik, Strugnell, and Starcky are sitting on published quickly in provisional form. Would you still be willing to go out and clear some of

10. J. M. Allegro to J. Muilenburg, December 24, 1957.

the fragments into journals? Please say nothing to anybody for the moment — it's a ticklish situation. But you will agree that something must be done, and that soon.

Then in a letter to Awni Dajani on March 2, 1958, John refers to the idea they had earlier discussed:

I have delayed taking further action about the Scrolls team and its enlargement: you will remember that I had in mind to put up a proposal to the Committee. I wanted to hear from you first about the present situation.

This letter mentioned that the BBC film they had made in September 1957, originally due to be screened at Christmas, had been put off until Easter 1958. By January 10, 1959, it had been put off five times:

Dear Awni,

Well, they've done it again. For the fifth time the BBC have put off showing that TV programme on the Scrolls: it was last due to go out on the 22nd of this month, and we had got as far as sending pictures and story to the Radio Times. There can be no reasonable doubt now that de Vaux's cronies in London are using their influence to kill the programme, as he wished. I should not be at all surprised if the Vatican has not commanded its contacts in the BBC, where they are numerous and powerful, to keep it off the screens.

My patience is exhausted, as I am sure yours is too. I will not have a French priest interfering in this way with British TV, and I am really very worried indeed now about the future of the Scrolls. It is clear that de Vaux will stop at nothing to control the Scrolls material. Somehow or other he must be removed from his present controlling position. Either he must be thrown out by the Jordan government, or be bypassed. I feel a special responsibility about this, since I am the only person on that team who is not playing de Vaux's game, willingly or unwittingly. The point is, how can it be done?

He had an action plan based on money:

Here, perhaps, is our opportunity. If *we* can raise the appeal for, say, a million dollars, *we* can buy the Scrolls on behalf of Jordan, to be kept in Jordan and to be edited as decreed by the committee, and *not* by de Vaux. In other words . . . bring in a large team to publish the stuff, from every country and every religious denomination. . . . *Everything* that is found will be published for the world, Church or no Church, for we shall see that no single denomination or party gets control or sees the material alone.

. . . I am sure that some millionaire in the States or elsewhere will put up the million dollars if we offer to call the collection by his name. . . . Then the Scrolls can stay in *Jordan* — and I think this is terribly important. I do not want to see that stuff scattered all over the world, and it would be worth considering whether, with the money, we might pay back those who have given some already, like Manchester, in order to keep what they bought of Cave Four in Jordan.

How to go about it? Well, obviously I have no authority to make the appeal, but I think I can say that I do have the ear of the world as no-one else of that Scrolls team. And the world knows that if I have a hand in that money, and the purchase and editing, nothing that passes through my hands will be suppressed for any reason. This should be made quite clear in the appeal — that the money will be spent by a committee of no one religious denomination or even nationality — in fact the committee that the Jordan Government set up in 1956, and which de Vaux has bypassed on every single occasion.

Quite frankly, I think it would be a ripe opportunity to take over the whole Museum, Scrolls and all, perhaps on the plea that the Government is dissatisfied with the way things are being done in the matter of the Scrolls, that they are not being published fast enough and there is some danger that they may never be seen at all.

This would cause a first class row, but the Jordan Government would find scholarship and the laymen on their side, for all are quite sick of the lack of information they are getting about the newly discovered stuff. To my mind it would clear the air considerably. Then when de Vaux and his cronies are yelping to the world that the material *is* being published as fast as possible, I will step in and say that it certainly is not, and that the copper scroll's contents have been purposely held back, even from the Jordan authorities, as being 'untrustworthy'. In short, you would have my complete support in everything you do which will get this stuff out honestly and quickly.

. . . I think we have a very good chance of pulling the thing off — loads of money in the bank for scrollering, an open team to break this Catholic monopoly, and a hell of a lot of prestige coming your and the Department's way. Remember, you are not putting out any anti-clerical propaganda in any way, merely insisting that from now on the Jordan authorities are going to take a firm hand in the publishing of the Scrolls. Nothing will possibly be suppressed. The present team is doing fine work, but it hasn't sufficient numbers or funds. . . . The Jordan govt. can always threaten to nationalize the Museum unless they can ensure that all is above board regarding the Scrolls.

His vision went further.

The Scrolls will form a bridge so much needed between Jew, Christian and Muslim *religiously*. Although each religion must preserve its own distinguishing marks and revelation, nevertheless, if through the Scrolls we see a common background and fount (which in fact we do), it should enable man to understand his fellow better and point a way to understanding and peace. This is a popular line, for men are indeed looking for some thread, however slender, on which they can fasten hope of reconciliation between the three great religions of the world. I, as a practising atheist or what-have-you, can say this and get away with it, where anybody of one of the faiths will only be accused of plugging his own line somewhere. . . . At least, I have no axe to grind, and am not afraid of publishing anything.[11]

Access to knowledge, freedom of speech, and a bridge to peace: a trinity of hope that fired John all his life. If, at that point in 1959, he had had the support of politicians or leaders of universities who had money and power available at the time to back his energy and enthusiasm. . . . But Awni Dajani was ill, and whether officialdom held him back, or he felt he could not make major changes amid the turmoil of the Arab-Israeli crisis, he did not reply.

Besides, John may have been over-simplifying the problem. He did not have the whole picture. The PAM archives show that the museum committee was busier than he thought over financial negotiations with various parties to finance the Cave 11 material. As John was not a museum trustee or a committee member, he was not aware of these negotiations. All he could see was a blockage on access to the Scrolls. He deduced that the church was imposing it and blamed de Vaux as editor-in-chief. Dajani may have known a good deal more than John about how busy de Vaux was.

John gives no proof that the Vatican had "numerous and powerful" contacts in the BBC: the letter indicates his frustration rather than evidence of a conspiracy. De Vaux wrote to John on March 22, 1959 — though the letter was wrongly delivered and John did not receive it until June 26 — asking him to submit his manuscript for *DJDJ V* by June 1960. He told him that they were currently at the proof stage with volumes II and III, expected to see Cross and

11. J. M. Allegro to A. Dajani, January 10, 1959.

Skehan's volume IV by the end of 1959, Milik's "large volume of texts" by June 1961, and the Starcky-Baillet and Strugnell editions at six-monthly intervals thereafter. The schedule did not go according to plan, but it does not suggest that in 1959 anything was being held back. De Vaux seemed to expect to wind down the PAM work as such, for he warned:

> I should tell you that this study will not be able to carry on in Jerusalem after the end of June 1960: this is in fact the last date set for the distribution of fragments among the Government, the Museum and the institutions that have bought them. Also, it is the date when the aid that Rockefeller gave for photographing the manuscripts will come to an end, and the Museum's own resources will not allow it to continue this service. Therefore the editors must gather before this date all the documents they need.[12]

Jordan counted the Scrolls as part of its cultural heritage. John, likewise, saw them as a national treasure, and in his letter to Dajani of January 10, 1959, encouraged him to think of taking control, raising money to buy all future finds and buy back existing pieces, and keeping them safely in Jordan. His overriding purpose was free access to the Scrolls for scholars everywhere: "*Everything* that is found will be published for the world, Church or no Church, for we shall see that no single denomination or party gets control or sees the material alone."

In 1961, John's friendship with the Jordanian Royal Family and the way he promoted Jordan's cultural heritage were rewarded with the title of Honorary Adviser on the Scrolls to the Government of Jordan. It was a way for the King and his officials to make the most, through John, of the publicity value of the Scrolls for Jordan, and to honor John for his contribution to this cause. He felt the title should help him secure Jordan's interest concerning the Scrolls among international scholars and institutions, allow him some influence on matters such as arranging scroll exhibitions, and give him the right to ask questions about the way the Scrolls were handled and kept at the museum. If he hoped it might help him persuade the government to stir the editing team into publishing more texts, he was to be disappointed.

De Vaux remained in charge of the editing and John continued to supply and amend material as he asked. At the same time he continued to chafe at the slow rate of publication. By 1966, de Vaux had decided to issue the volume prepared by John and Arnold Anderson ahead of those that were not yet ready, though as John wrote wearily, "The envisaged publication of my small

---

12. R. de Vaux to J. M. Allegro, March 22, 1959.

Portrait of John in 1965 from a print by Sara Doggart

section as a separate volume seems regrettable when so much more important material still awaits publication."[13]

The Challenge of Nationalization

The Jordanian government eventually decided to nationalize the PAM, but not until late 1966. By then John was becoming very concerned about the physical condition of the Scrolls and how the Jordanian authorities might preserve and protect them when they took over their care. He foresaw major problems for the Department of Antiquities. He made a swift trip to Jordan in September 1966, mainly to deliver manuscripts to de Vaux, and was concerned that in the three years since his last visit not much seemed to have been done to keep the fragments from deteriorating. Restoration of the ruins at Qumran was progressing much faster than work at the PAM. He wrote to Awni Dajani about this on September 13, 1966:

> I was able to visit Qumran again en route to Jerusalem and see the excellent work the lads are doing there. I was much impressed by its unobtrusiveness, and the care taken to make the new cement merge with the surrounding stone and mortar. It's a credit to your department.
>
> The situation in the Museum in Jerusalem is far less happy where the Scrolls are concerned and must give cause for grave concern. I chatted with Yusif [Joseph Sa'ad] and learned of his ill health and wish to have the tremendous responsibility of the care of the Scrolls lessened on his shoulders. Very clearly something urgent has to be done to ensure that adequate steps are taken to safeguard the fragments, and to stir up those responsible for the long overdue publication of the Cave Eleven material. I learned for the first time that Frank Cross has 'purchased' the rights on all the remainder of this cache but seems to have taken no steps towards preparing them for publication. These delays must not be allowed to continue, and after the end of the year, responsibility for seeing they do not will rest entirely on the heads of your Department and the Government. The Trustees having failed in their duties, the onus will fall upon your people, and the finger of accusation of the world will point unjustly at Jordan unless something is done soon.
>
> I shall prepare a paper on the whole subject of the future care of the Jordan Scrolls, and steps which need taking forthwith to oblige the scholars concerned to publish their documents. Also involved is a world appeal

13. JMA to de Vaux, May 26, 1966.

for money to prepare the published fragments for preservation (and I am by no means certain that binding them tightly between glass is correct — a great deal of scientific research on this problem is required), to enable them to be properly housed where all may see them and scholars may study them, and to enable further searches to be made under the direction of the Department of Antiquities for more.

Seeing the state of the Scrolls after a gap of three years had shocked him. As he later described to Prince Hassan,

> I discovered that virtually nothing had been done about preserving the parchments. Indeed, I saw glass plates containing our texts lying on top of one another, thus subjecting the fragile skins to unacceptable pressures. There is, of course, no temperature or humidity control possible in the Museum, and still the vast majority of the texts are unpublished. Some are still unstudied even. I found that all publication rights have now been 'bought' by interested parties, although little work on the editing seems to be under way. One important document was lying on a table covered with a loose sheet of glass. It had been there for years. The 'editor-by-purchased-right' had made a preliminary study and had gone away and left it some years ago.[14]

As Honorary Adviser, John felt it his duty to bring the problems to the attention of the Jordanian Ambassador, the Prime Minister of Jordan, and the King himself. During September 1966 he wrote to each of them. This is the report he sent the Prime Minister:

> MEMORANDUM from John Allegro, Honorary Adviser to H.M. Government of Jordan on the Dead Sea Scrolls.
> To: His Excellency, the Prime Minister.
>
> 21st September 1966
> On my recent brief visit to Jordan I was able to review the present situation with regard to the Dead Sea Scrolls now in the custody of the Palestine Archaeological Museum. Since I understand that control of this Museum is to be vested in the Government of Jordan from the end of this year, it is imperative that the present, most unsatisfactory situation should be fully appreciated by all concerned.
> The main problems requiring urgent attention fall into two sections:

14. J. M. Allegro to Prince Hassan, November 28, 1966.

I. The physical care of the manuscripts;

II. The arrangements for speedy publication of the texts.

I. The greater part of the thousands of fragments of parchment and papyrus scrolls are still unsecured, although they have been out of the caves for over fourteen years. Without expert preservative action it must be expected that these delicate pieces will deteriorate, and indeed some already show signs of this. The precise method of ensuring their preservation is still a matter of debate, some favouring the sealing of the glass plates in which they at present lie, others believing that a current of heat- and moisture-controlled air is the best way of arresting harmful bacteriological action in the skins. Much experimental work needs to be done, and opinions sought from as many competent authorities as possible.

II. The recent highly successful exhibition of the Jordanian Scrolls in the United States and Great Britain has focussed public attention once more on the importance of these documents for an understanding of world history. Much criticism has also been levelled at the seeming lethargic manner in which the publication of these vital and controversial texts has been handled. Indignation has also been forcibly expressed at the way in which the Trustees of the Palestine Archaeological Museum, in an effort to recoup their losses in rescuing the scrolls from their clandestine finders, have 'sold' the publication rights to the highest bidders.

Clearly, the Jordan Government cannot afford to incur such criticism when the takeover of the Museum comes into effect, and efforts should be made without delay to ensure that those scholars who have been entrusted with the publication of the Scrolls texts should complete their work without delay. Failure to achieve this within a specified time limit should forfeit the right of prime publication and the work offered to other scholars, regardless of any financial or other agreements entered into by the current Trustees.

Such incisive action on the part of H.M. Government will not only ensure the early publication of these important documents and show to the world that Jordan will not brook delay in the dissemination of information on whatever pretext, but will make the work of preservation of the fragments immediately possible.

The measures proposed above can best be administered by a single person in whom the Government should invest full authority to deal with the documents and their publication as he sees fit. He will need to work closely with the Director of the Museum, and one of his first tasks will be to contact as soon as possible the larger foundations with a view to acquiring the very large funds that the work of preservation, publication

and possible further archaeological exploration will require. This authority will preferably have an intimate knowledge of the Scrolls and have
worked firsthand on their piecing together and editing, and should be
able to deal with scholars in this field on an equal footing.

Already far too much time has been lost in tackling the very difficult
situation posed by the finding and custody of the Dead Sea Scrolls. The
grave responsibility for the care and publication of these documents will
shortly fall upon Jordan. I strongly urge that no time be lost in imple-
menting the measures proposed above, beginning with the appointment
of a Scrolls Authority with full executive powers.

To King Hussein, John emphasized the importance to Jordan of dealing
properly with the Scrolls:

> Frankly, Jordan is taking on a tremendous problem when it takes over the
> Museum at the end of the year. Years of neglect of the most vital measures
> for the preservation of these delicate fragments coupled with a strange
> lethargy about the matter of publishing the texts has brought the finger of
> criticism among laymen and scholars pointing accusingly at the Museum.
> Soon the Government itself will be standing in the line of fire. As you
> know, these Scrolls are not just any old piece of antiquity; their purport
> could change world history, and most of them are not yet published,
> some not even studied. The Scrolls Exhibition [January 1966, as described
> in chapter 9] by its very success focussed world attention onto the docu-
> ments and the country of their origin. Now Jordan will need to make it
> very plain to the world that she is going to take this job of custodianship
> very seriously, and will see that everything is safeguarded and published
> without fear or favour. I do hope you will call for the very speedy and ef-
> fective action the situation calls for.[15]

To the Ambassador, His Excellency Anwar Nuseibeh, he outlined the
first step in solving the problem: to appoint one person with overall responsibility for the threefold task of preservation, publication, and fund-raising.

> The problems allow of no simple answer, and the first step is to give some-
> one executive power to sort things out and at least begin the work of orga-
> nising research into the best method of preserving the fragments and of en-
> suring speedy publication of the texts. One of his first tasks is raising the
> money to do these things, and a very great deal of money will be required.[16]

15. J. M. Allegro to H.M. King Hussein, September 21, 1966.
16. J. M. Allegro to H.E. Anwar Nuseibeh, September 16, 1966.

It would be a difficult job, as he told Awni Dajani:

Whoever takes on this job of Scrolls Director will have his hands full. He'll not only have to bully the scholars into doing their job quickly or get out and let someone else do it, but he'll have to set about trying to get expert opinions on how to preserve the Scrolls. But first of all he'll need to find the money to do it all. I am sure with the full backing of the Government and the Department of Antiquities this ought to be possible, but it needs doing soon.[17]

Dajani responded by asking John to nominate an expert who could do a good job on the preservation of the Scrolls. John felt that no one person should be given authority for this task before there had been consultations on the different methods, since these varied so widely: from the British Museum technique of sealing the fragments between glass plates to the Israeli practice of exposing them to a heat- and humidity-controlled atmosphere.

So I would suggest the correct order of approach to this vital and urgent problem is:

(a) appoint an overall Director of Scrolls, whose concern would be the publication and archaeology of the Scrolls, as well as preservation problems;

(b) let that official take this preservation problem around a number of different institutions, if possible personally with samples of the manuscripts, and obtain as many different opinions as possible;

(c) authorise that official to approach the larger charitable foundations, like Ford and Gulbenkian, to supply the very large finances required for all future Scrolls work in Jordan. Facilities for further publication and study are necessary, and large-scale searches of the desert in Jordan are long overdue.

This impending takeover by H.M. Government offers an opportunity for long-term planning on the Scrolls. I suggest that the immediate course of action, in advance of the takeover date, is to convene a meeting of, say, yourself, the Minister of the Government concerned, the Director of the Palestine Archaeological Museum (or Director-designate, if a change is contemplated), and myself as Honorary Scrolls Adviser to the Government. We could then discuss the immediate and long-term requirements

17. JMA to Dajani, September 21, 1966.

and at the end of the conference issue a statement outlining the Government's intentions. These will include the urgent measures to be taken for the preservation of the fragments and the provisions for future editing work on the Scrolls, emphasising the completely non-sectarian and non-political approach of the new custodianship.

The need for large sums of money might at the same time be stated, and the authorisation of an acting Scrolls Director to begin negotiations for finding that money. This person might also be authorised to seek advice from various experts on conservation on the best ways of preserving the Jordanian Scrolls, since no time should be lost in this all-important matter.[18]

Next day John wrote in the same terms to the Jordanian Ambassador, who wished him luck. Seven weeks later nothing had been done. On November 28, 1966, John wrote to H.R.H. Prince Hassan, who was currently studying at Oxford, describing the situation as he saw it and asking him to help persuade the authorities of the urgency of the case:

This is the kind of haphazard treatment of the Scrolls that I have been bemoaning in public for some time. But whereas I could and did blame the Museum trustees for lack of drive and a sense of urgency in the handling of these vastly important manuscripts and in instituting further archaeological searches, after the end of the year the Jordan Government will have put itself in the firing line. I cannot think that the Government is aware of the state of affairs, although I have tried to bring the matter to its attention over the years since I was appointed honorary Scrolls Adviser, and since my return I have written to Dajani and H. M. about the urgency of the matter.

Again he outlined his proposals: a meeting to discuss long and short-term policy and the appointment of a full-time Scrolls Director. "All this I have suggested in my letters to H. M. and Dajani, but it could do with restating on the spot." Since Dajani and Saʿad both wanted to leave or retire, "if we are not careful the Government is going to take over a Museum and all its problems with nobody on hand knowing the first thing about them."

As an outsider, an adviser without executive power, John was endlessly frustrated and deeply worried about the treatment of the Scrolls on all fronts. His aim remained to safeguard the Scrolls as part of Jordan's heritage and make them available for study by scholars everywhere. He believed that since

18. JMA to Dajani, October 8, 1966.

they were found in Jordan they belonged to Jordan, and the Jordanian government should look after them. Because he saw them mishandled and access blocked by de Vaux and the Trustees, he wished to have them removed from their control.

Since 1959 John had been developing plans to put the preservation and publication of the Scrolls on a sound footing, with transparent methods of funding and control. For himself, he would have hoped to continue as adviser and as one who presented the issues to the outside world, because he was used to dealing with the press and publicity and believed that the Scrolls mattered to people at large. At no time — lest this be suspected — did he think he could ever step into de Vaux's shoes, or try to tell a scholar of Milik's stature what to do, or become Scrolls Director himself. He did not seem confident that any expert, least of all he, had the technical knowledge to know how best to preserve the Scrolls from deterioration. The directorship itself would have been a full-time post in Jordan; in the mid-1960s John was settled at Manchester University and also enjoying the public interest aroused by the Dead Sea Scrolls Exhibition and his various books, while the family was thoroughly settled into their Derbyshire home. The question of the Scrolls directorship never came up at home, and had it done so, Joan would have squashed it flat.

So why didn't the authorities act sooner on the treatment of the Scrolls? Maybe the question of financial support was much more complicated than John knew, or bureaucratic control was too tightly knotted. Or, as he guessed himself, the political situation was too tense for any change to be contemplated. As he admitted to Prince Hassan, "I know too well that your thoughts must just now be occupied with more urgent problems at home."[19] Nothing at all came of John's plans for Jordan and its Scrolls, for nationalization was hardly complete before Israeli forces overran East Jerusalem and appropriated the Palestine Archaeological Museum with the rest of the city.

The Dispute over the Title of *DJDJ V*

As a footnote to the story of *Discoveries in the Judaean Desert of Jordan*, in 1967 the publishers dropped the last two words from the title of the series. All volumes subsequent to I, II, III, and V became *Discoveries in the Judaean Desert*, omitting reference to Jordan, because Israel had taken over the Palestine Archaeological Museum and also overrun much of the Judean desert. The publishers foresaw that the series would be continuing "under Israeli

19. JMA to H.R.H Prince Hassan, November 28, 1966.

auspices." John was outraged. In his eyes the new title was a desecration of Jordanian heritage. He learned of the change from a casual postscript in a letter of September 20, 1967, about page heads from the Clarendon Press (the section of Oxford University Press responsible for producing the series):

> P.S. I'm glad to find that de Vaux has emerged unscathed from the Middle Eastern war. In fact he seems to have fixed it so that if we simply remove the words 'of Jordan' from the title the series can go on under Israeli auspices.

It seems unlikely that de Vaux, any more than John, would have willingly conceded anything to Israel, but John assumed he had and wrote back immediately:

> To change the title of the series in the way you suggest is to acknowledge a change in the political status of the Judaean Desert which is by no means generally accepted or, indeed, likely to be so. Had the series not yet begun, it would have been a different matter, but a deliberate change now would be to make a statement that the Press has no right to make and which I, as author, cannot possibly accept. Just what you mean by 'the series can go on under Israeli auspices' I cannot understand. The documents that have recently been looted from the Palestine Archaeological Museum are still legally Jordanian, and I cannot see how the arrangements for publication that have already been entered into by the Press are in any way affected.
>
> I must make it clear that in no circumstances can I allow this volume to carry any contribution by an Israeli official or scholar, nor any acknowledgement to Israel in any part of the book for any reason whatsoever. Mr Anderson, as joint contributor, is equally adamant on this point.
>
> I should appreciate receiving an assurance on this matter at your earliest convenience, and confirmation that the title of the work will remain unchanged. No further work on the volume will be possible until such assurances are received.[20]

He evidently felt no compunction to consult de Vaux. The publishers' representative, rather puzzled, suggested that surely it was better to get the work out and published by compromising over the title than to hold it back yet again:

> Our concern (as I am sure it must be yours) is not to take sides in the Middle Eastern conflict, but to publish this volume as quickly as possible and in a way that will not jeopardise the future of the Museum. To

20. J. M. Allegro to the Clarendon Press, September 20, 1967.

achieve this, surely the modification of the title is justified. It attributes nothing to Israel, but merely recognises the undeniable, and perfectly neutral, fact that the status of the Judaean Desert is at present subject to dispute. With these considerations in mind may I appeal to you not to press your objection?[21]

However, as Honorary Adviser to the Jordanian government, naturally John felt he must uphold Jordan's position at this time of inflamed sensitivity between Israel and Jordan. He replied, "We are still very firmly of the mind that any alteration to the title in the way you suggest is a positive acknowledgement of a territorial claim by a foreign country. As I said previously, had the title not contained the words 'of Jordan' on previous volumes there would have been no difficulty. As it is, the omission would certainly be noticed and, particularly in view of the rather special position of the Clarendon Press in the world, some significance regarding our Government's intentions in the future read into the action."[22] He held that the West Bank was still legally Jordanian territory and that copyright of the documents and archeological remains in the Museum was still vested in H.M. Government of Jordan, as he had confirmed in writing with the Minister of Tourism and Antiquities three months earlier, so there was no question of doing anything on Israeli sufferance or under Israeli auspices.

The Clarendon Press assured him they intended to do what the Jordanian government told them: While de Vaux remained Chief Editor "it is not for us to ignore his instructions. On the other hand, since our agreement is with the Museum it is in the final resort with the Jordanian Government (it is in fact signed by the 'President of Tourism Authority and Antiquities'). So we can without hesitation give you an assurance that we shall do whatever the Jordanian Government instructs us to do with regard to the title of the volume."[23]

The Jordanian Minister of Tourism and Antiquities confirmed to them on October 29, 1967, that the agreement concluded with the PAM trustees, "through which you have been given the right of publication of the Dead Sea Scrolls under the title of: DISCOVERIES IN THE JUDAEAN DESERT OF JORDAN," was still binding now that the government of Jordan had taken over the administration of the museum, and there should be no change in the title. The Clarendon Press seemed to be under pressure from the Jordanian authorities, Israeli authorities, de Vaux, and John at the same time.

In the end the publishers discovered that their copy of the agreement

21. Clarendon Press to JMA, September 27, 1967.
22. JMA to Clarendon Press, September 28, 1967.
23. Clarendon Press to JMA, October 2, 1967.

gave the title as *Discoveries in the Judaean Desert* after all, but their representative admitted, "Of course this doesn't affect the substance of the case. I was able to discuss the problem with Father de Vaux on 25 October and we agreed to print in Mr. Allegro's volume the full title of the series *Discoveries in the Judaean Desert of Jordan*."[24] However, after de Vaux's death, the title reverted to *Discoveries in the Judaean Desert*. The whole episode serves mainly to show how John felt he must represent the political interests of the Kingdom of Jordan. His interest was less to take personal control of the Scrolls than to jump into the fray on behalf of Jordan.

24. Clarendon Press to JMA, November 1, 1967.

CHAPTER 9

Questions from the
Dead Sea Scrolls Exhibition

On December 16, 1965, the Dead Sea Scrolls Exhibition opened at the British Museum to national acclaim. John had been negotiating for years to persuade the Jordanian government to let the Scrolls out of the country. Now at last, after touring America and Canada, the exhibition came to Britain under the joint patronage of Queen Elizabeth II and King Hussein. It was set out in four parts: the discovery of the Scrolls, the people of the Scrolls, the Scrolls themselves, and modern Scrolls research.

John had spent a long time — years rather than months — discussing the choice of exhibits with the Jordanian Department of Antiquities. He planned to include technical information on handling and treating the scrolls, as he had explained to Dr. Reed at the University of Leeds on March 8, 1962: "We shall wish to show how science has played a part in the work on the Scrolls, and it would be rather nice if you and your colleagues could provide us with something tangible as an illustration of your own work on the fragments."

Frank Moore Cross wrote the introductory notes for the exhibition pamphlet, and John delivered the inaugural public lecture at the British Museum. Staged in succession at London, Manchester, Edinburgh, and Cardiff, the exhibition was phenomenally popular. The only problem with its presentation arose in Manchester, where the John Rylands Museum proved far too cramped to accommodate the numbers who wanted to see the scrolls, and people grumbled about the queues. The display included fourteen scrolls or parts of scrolls, documents and artifacts from the time of Bar Kokhba's revolt, Byzantine remains from Khirbet Mird, and an Aramaic legal document on papyrus from the fourth century B.C.

In the weeks before the exhibition opened, John wrote article after article. Journals that ranged from *The Times* to *The Lady* ran features on the Scrolls. *The Spectator* commented, "The Dead Sea Scrolls attracted attention at the British Museum, and Mr John Allegro wrote so many articles on the subject that it was said he ought to change his name to Fortissimo." There were also radio interviews, and his lectures packed public halls all over the country. Everyone was talking, everyone wanted to see the exhibition; whatever John said stoked up a gratifying blaze of controversy. John rode high on all this and loved the uproar.

In the lecture at the British Museum on December 16, 1965, John asked questions — open questions, urgent questions, demanding that people question their own assumptions about religion. He urged the listeners: Never be fobbed off with insufficient answers; have the courage to go on asking questions.

His theme was the importance of the Scrolls to biblical studies. "We are on the verge of a tremendous breakthrough down the whole New Testament front," he said, "at the end of which we are likely to see New Testament Christianity emerging as a kind of neo-Essenism stemming directly from the people of the Scrolls." But, he added, the breakthrough was jeopardized by religious and academic prejudice. Prejudice had led to a partial boycott of scrolls research, to inexcusable delay in publication, and to refusal to ask questions.

He repeated the view he had set out in his book *The Dead Sea Scrolls*: The Scrolls were important not just as two-thousand-year-old scraps of parchment but as windows into the life and thought of our ancestors, people whose ideas shaped our culture and history. So understanding what the Scrolls were about mattered to everybody. But he thought they mattered more than many scholars wanted to admit. While others looked on the Qumran community of Essenes as an interesting but esoteric sect as different from the Christians as they could possibly be, John saw Essenism as the womb of Christianity and thought the similarities intrinsic.

He reminded listeners of the correspondences that he had first set out in his book. Essenes and early Christians shared root and branch ideas and practices. Both upheld community rules of poverty and sharing. They felt the coming of the Kingdom of God was imminent. They had many common practices, such as healing and exorcism, sacred meals, baptism, and the inner council of twelve. Then there was the language: the imagery of light and dark, the Word, the cornerstone, the meek, the many poor in spirit, Son of God, Breath of God, and so on. They took a similar view of history — not as a linear sequence of events so much as a cycle fulfilling Old Testament prophecy, which in turn drew on age-old mythology. Abraham, Moses, Joshua, and Jesus all relived the cycle of transgression, atonement, and redemption at the head of the Chosen People.

There were other historical parallels. In Luke 3, John the Baptist opposed Herod Antipas, who had married his sister-in-law Salome, as (in John Allegro's view) the Teacher of Righteousness had opposed Jannaeus, who also married a sister-in-law called Salome. The crucifixions of around A.D. 27 seemed to echo those of 88 B.C. The reference in Acts 9 to Saul's visit to Damascus could well have reflected the Qumran community's exile there at the time the sect was first formed — though it could be that the Damascus of the Scrolls was a cryptic or symbolic reference to Qumran itself. John felt it was time to drop the usual approach to biblical history — the literal and linear approach normally assumed for more recent and better documented history. The written history of the day was what people thought important enough to write down, and two thousand years ago their interpretation of events seemed to be shaped by prophecy and biblical precedent.

John also felt it was time to ask questions about the mythology underlying biblical stories. He used a fairly broad definition of mythology — the explanation in story form of cosmic phenomena or major events. People had long been looking at various religions in the light of mythology, especially since the publication in 1922 of Sir James Frazer's encyclopedic study in magic and religion, *The Golden Bough.* However, they usually studied other religions; few people openly applied the same outlook to Christianity. John had no doubt that it should and did apply. Essenism, he posited, was the matrix of the Christian myth.

But that did not make it a blueprint for Christianity. John the Baptist and Jesus might have grown up with or been schooled in Essene traditions, but the religion that grew out of their teaching was not Essenism, nor a copy of Essenism. There were basic differences in outlook and in their conception of the central figure. The Scrolls indicated that the Teacher of Righteousness may well have been crucified and was probably expected to return from the dead. But in no way was he divine, nor was his resurrection to be part of the general Last Days, while Christ was a superhuman figure who had apparently risen again only three days after his death. The Teacher spoke to fanatical purists and expected all Gentiles to be exterminated at the apocalypse; Jesus spoke to sinners and Gentiles and included them all in a very different kingdom of God.

The similarities were indisputable but the differences were fundamental. John had pointed this out in the first edition of *The Dead Sea Scrolls;* he went on saying it and he went on asking, Why? What happened, between the sacking of Qumran and the time that Christianity was adopted as part of the establishment, to turn a fiercely exclusive, inward-looking sect of Judaism into a broad-based religion, centering on a supernatural figure, which could appeal to many nations in many ages? The answer for many Christians, who wished to look no further than the church's own front door, was that Jesus Christ happened and, being the Son of God, he was the answer to everything.

To the end of his life, John found it hard to believe that thinking people, many of whom had studied as far as or further than he had himself, came back with this answer. For his own part, he had slipped out of the emotional shackles of the church during his Methodist training, as soon as he began asking where in the origins of language and philosophy such ideas came from and who had the authority to impose them on him. He had no time for answers that begged the questions; he saw himself as a truth-seeker whose job was to ask the questions and he expected other scholars to share the same approach. Maybe he did not fully understand how religion could still keep its grip on people's minds and hearts in a scientific age or why people who were accustomed to think deeply about everything else should so obediently accept the authority of the church.

So now he asked why people in first-century Palestine and beyond accepted Jesus as Messiah, and why they were impressed by his appeal to people of all nations and all walks of life. Jesus may have been a charismatic preacher and skilled healer, but John felt the gospels failed to give the whole picture. So much in them did not ring true. Who were the enemies, Romans or other Jews? Weren't the chief protagonists in the story Jews? When Jew strove against Jew, and the emperor played one faction against another until in the end he destroyed Jerusalem through siege and slaughter, it seemed unlikely that a Galilean preaching brotherly love and taxes for the Romans could have made his voice heard.

The Scrolls make no mention of Jesus, and the New Testament does not apparently refer to the Essenes. Is it really likely that two such similar organizations lived closely together in a small country without recognizing each other's existence? Why was Essenism nowhere to be found in the New Testament, though Sadducees, Pharisees, and other groups such as Hellenists and Herodians were mentioned? Had the Romans completely suppressed it, or had Christianity completely supplanted it? Is it possible that no Christianity and no Christ in fact existed in Palestine before the Essenes were driven away at the failure of the first Jewish revolt in A.D. 70?

Or was Essenism still there? In the scroll commentaries he had been studying, biblical passages were enriched for the sectarian readers by puns, derivations, and other forms of word-play, "which, being interpreted, refer to. . . ." Could there be similar word-play in the gospels? After all, there are parables, which hold within them deeper meanings. As Jesus tells his disciples: "To you has been given the secret of the kingdom of God, but for those outside, everything comes in parables, in order that they may indeed look but not perceive, and may indeed listen, but not understand" (Mark 4:11-12). Could some of the Jesus stories be Essene creations that most people would be likely to take at face value but some, the chosen few, could interpret as referring to something else entirely?

To early Jewish writers, punning was less a low form of wit than a legitimate form of exegesis. "Since every word of Scripture was divinely inspired," John wrote, "it followed that words looking and sounding similar to those of the sacred text might also have some special significance. Such similarities were unlikely to be accidental. Rightly understood, they too could convey some hidden truth. The Old Testament abounds in this kind of word-play. Many of the stories about the origins of tribes or persons depend on puns made on the proper names concerned. Thus in Genesis 25 the second twin to emerge from Rebekah's womb was called Jacob *(Ya'aqob)* 'because he had taken hold of Esau's heel' *('aqeb)*."[1]

With scriptural word-play in mind, John looked again at the "Caiaphas" document, 4Q Therapeia. It appeared to be a clinical report. John's translation, which he eventually published in *The Dead Sea Scrolls and the Christian Myth,* begins: "The report of the Caiaphas *(Qayy'pha),* being an account of his rounds of the afflicted (among) the guests; supplies of medicines . . ." and ends "Eli is witness, dictated by Omriel, Qp *(Qayy'pha)."* The language was "a mixture of transliterated Greek, Aramaic and grammatically irregular Hebrew, giving the inescapable impression of deliberate obscurantism, not entirely unfamiliar in medical writing."[2] Some later translators have failed to see the medical connection and conclude that the tag is only a writing exercise by someone who was not very good at Hebrew. Others have agreed with the medical interpretation in general, though disputing certain details, but thought it chiefly significant as an early Jewish medical text rather than a clue to early Christian activities.[3]

For John, however, the decipherment of *caiaphas* as "physiognomist" was to prove pivotal in his understanding of the Qumran sect. The significance is that the *caiaphas* is the scrutinizer, the physiognomist, who examines the afflictions of people's minds and bodies to find out what infections or bad spirits need to be cured by either medicine or exorcism — for the healing arts

1. J. M. Allegro, draft BBC radio script, February 1966.

2. J. M. Allegro, *The Dead Sea Scrolls and the Christian Myth* (Newton Abbott: Westbridge Books, 1979), p. 235.

3. J. H. Charlesworth, *The Discovery of a Dead Sea Scroll (4Q Therapeia),* ICASALS Publication No. 85-1 (Lubbock, Tex.: Texas Tech University, 1985).

are spiritual as well as herbal. In the Qumran community he is also the official who examines applicants for membership. Caiaphas is a job title — but the same consonants also make *cephas,* Simon Peter's other name in Aramaic, whose Greek translation, derived from *petra,* a rock, gives rise to the alternative and better-known pun from Matthew 16. So Peter is principally the scrutinizer, one of the chief officials of the Essene community, before he becomes labeled as the rock on which the church is built.

Can we then be sure he is a real individual, or is his name just a job title around which stories are woven? Could other New Testament names and titles carry similar literary rather than historical significance? At first sight one would answer no; the gospel characters are full of quirks that make them sound human, and the more one reads their tales the more they seem like familiar friends. Yet, if the narratives are webs of myth, history, prophecy, and folk-tale, could stories based on names also be woven in? John began to decode other names. "Iscariot," the second name of the disciple Judas, who "had the common purse" (John 13:29), could be from *ish sakharioth,* man of wages, the bursar of the community. "Boanerges," the name Jesus gave to the brothers James and John, may have derived from *baney regesh,* judges who had powers of divining truth. If *kharash* can mean "magician, wonder-worker" as well as "carpenter" and can also be read as *kheresh,* "deaf-mute," then Jesus' father Joseph the carpenter and John the Baptist's father Zechariah, whom the angel struck dumb (Luke 1:20), could equally have been magicians.

It all sounds far too contrived. When you start unraveling puns, how long is the resulting piece of string? Yet even without distorted names, the gospels seem to be highly contrived literary works. We know that word-play was an important though intricate means of exegesis for Jews schooled in Bible study. To the learned few, word-play may have enriched the text, as in our day we recognize how metaphor, rhyme, and alliteration can bind and strengthen English poetry.

John went further. He wondered whether Essene terms were not just being spun into stories but deliberately disguised as everyday tales that ordinary people would like and Roman officials — thought-police — would dismiss. If so, why? Why should it be important to disguise official titles? What were they really trying to hide? The Essenism of the Qumran community seemed to have disappeared from public view. Were its proponents all dead, or hiding among the caves, or were they living underground, as it were, among their lay brethren of the towns and villages, keeping their lore alive by secret meetings and secret messages?

At first John did not think such questions would take him very far. He had to agree that on the face of it the idea of the gospels as cover-up stories seemed far-fetched. The most searching of his critics, Geza Vermes, pointed out in *The Daily Telegraph* of March 9, 1966, that not only was the cover-up idea intrinsically improbable, but some of John's word derivations had never actually been found in Jewish literature of the period. But John kept on looking at words and finding links, and gradually he found the links growing into new webs of significance. For obviously, in a Roman world when all hope of messianic rescue was past, an esoteric Judaic sect would have to either adapt or die; to survive at all it had to present itself in Roman-friendly terms, and to grow it had to appeal to all the Gentile nations that Rome bound together. It had to render unto Caesar whatever would ensure Caesar's approval.

Did the whole sect go along with this? What happened to the purists?

At the British Museum lecture, as it was subsequently reported in *The Sunday Times* on December 21, 1965, John put it this way:

> It used to be maintained that the Essenes were nowhere mentioned in the New Testament. In fact it is now possible to show that Essene titles and self-description are woven right through the fabric of the New Testament myths, although in an understandably disguised form. For example, when it is said that Jesus counted gluttons, winebibbers, harlots and publicans as his friends, these words simply represent word-plays on the Hebrew and Aramaic titles and descriptions of the Essenes. The derogatory connotation given them as a result of this word-play on the part of the Christian storytellers symbolises the whole function of the New Testament, to adapt this strictly exclusive Jewish sect to the needs of people outside the pale of the non-Jewish world.

The whole function? For John the central issue was the unreality of the gospel story. Writing in *The Spectator,* he asked:

> Did the Jesus story owe anything to the Teacher of Righteousness one hundred years before? Can the differences be explained other than by pleading the divine nature of Jesus Christ? Have the Scrolls provided any contemporary evidence to support the otherwise uncorroborated witness of the New Testament to the very existence of Jesus, let alone the historicity of the miracle stories?
>
> It becomes in the light of the Scrolls more and more inconceivable how such a pro-Gentile gospel could have been openly preached in Jerusalem around the time of Pontius Pilate . . . the Scrolls only emphasise the unreality of the situation presented by the Gospels and the Acts.[4]

4. J. M. Allegro in *The Spectator,* December 3, 1965.

And in the *New Statesman* of December 17, 1965, answering critics who sought to reassure people that Christianity remained untainted by Essenism, John wrote:

> The differences are indeed striking. Perhaps it may have occurred to those whose minds were being set at rest to ask just how a Jewish rabbi of the first century, leader of a group that seemed to have so much in common with the Essenes in matters of discipline and doctrine, could have been in other respects so very different. Indeed, humanly speaking, it is difficult to understand how this dangerous freethinker, this bosom companion of the hated Gentile, could have survived three weeks of public appearances among people already seething with revolt, let alone three years. . . . Unfortunately, by refusing to compromise their religious conception of Jesus as a completely unique God-man, the Christian scholars are in danger of erecting in their minds a mental barrier against the one line of enquiry that could lead to the long-awaited breakthrough in New Testament study.

The church fired back.

There was noisy rebuttal on BBC radio against "this wild assertion that Jesus was a myth."[5] In the parishes there was outrage: "The source of Christian strength is faith in Jesus Christ. Christianity has been battered from outside and betrayed from within the churches, but it is going to take more than a load of ancient writings to sweep it away."[6]

In a letter to *The Times* of December 21, 1965, eight eminent professors stated the orthodox line: "Nothing that appears in the Scrolls hitherto discovered throws any doubt on the originality of Christianity. The Scrolls contain no reference or allusion to any Christian doctrine except such as can be traced to the Old Testament or can be found in Jewish thought of the intertestamental period; nor is there any hint that the Rightful Teacher may have been regarded as in any sense divine."

Professor Rowley, one of the signatories, restated his denial in the *British Weekly* of January 6, 1966: "The Scrolls tell us about the Teacher of Righteousness and about the sect, about the hopes and aspirations of men in the world into which Jesus came, and for these they are to be prized. They shed light on the New Testament, but they do not explain it, and there is no evidence to connect Jesus directly with the sect."

Some acted the ostrich: "God has been forced to give deeper esoteric

5. BBC, December 29, 1965.
6. *Batley News,* November 26, 1965.

truths into the keeping of chosen groups of people in order to protect them from destructive powers of evil. He [Allegro] represents a great evil. . . . The discovery of the Dead Sea Scrolls is only one of such documents which will be allowed to be discussed when the time is ripe."[7]

Others argued with hindsight: Essenism had died, but Christianity had survived and spread, thanks to the unique authority of Jesus Christ. Or thanks to political expediency, for the Emperor Constantine had found he might safely promote Christianity as a respectable form of personal salvation; it was less likely than other mass religions to lead to insurrection and moreover did not demand the mutilation of little boys by circumcision. Constantine made sure that from the fourth century onwards the church had the authority to suppress criticism.[8]

On a less worldly side, the *Daily Mail* pointed out that even if it were proved a myth, Christianity answered the human condition with spiritual if not historical truth, and people needed myths.[9] *The Scotsman* accepted the parallels between Essenism and Christianity but sensibly separated history and theology: "The scrolls portray for us, in vivid but authentic colours, the environment whose spiritual idiom John and Jesus spoke; whose concepts they developed and transmuted and whose religious ideas served largely as the seedbed of the New Testament. . . . There is there no trace of any of the cardinal theological concepts: the incarnate Godhead, Original Sin, Redemption through the Cross and the like, which make Christianity a distinctive faith."[10]

The British Weekly suggested that preaching peace was not so unlikely, in Galilee if not Jerusalem; and John had overlooked the essential characteristic of Christ: "It is well recognised that the virgin birth, crucifixion and miracle stories owe a great deal to Old Testament prophecy and to folk myth and legend. Mr Allegro misses the point that Jesus Christ is the Son of God sent to redeem the world and bring Gentiles to God."[11]

And Professor F. F. Bruce supposed very reasonably that Jesus had deliberately chosen to take a different outlook from the Essenes: "Their separation, in which they out-Phariseed the Pharisees, was as far removed from the way of Jesus as can well be imagined, and their conception of the Messiah was among those that Jesus deliberately rejected in favour of the way of the suffering Son of Man."[12]

7. *Mercury and Advertiser,* January 13, 1966.
8. A. Samuel, Letter to the Editor, *New Statesman,* January 7, 1966.
9. *Daily Mail,* December 29, 1965.
10. *The Scotsman,* March 29, 1966.
11. *British Weekly,* December 20, 1965.
12. *Church of England Newspaper,* December 10, 1965.

John affirmed that both Essenism and Christianity are rooted in Judaism. In his view, the New Testament represents the reworking of one into the other. In a radio talk he explained:

> [T]he similarities are infinitely more important than the differences . . . the differences between the two creeds represent precisely the kind of mutation that Judaism and Essenism would have had to undergo in order to appeal to the Gentile communities within the Roman Empire.
>
> The whole work is propaganda material, designed to teach in popular form some extraordinary religious ideas to people on the fringes of Palestine, some of whom were not even Jews — people, in fact, for whom Essenism proper held out no greater promise than to have their throats cut on Judgment Day.
>
> Could it be that the religion of the Gospels was after all Essenism adapted to suit the needs of members who under the old dispensation could have no hope of participating in the coming millennium of peace and plenty? How much of this new development was owing to the genius or inspiration of one man, and how far is the picture of his life and ministry as depicted in the Gospels an historic record of the origins of the movement?[13]

What were these "extraordinary religious ideas" that he was uncovering? He went on, broaching them for the first time in public:

> The New Testament is full of references to Essenism — indeed it *is* Essenism. But these references lie, as I've said, under the surface. As it stands the New Testament is a kind of cover document for the real thing. It's innocuous enough on the surface not to offend the Roman enemies if it fell into their hands. Indeed, it falls over backwards time and time again to make the Gentiles the real heroes. Even Pilate is made to wash his hands and the Jews to accept the blame for the Master's death. But under the surface we find a very different outlook. Here is an Essenism more exclusive even than we see in the Scrolls. This is the real stuff of occult Essenism — demonology, raising of the dead, Aramaic incantations, the secret names of the angels by which all kinds of magic could be worked. The whole have been woven together with word-play and Biblical allusion to present a myth which seemed so real to the uninitiated that it became early on accepted as history.
>
> In fact the Scrolls give us the clue to the spurious chronology of the Je-

---

13. JMA, draft BBC radio script, February 1966.

sus story that put him in the time of Pontius Pilate. Even the names of the enemies and companions of Jesus are word-plays or puns on Essene titles and self-descriptions. In short, nothing in the Gospels and Acts is what it seems. The Scrolls have given us the key at last to unlock the real truth.

"Nothing in the Gospels and Acts is what it seems." Once he started to look for clues in names and titles, he found them everywhere. If you accept that words can have different meanings or shades of meaning in different contexts, your subject-matter is fluid; it can take all shapes. Powered by speculation, it can reach hidden truths. All innovation depends on speculation. But in the case of philology — speculation about the derivation of words — it can be hard to test objectively. John was at the speculative stage and carried along by the excitement of discovery; the time for testing would come later. As he had written in October 1965 to Geoffrey Bridson of the BBC, who was planning a radio program about the Scrolls to coincide with the Dead Sea Scrolls Exhibition, he was on the brink of "a tremendous breakthrough in New Testament studies, with just about everything collapsing on every side. . . . As you can imagine, once the cracks begin to open wide there is practically nothing in this extremely brittle set-up that doesn't give."

CHAPTER 10

A Grand, Unifying Theory of Religion

The Sacred Mushroom and the Cross ruined John's career.

The book was the culmination of twenty years' study, for it grew out of everything he had learned about the development of Semitic and proto-Semitic languages. He meant it to launch his name upon history as a world thinker. He hoped it would illuminate the origins of thought and language, so that people could better understand where they came from, shed the trappings of religion, and take true responsibility for what they did to each other and their world.

None of this got past the initial shock-waves. The mushroom cloud spread more derision than enlightenment.

This chapter outlines the views that John elaborated in his controversial book. Chapter 11 takes a further look at his reasoning and at the questions, criticisms, and reactions it provoked.

Overview

Underpinning *The Sacred Mushroom* is the idea that fertility must be of fundamental importance to primitive religion, as it is to life. John set out this concept in a preliminary plan of the book, sent to the publishers Hodder and Stoughton, Ltd., on October 23, 1968:

> The most important thing in life was life itself, and life is rain. The reasoning is simple. Rain begets vegetation on the earth as spermatozoa beget offspring in the womb. God, the Creator, the source of rain, must

185

therefore be the sperm of creation and the heavenly penis from which it spills. The storm is the orgasm of God. The drops of rain are the 'words' of God.

Earth is the womb of creation. Through her furrows, her labia, she receives the Lord's seed, and deep within her uterus there burn the eternal fires of fermentation.

In a climate of extremes, baking heat punctuated by violent rainstorms, people eking their living from crops must be especially attuned to the weather. Season after season, rain brought life; plants and animals were born, fed, grew, and died. But not every season: In a dry spring there was no rebirth and everyone suffered. Why should the season fail them?

It is logical to assume that people, seeking reasons for life as people do, should imagine an almighty power in control of their fortunes and should imagine that power or others, benevolent or malign, playing with their world. And then should seek to influence the power in order to propitiate it or partake of it. To do this they needed to understand the nature of the divine power. They sought understanding through meditation, fasting, or, more speedily, through hallucinatory drugs such as those found in certain fungi. They believed these drugs could bring them the key to divine knowledge, knowledge that controlled the fertility of human, beast, and earth.

That, in simplest terms, was the centrality of fertility to ancient religion.

Where did the evidence come from?

The first religious poems were written down in Sumer about 2800 B.C., but drawings, carvings, and pictograms from long before that date show the central importance of fertility to religious thought. At first the ideas and practices remained unwritten: oral traditions, rites, and legends that were depicted in artistic form and resurfaced in various guises in the mythologies of different cultures. The development of writing brought more tangible evidence.

In *The Sacred Mushroom and the Cross,* John set out to "trace the expression of this simple philosophy through the sacred literature of the ancient world. The source of this breakthrough has been the oft-attempted but hitherto inconclusive search for a common denominator to the language groups of Sumerian, Indo-European, and Semitic. It is now possible to decipher some important proper names in the old hymns and epics in all these literatures, and to check and cross-check our results with the other languages."[1]

---

1. Letter from J. M. Allegro to Hodder and Stoughton, October 23, 1968.

By the 1960s, scholars had amassed a great deal of information about ancient Sumer, the rich alluvial plain between the Tigris and the Euphrates. Here, during the fourth millennium B.C., writing developed from pictograms through cuneiform, and its development is traced on thousands of baked clay tablets left in the libraries of temples and palaces. For Sumer was a wealthy and highly organized society, with power and culture in the hands of priests and kings. The king was the god's bailiff, responsible for ensuring productivity. Temples were centers of justice and administration, learning and theology, and those at Nippur and Uruk housed rich libraries. The literature inscribed on the tablets in these libraries covers three thousand years of thought on subjects that include theology, botany, and mathematics, and it shows the early history of the written word. Of particular value to philologists are the word-lists matching Sumerian vocabulary to that of its northern neighbor Akkad, lists that may have been used for teaching or in commerce between the two countries.

The tablets show how Sumerian pictograms developed into cuneiform. Each of the three hundred or so early cuneiform symbols, like the pictograms they replaced, seemed to have several different sounds and meanings. Gradually these were standardized, as patterns emerged for word structure and variation.

As John explained it, the Sumerian vocabulary was made up of strings of phonemes, or word-bricks, and the most basic bricks resisted phonetic change. Many passed virtually unchanged into successive languages. John suggested that with them went the concepts they signified. To these word-bricks we can trace Indo-European and Semitic verbal roots, even though different styles and sound-patterns grew up around them. They included some names and religious terms, which were presumably of special importance. So where they recur in other ancient languages, we can begin to trace them right back to their source. The story of how language spread from Sumer through Akkadian into other Semitic and Indo-European languages is also the story of the spread of religious ideas.

The ideas were carried in stories and became so deeply embedded in myth or metaphor that in time people remembered the stories rather than the original ideas. To allot the stories a time and place in history helped people relate to them and lent them solidity. This appealed to rational minds that liked to take a linear, cause-and-effect view of events, but it often changed their significance over time.

John set out to understand where it all came from primarily through analyzing words. Words express ideas; the development of writing shows the development of ideas. As he explained:

A written word is more than a symbol: it is an expression of an idea. To penetrate to its inner meaning is to look into the mind of the man who wrote it. Later generations may give different meanings to that symbol, extending its range of reference far beyond the original intention, but if we can trace the original significance, then it should be possible to follow the trail by which it developed.[2]

The trail led back, again and again, he suggested, to a mushroom cult: "The isolation of the names and epithets of the sacred mushroom opens the door into the secret chambers of the mystery cults, which depended for their mystic hallucinatory experiences on the drugs found in the fungus. . . . Above all, those mushroom epithets and holy invocations that the Christian cryptographers wove into the stories of Jesus and his companions can now be recognized, and the main features of the Christian myth laid bare."[3] He admitted that direct references to mushrooms themselves are rare in biblical, Near Eastern, and even Greek literature but suggested that the sacred mushroom was often classed with or confused with the mandrake, a notorious aphrodisiac of demonic power.[4]

Names changed least: They were the most sacred of words, for to call on the god by name was to invoke its power. Through exploring the names of the gods and the names associated with the drug cult, especially those for the sacred mushroom, John thought he could trace the old fertility religion back to Sumer, as he explained:

> Even gods as different as Zeus and Yahweh embody the same fundamental conception as the fertility deity, for their names and origin are precisely the same. . . . Languages so apparently different as Greek and Hebrew, when they can be shown to derive from a common fount, point to a communality of culture at some early stage. All roads in the Near East lead back to the Mesopotamian basin, to ancient Sumer. Similarly, the most important of the religions and mythologies of that area, and probably far beyond, are reaching back to the mushroom cult of Sumer and her successors. Therefore to understand the origins of Christianity we must look not only at the Old Testament, New Testament, apocrypha and Dead Sea Scrolls, but to Sumerian texts and the classical writings of Asia Minor, Greece and Rome.[5]

2. J. M. Allegro, *The Sacred Mushroom and the Cross* (London: Hodder and Stoughton, 1970), p. xvii.

3. Allegro, *Sacred Mushroom*, p. xviii.

4. Allegro, *Sacred Mushroom*, pp. 40-41.

5. Allegro, *Sacred Mushroom*, p. xvi.

Corroboration from Classical Texts

For evidence about how people in the first century A.D. were thinking, John used contemporary writers, mainly Pliny the Elder, Dioscorides, and Josephus. There was certainly much interest in healing, spiritual and physical, and in the use of drugs. John related it straight back to Sumerian origins. Dioscorides' *De Materia Medica* lists commonly used drugs and classifies them according to their vegetable, animal, or mineral origin. Pliny (A.D. 23-79) includes in his *Natural History* not only a description of medicinal plants but also stories about them from popular mythology and folklore. Pliny and Dioscorides both cite among their sources the "magi" or "prophetae" who were the drug-peddlers and seers of the ancient world. Josephus, at about the same time, writes in his *Jewish Antiquities* and *The Jewish War* about the state of his nation and its contemporary history. Of the Essenes, he says they have "an extraordinary interest in the writings of the ancients, singling out in particular those which make for the welfare of the soul and body; with the help of these, and with a view to the treatment of diseases, they investigate medicinal roots and the properties of stones."[6] He also describes the practice of exorcism, that is, drawing out demons through the nose by using drugs and incantations, a method ascribed to Solomon.

The Sumerians knew the plants that brought healing as well as hallucination. The earliest known medical text is a Sumerian tablet from about 3000 B.C., listing herbal medicines. There is a direct link here to the Essenes, whose name, *assayim*, derives from the Sumerian A-ZU or I-ZU: physician, prophet, seer.[7] Part of the Essenes' "secret lore" was to know the names of the demons that cause illness and of the angels that cure it, and part of their skill was to divine people's astrological character, the share of light and dark allotted to each person at birth. Among the Essene scrolls from the Dead Sea is a coded astrological chart showing the characteristics of people born under the different signs of the zodiac. To administer drugs in the correct doses, healers needed to know the nature of the patient; the people who divined this were astrologers. So the arts of medicine and astrology went hand in hand and had been passed on from ancient times through successive generations to the magi of Pliny and the New Testament.

6. Josephus, *The Jewish War*, 2.36.
7. Allegro, *Sacred Mushroom*, p. 30.

The Technique of Analyzing Words

John's technique is to analyze Sumerian words in which phonemes recur in different contexts but with related meanings. He shows how these phonemes pass into Semitic or Indo-European languages or both, carrying their basic meaning with them and carrying their religious significance into the myths and rituals of different religions. Unlike John's other books, *The Sacred Mushroom and the Cross* is difficult to read and difficult to summarize, even without the 142 pages of notes that form the bulk of his evidence, because he follows clues that criss-cross different cultures and lead into many-layered webs of association. John was thirty years too early to make a computer program for his research. Here are a few examples to show the reasoning behind his etymology.

As an example, John looked at the phoneme U, which he took as one of the most basic and essential word-bricks in Sumerian. In philological terms, it was the key to the whole fertility concept. U signifies "god" or "seed." It appears with different cuneiform symbols all related to the idea of fecundity: semen, seed, word, power, storm. As IÀ-U, literally "strong water of fecundity," it forms the root of *Zeus* and *Yahweh*. Linking phonemes together, John suggested how other words could be built up with associated meanings. He took care to put an asterisk in front of words that were his own constructions but that had not yet been found in any Sumerian text so far discovered. These asterisks show where imagination had to leap the gaps in the evidence. For example, by adding IÀ-U to SHU, "to save," he formed *IÀ-U-ŠU-A, "semen that saves" — the name *Joshua*, whose Greek equivalent is *Jesus*. Adding NU, "seed," this would become *IÀ-U-NU-šuš — *Dionysus,* and the Greek *Nosios,* healer, an epithet of Zeus. The Bacchic cry *Eleleu,* the Hebrew *Elohim, Hallelujah,* and *Elijah,* all come from this sacred phoneme U. *Eleleu* is associated with one of the most famous fertility festivals of all, the Dionysiac Easter revels or *Anthesteria*. There the Maenads rampaged in drug-induced frenzy, and girls (or men dressed as girls) carried the unmistakably phallic thyrsus, an ivy-covered rod tipped with a vine-cluster. The third day of the Anthesteria is called *Khutroi,* a Greek name related to the Semitic mushroom word *kotereth*. The name Anthesteria itself may be from the Sumerian *ANTA-AShTAR, "penile erection."[8]

8. Allegro, *Sacred Mushroom,* p. 157.

Mushroom Names

Here are some examples from the book of the most common Sumerian mushroom names on which, according to John, part of the mythology of the New Testament is based. Some are the Sumerian originals found extant in texts or inscriptions, and some are reconstructed from transliterated words in other dialects or built up on preexisting patterns. Again, the constructed forms are denoted by an asterisk.[9]

BALAG
kur-kur
SIPA
*BALAG-ANTA
*TAB-BA-RI-GI

BALAG means both "mushroom" and "crown of the penis." Supplemented by ANTA, "raised," it would form *BALAG-ANTA. By dropping LA, or assimilating it to the following consonant, it gives *paqqu'a*, a Hebrew name for the mushroom, and the *Bacchantes*, the Greek name for the followers of Dionysus.[10] The BAL syllable incorporates Sumerian AL, "drill," "borer," and becomes in Semitic *ba'al*, "lord," "husband" and the name of the Canaanite god *Baal*, as well as Latin and English *phallus*.[11]

KUR means "mountain" or "conical object" and may underlie the Greek *korkoron*, a type of chicory whose name Pliny appears to confuse with *kirkaion*, "mandrake." He says that people use the juice of this plant to anoint themselves, and "so great are its health-giving properties that some call it Chreston."[12]

SIPA appears to mean both "shepherd" and "penis," with the idea of the protector and promoter of fecundity, a combined role for kings, priests, and farmers alike. *SIPA-UD would then mean "penis of the storm" and could become the Semitic *Sabaoth*, an epithet of Yahweh, and in Phrygian the name of the god *Sabazios*.[13]

*AB-BA-TAB-BA-RI-GI, John suggests, is the Sumerian mushroom name underlying the Aramaic *'abba'debareqi'a'*, customarily translated, "O my father who art in heaven" but more accurately the Gnostic invocation used to summon beneficent spirits against disease and misfortune: *abracadabra*.[14]

9. Allegro, *Sacred Mushroom*, p. 50.
10. Allegro, *Sacred Mushroom*, p. 52.
11. Allegro, *Sacred Mushroom*, p. 24.
12. Pliny, *Natural History*, XX.74.
13. Allegro, *Sacred Mushroom*, p. 24.
14. Allegro, *Sacred Mushroom*, pp. 160-61.

The Fertility Concept in Ancient Sumer

John identified the most important elements in the fertility concept as the generative rain or dew, the underground source of fecundity, and the cycle of death and rebirth. The most important practices focusing on this concept include propitiation by gift or sacrifice and atonement for taking the fruits of the fertile earth. All life derives from God, but some life-forms have more of God's life-force in them than others. People choose things to give back to God that would be most pleasing to God — those containing the strongest divine essence. In the first-born or the first fruits it is especially strong. It is the first-born or first-reaped that is returned to God as sacrifice or gift, in atonement or propitiation.

Rain, Dew, and the Sea of Knowledge

The word of God, the seed of God, comes as rain to impregnate the womb of earth. God's seed forms a reservoir of potency underground. This is the "sea of knowledge" and the source of all wisdom. Plants that can tap this source of knowledge produce hallucinatory drugs, and to partake in the drugs is to ingest the knowledge of God: divine omniscience. Swifter than meditating and more decisive than fasting, drug-taking is the direct line to God. Some of the most effective drugs come from fungi, in particular *amanita muscaria* or fly agaric.

Pliny describes dew, brought by the morning star, as the most powerful conceptual fluid of Nature: "Its influence is the cause of the birth of all things upon the earth; at its rising it scatters a genital dew with which it not only fills the conceptual organs of the earth but also stimulates those of all animals."[15]

It also gives rise to the bread from heaven, manna — or mushrooms, since they can spring up overnight and appear with the morning dew. To eat this heavenly gift bestows power over storms, like that of the Dioscouroi or of Jesus.[16]

Death and Resurrection

Death and rebirth in nature underlie the most ancient myths of humankind. For example, in Greek myth, Persephone visits the underworld for part of the

15. Pliny, *Natural History*, II.38.
16. Allegro, *Sacred Mushroom*, pp. 109-17.

year but reappears each spring. John traces her name to the Sumerian *BAR-SIB-U-NI, "container of fecundity." In Greek her alternative name, *Kore*, comes from the Hebrew *qore*, "spindle-rod," which John derives from the Sumerian *GU-RI, "phallus." Her consort in the underworld is the Greek god *Plouton*, Roman *Pluto*, which John argues, taking phonetic variation into account, may come from Sumerian *BURU-TUN, "deliverer of the womb."[17]

Mandrakes and Mushrooms

The mandrake is famous as an aphrodisiac, and its English name comes via Greek *mandragoras*, which John derives from Sumerian *NAM-TAR-AGAR, "demon/fate-plant of the field." NAM-TAR also gives *nektar*, another food of the gods. Among the mandrake's other Greek names are, as mentioned above, *Kirkaia*, from KUR-KUR, "double cone," another mushroom epithet. These names, and many other references to the mandrake's characteristics, lead John to identify it with the sacred mushroom itself. A liturgist of ancient Syria, about 1400 B.C., cries to Baal to send a compensatory offering for having pulled up a mandrake; the offering he asks for is in Ugaritic '-r-b-d-d, from the Sumerian *URUBAD-BAD, "furrow-appeaser"; both words are related to the Greek *orobadion*, a mushroom name.[18] Compensation for the harvest of crops (or mushrooms, or mandrakes) by offering sacrifice is a fundamental concept in fertility religion.

Why Mushrooms?

If you look for it, mushrooms are full of phallic imagery. They first appear as an egg-shaped bud, grow quickly into a red-tipped shaft, spread out, die down, and appear to rise again within a few days. According to John, the story of the virgin birth, which recurs in many mythologies all over the world, may derive from the way mushrooms sprout from the soil after rain without any apparent seed. They produce a sticky mucus, which he suggests is symbolic of the god's semen and a potent source of fertility. Other emanations of the same substance in rain, dew, spittle, sap, or resin have similar effect. The Sumerian MAŠ and ŠEM, "semen" or "resin," was used as an epithet for a priest, the anointed one.[19]

17. Allegro, *Sacred Mushroom*, pp. 152-53.
18. Allegro, *Sacred Mushroom*, pp. 169-70.
19. Allegro, *Sacred Mushroom*, p. 60.

Mushroom cults are well attested worldwide and can probably be identified with the *soma* cults found as far apart as India, Siberia, and South America, which have been extensively studied by R. G. Wasson.[20] Folknames for the mushroom proliferate wherever it is used; they get woven into countless stories where their original significance may be perverted, distracted, or lost. Sometimes the word-root, sometimes the characteristics, themes, or incidents of the associated story give the clue to the original idea. For example, to develop the theory described in chapter 9 on the names of the apostle Peter, the obvious derivation of "Peter" is *petra*, "rock" with its Aramaic equivalent *cephas*. But *pitro* is a Semitic term for a mushroom; while *cephas* is related to the Latin *cepa*, mushroom, and also to the Essene title *caiaphas* for a physiognomist or seer skilled in diagnosis and healing. So John reasons that the name does not necessarily belong to any individual, but to an Essene official, whose special skill lay in the secret and sacred mushroom lore that the sect kept alive through violent times. And he suggests that Peter's patronymic *Bar-jonah* may derive from the Sumerian BÁR-IÀ-U-NÁ, "womb or fertility," related to the Greek *Paian,* an epithet of Apollo, and *paeonia* — not our common garden peony but what Pliny described as a wild bush bearing small egg-shaped (mushroom-shaped) buds.[21] But if that were ever true, the significance of the name was soon completely suppressed or lost, so that we assume the name *Bar-jonah* simply referred to the father of a man called Peter and would no sooner associate him with a mushroom cult than we would Little Red Riding Hood.

We can follow the etymology more readily in the development of the Sumerian BA-LAG-ush, which can mean either "phallus" or "mushroom." As we have seen, in Hebrew it drops the LA to become *paqq'ah* and hence *Bacchus*. Bacchus' Greek name is *Dionysus,* the god of fertility whose woodland revels sound more than likely to have involved hallucinogenic fungi.[22]

Amanita muscaria, the fly agaric mushroom, has a red cap flecked with white. In the Old Testament, similar coloring is associated with rough red-headed Esau and with Joseph's coat. The Sumerian BAR-DARA for "reddish or spotted skin," becomes the Greek *pather* (panther, with mottled coat) and *panderos,* an alternative name for *akanthos*, which Pliny calls a type of thorn-bush "with a reddish root and a head like a thyrsus." Through word-play, this could also give *paideros,* the beloved disciple.[23]

20. R. G. Wasson, *Soma: Divine Mushroom of Immortality* (New York: Harcourt, Brace & World, 1968); *Sacred Mushroom,* p. 39 and notes on p. 229.

21. Allegro, *Sacred Mushroom,* p. 18.

22. Allegro, *Sacred Mushroom,* p. 86.

23. Allegro, *Sacred Mushroom,* pp. 118-32.

The garden theme that recurs throughout the Bible may have a mushroom derivation, for the Sumerian GAN can mean either "field," "garden," or "the red canopy of the mushroom." It is found in the drug name *kannabis* and the Arabic *gannati-nna'imi*, which can be read as "garden of delight" and may derive from Sumerian *GAN-NA-IM-A-AN. *Na'iman* is another name for the Greek god Adonis, consort to the mother goddess of fertility. Jerome in the fourth century A.D., and J. G. Frazer in the twentieth, identified Adonis with Tammuz (Sumerian DUMUZI, "Son of Life"), the corn-spirit or Mesopotamian god of harvest.[24] Tammuz's festival fell at the beginning of the cereal harvest. Like Easter, it celebrated the dying and rising of a god, in this case the resurrection of the life-giving corn. Jerome recorded rituals still practiced in his lifetime to hasten the germination of seed in a grove dedicated to Tammuz, that is, in the gardens of Adonis, at Bethlehem.[25]

John suggests that *GAN-NÁ-IM-A-AN may mean "canopy stretched across the heavens," and speculates that the image may recall the shape of the mushroom.[26] He maintains that Sumerian cosmography was based on the picture of the strong man holding up the arch of heaven: the mushroom symbol writ large in the form of Atlas or writ small as the archetypal phallic stem piercing the archetypal groin.[27] This does, to put it mildly, strain the credulity. Possibly the Sumerian subconscious worked with such images, but to prove it a conscious process would be impossible. Atlas holding up the sky was a Greek myth, quite probably based on a similar myth from earlier times; no one need have thought he looked like a mushroom, nor that a mushroom was doing the same job.[28]

John believed absolutely in his research. He believed that through analyzing the earliest written languages he had uncovered the fertility religion that shaped their conception of the world. People's language showed how they thought, what was important to them, what they considered worth writing down. It showed how their lives were governed by the fertility of the earth, so that their highest endeavor was to learn how to influence the gods who controlled it. The language of the ancients was the thought of the ancients made tangible and transmissible. Many of its root elements have been transfigured through the alphabets of many races, and the imagery of the first concepts has elaborated into succeeding mythologies. Language and thought have grown and taken wing; they are powerful creatures, and few of

24. J. G. Frazer, Chapter 32 in *The Golden Bough* (London: Macmillan, 1922).
25. Allegro, *Sacred Mushroom*, p. 177.
26. Allegro, *Sacred Mushroom*, pp. 178-90.
27. Allegro, *Sacred Mushroom*, p. 134.
28. Allegro, *Sacred Mushroom*, p. 139.

us now recognize any particular religious framework to our words and reasoning. But the roots of Western religion still reach down to Sumerian concepts of fertility through layers of mythology. By tracing the development of thought through language, John believed he had found a grand, unifying theory of religion.

That was the general idea; the difficulties lay in the detail.

CHAPTER 11

Questioning
The Sacred Mushroom and the Cross

Specifically, the difficulties of explaining this grand, unifying theory of religion lay in applying the details of an ancient drug cult to first-century Palestine. It is easy to imagine that three thousand years earlier, in a world dominated by the natural forces of sun and storm, people felt their fortunes and their lives caught up in the power of these forces and tried to appease the destructive elements while propitiating the good ones. They lived in a world with spirits in it: gods and lesser gods, angels and demons. Clay and flesh were not everything: Magic gave an extra dimension to the world, so they used magical means to communicate with the spirits. There was imitative magic, propitiatory magic, divinatory magic, and the magic of summoning by name. Some, shaman-like, could leave their body altogether, and the drug that most helped them to do this was the hallucinogen from the mushroom. So, in John's view, they would have held the mushroom in particular reverence.

But it is more difficult to imagine this going on in Jesus' day. Was mushroom lore carried through Old Testament times to the first century A.D.? Neither the Bible nor the Dead Sea Scrolls hint that it was among the secret teachings of the Essenes, so how could we test John's theory? To say that it was occult knowledge, therefore deliberately encrypted, is to invite cynicism on several fronts. How would the recipients know they had deciphered the code correctly? What would they do with the knowledge? Couldn't such an elaborate technique make almost anything hide almost anything else? Couldn't anyone but the intended recipients crack the code? How were so many people fooled on such a massive scale for so long?

John thought the invocations were being deliberately woven into the story and deliberately mistranslated or punned upon by those he calls "the cryptographers." And he was sure that when the meanings of the secret names were unlocked, the whole edifice would crumble:

> We must be in no doubt of the effect that importing a new, mushroom element into the New Testament picture must have on our understanding of the origin and nature of Christianity. It needed only the decipherment of one of the strange, non-Greek phrases in such terms to upset the whole previous picture of the beginning and growth of the Church. If, for instance, 'Boanerges' is correctly to be explained as a name of the sacred fungus, and the impossible 'translation' appended in the text, 'Sons of Thunder', is equally relevant to the mushroom, then the validity of the whole New Testament story is immediately undermined. For the pseudo-translation demonstrates an intention of deceit, and since mushrooms appear nowhere in the 'surface' tale of Jesus, it follows that the secret reference to the cult must be the true relevance of the whole. If the writers have gone to the trouble of concealing by ingenious literary devices, here, and as we have seen, in many cases elsewhere, secret names of the mushroom, not only must its worship have been central to the religion, but the exigencies of the time must have demanded that they should be transmitted among the initiates and their successors in a way that would not bring their enemies down upon them. It therefore follows that the 'surface' details of the story, names, places and possibly doctrinal teachings must be equally as false as the pseudo-renderings of the secret names.

> One immediate result of the cracking of the already very fragile skin of the New Testament story is that all those doubts about its details which have so exercised scholars over the years are brought sharply back into focus. There have always been extreme difficulties in understanding the story of Jesus. There are in the New Testament picture many kinds of problems posed on historical, geographical, topographical, social, and religious grounds, which have never been resolved. But to the Christian scholar they have always seemed of less relevance than the apparently incontrovertible fact of the existence of one, semi-divine man who set the whole Christian movement in motion, and without whose existence the inauguration of the Church would seem inexplicable. But if it now transpires that Christianity was only a latter-day manifestation of a religious movement that had been in existence for thousands of years, and in that particular mystery-cult form for centuries before the turn of the era, then the necessity for a founder-figure fades away, and the problems that have beset the exegete become far more urgent. The improbable nature of the tale, quite apart from the 'miracle' stories, the extraordinarily liberal attitude of the central figure towards the Jewish 'quislings' of the time, his

friendly disposition towards the most hated enemies of his people, his equivocation about paying taxes to the Roman government, the howling of the Jewish citizens for the blood of one of their own people at the hands of the occupying power, features of the Gospel story which have never rung true, now can be understood for what they have always been: parts of a deliberate attempt to mislead the authorities into whose hands it was known the New Testament documents would fall. The New Testament was a 'hoax', but nevertheless a deadly serious and extremely dangerous attempt to transmit to the scattered faithful secrets which the Christians dare not permit to fall into unauthorized hands but to whose preservation they were irrevocably committed by sacred oaths.

Let it be repeated: If even one only of the mushroom references of the cryptic phrases of the New Testament were correct, then a new element has to be reckoned with in the nature and origin of the Christian religion. This new element, furthermore, is the key that fits the phenomenon of Christianity firmly into the surrounding mystery cult pattern of the Near East; but it does so at the cost of the validity of the surface story which knows nothing ostensibly of mushroom cults and which offers for its sacred cultic titles and invocations deliberately false 'translations'.[1]

The hoax theory seems fantastic. But, for many people, so does the tale of the god-man with supernatural powers that millions of Christians have swallowed over the centuries. John believed that philology had given him the key to the origin of Near Eastern and European religions. But how sound was the key?

One problem in studying ancient languages is to know exactly what meaning people attached to a word or part of a word at any one time. Languages evolve over time through circumstance and through contact with other languages. John supposed the root meanings would persist with the root phonemes, but is this true? As the first written pictograms became increasingly stylized cuneiform symbols, and the symbols became tools for making an almost infinite number of words that carried little or none of their original connotation, so words develop significance according to circumstance and may lose their original connotation.

For example, as previously mentioned, John suggests that the Sumerian mushroom title *AB-BA-TAB-BA-RI-GI became the Aramaic invocation 'abba'debareqi'a', which was used as "abracadabra" by the Gnostic physician Q. Serenus Sammonicus to summon beneficial spirits against disease and

1. John M. Allegro, *The Sacred Mushroom and the Cross* (London: Hodder and Stoughton, 1970), pp. 192-94.

misfortune — one of many similar incantations, mostly based on the names of demons, known to the Gnostic sect. It is more commonly translated as "Our Father who art in heaven."[2] Did Serenus know he was invoking the name of a sacred mushroom? He may have, for the Gnostics, like the Essenes, studied the lore of healing and divination and passed it one to another through secret rites. But it would be hard to prove.

Did the Maenads chanting their paean *"Eleleu, eleleu,"* like the Israelites calling on Elohim or the Christians exclaiming "Hallelujah," realize they were using the Sumerian name for semen, the water of fecundity, E-LA-UIA? Jesus' cry, *"Eloi, eloi, lama sabachthani"* rends any parent's heart when translated, "Father, father, why hast thou forsaken me?" But did the evangelist who wrote it down know it came from an invocation of the sacred mushroom, E-LA-UIA, E-LA-UIA, *LI-MAShBA(LA)GANTA?

If they didn't know, then the original meaning was lost, and so was its significance at the time it was spoken. Though known to be holy, the words may have lost their original connotation entirely.

The same question applies to other religious concepts. John says. "The Christians saw their Christ . . . as the divinely sent substitute offering for the rape of the fungus harvest. He is 'raised up' as the 'little cross' [i.e. mushroom], sacrificed, returns to earth whence he came, and then resurrected to new life. He is a microcosm of the natural order."[3] The death-and-resurrection concept, fundamental to so many myths, fits the Easter story in general terms. But does the explicit link to the mushroom cult remain directly relevant? If the idea of an atoning sacrifice is deeply rooted in every succeeding religion, do its followers have to be conscious of the earlier forms the sacrifice took? Again, in general terms *The Sacred Mushroom and the Cross* may cast light on the development of many religions including Christianity; the difficulties lie in the detail.

The ideas in *The Sacred Mushroom and the Cross* about deliberate concealment throw up major questions. If the New Testament is full of hidden mushroom references, how could we be sure that they had been hidden there deliberately? Perhaps they were phrases whose meaning had changed entirely over centuries, phrases that people chanted because they knew them to be holy without knowing why. Can religious rites such as processing through the Temple to the Holy of Holies really be conscious imitations of sexual intercourse? They cannot, of course — they have their own significance in dignity and reverence. So if the original meaning related to a fertility rite, does the original meaning matter anymore?

2. Allegro, *Sacred Mushroom,* p. 160.
3. Allegro, *Sacred Mushroom,* p. 171.

And how could the nature of Christianity have come to be misunderstood so colossally in such a short time? John explored this question in later books, especially *The Dead Sea Scrolls and the Christian Myth,* but not at all adequately in *The Sacred Mushroom and the Cross.*

However, his evidence mounted. Trays of index cards and reams of notes piled up among the dictionaries and concordances in his study. He emerged from behind the barricade for meals and for a daily walk, five brisk miles along empty lanes, with or without Joan. He hardly glanced at the countryside; he was too busy expounding theories either aloud or in his head to bother where his feet went. Joan patiently accepted her role as sounding board. She marveled at his ingenuity and let the expostulations bounce off her. He was always expostulating these days: the church, the university, Israel, de Vaux, bureaucracy, politicians of every color. While John went in for full-scale iconoclasm, Joan got on with running the home and family. She also lectured part-time in accountancy at Salford University and welcomed the part-time independence this offered.

In John's opinion, his theory established that the church was irrelevant to modern civilization. He concludes his book:

> [N]ow that we no longer need to view the Bible through the mists of piety, does it really matter in the twentieth century whether the adherents of this strange Judaeo-Christian drug cult thought their community ethics valid for the world at large, or not? If some aspects of the 'Christian' ethic still seem worthwhile today, does it add to their authority that they were promulgated two thousand years ago by worshippers of the *Amanita muscaria?*[4]

In John's eyes the church stood for an evasion of responsibility. He detested the idea that anyone could avoid his or her moral responsibility by handing the issue to priests or, even without priests, to a conveniently external divine arbiter. Though Christians felt they came to know truth and justice through Christ, John thought it none of Christ's business: Morality should be an issue between men and women; grown-up people should take responsibility for doing right by others. To share the responsibility with a god would be to dilute or avoid it. Surely, he thought, people had outgrown the need to rest their moral judgment on folk tales?

---

4. Allegro, *Sacred Mushroom,* p. 205.

Reaction

The publishers looked forward to hot debate and sizzling sales.

"Not since the great 'Apes versus Angels' debate started by Charles Darwin has there been a book that will set the country talking to such an extent. Its persuasive, documented theory that the New Testament is in fact the cover story of an ancient fertility cult outlawed by Rome, is one that could shatter our whole established belief." That was some of the pre-publication promotion for *The Sacred Mushroom and the Cross* in March 1970.

To spark off the debate and prime the market, Hodder and Stoughton sold the serial rights to the *Sunday Mirror*. The first installment came out on April 5, 1970.

Serialization in the *Sunday Mirror* meant money and fame. It certainly stirred up popular interest. It was scarcely the way to command respect among thinkers and scholars. On the other hand, John suspected with reason that the Establishment would detest his theories and do their best to choke the life out of them at birth; if he approached an academic journal first he would get no further. He went along with the publishers in choosing the publicity trail, and it did his reputation no good at all.

In his *Sunday Mirror* introduction on April 5, 1970, John set out the stark bones of the theory:

> Thousands of years before Christianity, secret cults arose which worshipped the sacred mushroom — the *amanita muscaria* — which, for various reasons (including its shape and power as a drug) came to be regarded as a symbol of God on earth. When the secrets of the cult had to be written down, it was done in the form of codes hidden in folk tales.
>
> This is the basic origin of the stories of the New Testament. They were a literary device to spread the rites of mushroom worship to the faithful. . . . The stories of the Gospels and Acts were a deliberate hoax.
>
> Through studying Sumerian cuneiform texts which go back to 3500 B.C., we can trace the proper names and words used in the Bible back to their original meanings.
>
> The cult forgot or purged from their memories the one supreme secret on which their whole religious and ecstatic experience depended [the source of the drug. John then explained how his clues lay in the hitherto inexplicable names and nicknames given to some principal New Testament characters such as Boanerges or Barnabas.]
>
> Concealed within the nicknames and their 'translations' are names of the sacred mushroom, the sect's 'Christ'. The deliberately deceptive na-

ture of the mistranslation puts the lie to the whole of the 'cover story' of the man Jesus.

The gospels a deliberate hoax? A forgotten secret? Bewildering.

Then the book came out. The reaction was almost universal outrage. Much of it came in terms such as "one long gush of phallic drivel" (*The Times Literary Supplement,* June 10, 1970); "rich indulgence in the wildest flights of uncontrolled fantasy" (*Daily Telegraph,* May 21, 1970); "a vivid but sick imagination that appears to see sex everywhere" (*Baptist Times,* May 28, 1970); "All right, so Jesus was a mushroom. But who made the first mushroom?" (*Sunday Mirror,* May 31, 1970).

John expected that sort of thing, though he was disappointed in the *TLS.* What he did not expect was the unanimous denial from fifteen eminent professors in *The Times* of May 16, 1970:

> Sir,
>
> A good deal of publicity has recently been given to a book *(The Sacred Mushroom and the Cross)* by Mr John Allegro, formerly a lecturer at Manchester University. This is a work upon which scholars would not normally wish to comment. But the undersigned, specialists in a number of relevant disciplines and men of several faiths and none, feel it their duty to let it be known that the book is not based on any philological or other evidence which they can regard as scholarly. In their view this work is an essay in fantasy rather than philology.

This time the assault shook him. When de Vaux and the rest had used the same tactic — a letter to *The Times* — back in 1956, John had been astonished, and anxious mainly for his job. By 1970 he had resigned from the university anyway. But he had staked his reputation on *The Sacred Mushroom* and realized his credibility in the eyes of the world was under attack. From years and years of sifting word-dust, tracing threads, untying and retying knots of sound and meaning, he had produced this grand astonishing theory that, in his view, ought to sweep away people's old assumptions about their past, give them a clear view of a godless and truly moral present, and provide a rich field for future philological research. He wrote about it to André Dupont-Sommer, who had suffered similar vilification in 1952 for suggesting that the Scrolls' Teacher of Righteousness might prefigure Jesus:

> Of course, I expected a storm of abuse from all sides, particularly from those who have never read the book. But never, even in my wildest flights of imagination, did I anticipate the reaction from the British Academic

Establishment in the manner of this letter from [Professor Godfrey] Driver and fourteen of his cronies to *The Times*. To say that this book is not 'scholarly' and is 'an essay in fantasy rather than philology' without offering any real objective criticism stems from sheer emotion and not from reasoned critical assessment. It is what one might expect from ecclesiastics, but hardly from the British Academy.

I have waited in vain for some British scholar to have the courage to answer this libellous assault upon my integrity, although two letters (from laymen) have appeared, expressing astonishment that academics should treat me and my work in this cavalier fashion. I hoped that somebody with some specialist knowledge in the field covered by the book might conceivably have written saying that although he did not commit himself to agreeing with my conclusions, he nevertheless appreciated the vast amount of highly scholarly work represented by *The Sacred Mushroom,* and that the philological approach attempted by the author to the myths of the ancient Near East was correct and fruitful potentially. Furthermore, that the link between Sumerian and the Indo-European and Semitic languages, if sustained by further research on similar lines, could be extremely important for future studies in our field and human relationships between East and West generally.

I have, as I say, waited in vain. Doubtless in due course somebody here might dare to stem the current tide of denigrating me and my work, but he will have to risk his professional standing by seeming to support me. You are not unaware of the power of the Establishment!

. . . How swift everyone is to criticize someone who publishes his work, but strangely tolerant of scholars who prefer to say nothing and hold onto valuable material to prevent others seeing it! It is a strange world, this academic rat race.[5]

John asked Dupont-Sommer to write such a letter in his support. It is a measure of his hurt that Allegro the iconoclast, who commanded attention but never begged for anything, had to ask for help. There is no evidence that Dupont-Sommer agreed.

The "two laymen" that John referred to had complained to *The Times* that it was unfair for the professors to condemn John for their own lack of imagination. They pointed out that the stories of Freud and Einstein, whose theories had been dismissed as fantastic in their day, should have shown us that fantasy and mythology could provide undreamt-of insight. Theirs was

5. John M. Allegro to André Dupont-Sommer, June 25, 1970.

the sort of reaction John had hoped for: a stirring of interest among people at large, an opening of minds to debate and reappraisal.

John responded immediately to the letter in *The Times:*

26 May 1970

Sir

It is difficult to judge what motives underlie the extraordinary letter you publish in your columns today, nor what scholarly purpose it is meant to accomplish. It condemns many years of intensive research in Near Eastern and classical studies with no more justification than that it seems to its learned signatories as 'an essay in fantasy'.

My working is fully set out in the notes of *The Sacred Mushroom and the Cross,* and I am quite prepared that the many important advances in our knowledge that the book offers should be measured against equally objective and scholarly criticism. Perhaps when these scholars have actually read and studied the book they will feel better able to offer the world a balanced judgment less clouded with emotion and more in accord with their responsibility to the centres of learning they adorn.

Tetchiness did not help much. John seriously considered suing for defamation. It was what his publishers advised — ostensibly on the ground that the professors had sought to impugn his scholarship without showing evidence or cause, though presumably because Hodder wanted yet more publicity. However, after a few days' reflection John drew back. His solicitors had agreed that *The Times* letter had been damaging and defamatory, but not unequivocally libelous; legal action would be lengthy, expensive, and probably unsuccessful.

Some questioning voices spoke up in John's support. *The Humanist* of July 1970 called in the theories of J. M. Robertson and Robert Graves about the importance of soma and other drugs in religious rites. In his foreword to the 1960 Penguin revised edition of *The Greek Myths,* Graves had said that he was convinced that the followers of Dionysus drugged themselves into frenzy on a far stronger potion than wine or ivy-ale, "namely a raw mushroom, *amanita muscaria,* which induces hallucinations, senseless rioting, prophetic sight, erotic energy, and remarkable muscular strength." He also identified the food of the gods, ambrosia and nectar, with this type of mushroom. Graves noted the unmistakable correspondences between the worship of Dionysus and that of Tlaloc, the mushroom-god of some Central American Indian cultures, asked how they could have come about and called for "any expert help in solving the problem." But he declined to discuss *The Sacred Mushroom and the Cross;* in the *New Statesman* of May 1970 he said he was skeptical about John's botanical accuracy.

The *Toronto Telegraph* of June 20, 1970, offered a refreshing appraisal. Boldly for the day — for the rising tide of hedonism had only just begun — it suggested that people should be less puritanical about the idea of sex in religion, and that John's theory only reflected the lack of inhibition that ancient fertility cults displayed. It also declared that to separate theology from religion as John did was to contribute to the freedom of thought. On the other hand, belief evolves: the origin of a religion comes to be less important to the believer than its accrued meanings. This was exactly the sort of debate that John wanted. But who read the *Toronto Telegraph* outside Toronto?

The *Freethinker* of June 27, 1970, argued in John's favor that the book merited careful analysis and that the professors' condemnation was grossly unfair. Sumerian etymology would repay investigation, and when more tablets were discovered, John's speculative word-juggling could be tested objectively. The idea of a common ancestry among the gods of the Near Eastern fertility cults made sense as a common denominator between the mythologies of Christianity and the cults of Baal and Essenism, as well as a vast range of related mythologies. The matter that did need more investigation was the identification of the holy plant with *amanita muscaria,* for other fungi with similar properties were more readily available in the region. But it would certainly be worth investigating.

R. Gordon Wasson, who had studied mushroom cults widely from Central America to India, identified the soma of Vedic worship with *amanita muscaria.* He wrote in the *Times Literary Supplement* of September 25, 1970, that people in the Near and Middle East did indeed use soma during the third and second millennia B.C.: Their art and folklore were full of this "marvellous herb" linked with the Tree of Life. However, he had found no evidence that it was used later than 1000 B.C.

There was also debate in Chicago. The *Daily News* pointed out, "Allegro is disturbed that the sexual aspects of his argument should have been seized on to the exclusion of the rest. To him it is a clearing of the intellectual decks without which man will be lost."[6]

But the *Chicago Sun-Times* prevailed, writing, "The core thesis, however ingenious and sensational, is raw or sometimes wild and rampant conjecture, which has no basis in history and hardly any in philology. Much of the book is an exercise in the most arbitrary reasoning and fanciful deductions and, as such, is a disservice to serious scholarship." It accepted that a few of the in-

6. *Chicago Daily News,* August 15, 1970.

sights into fertility cults were worth pursuing, "but to jump from that to conclusions which, he claims, have abolished the authenticity of the Judaeo-Christian heritage and its ethical system is his final, rashly prescriptive, non-sequitur."[7]

Christians who felt to the depths of their souls that they lived and breathed through God and the Son of God were never going to follow the cold reasoning of an etymologist. Their religion was not just a set of ideas but a way of thinking. Even for people willing to accept that fertility rites, phallic symbolism, and hallucinatory drugs had a part in many religions including Christianity, the mushroom was not the whole story. However vast the amount of philological evidence, Christians could not accept that the New Testament was little more than a cover-story for the drug-crazed followers of a fungus cult.

The *Canberra Times* of August 28, 1970, suggested in a most thoughtful way that there was more to religion than its historical origins; that people could reinterpret religious teaching to create their own perfectly valid ideals:

> Perhaps Allegro is correct in his linguistic conclusions and perhaps the criticisms only reflect an extreme suppression of sexuality. One can accept Allegro's philology, and instead of arguing that tracing biblical names and events to a source in fertility cults necessarily means the debunking of Christianity, it can equally well be pointed out that what is perceived at the instructional level can find its highest dignity in the Christian gospels.

The *Canadian Churchman* of September 1970 gave a fair appraisal of John's main themes: how religion developed, how secret codes could be embedded in stories, how the key was the mushroom, the phallic symbol of fertility. But it made the point that magic words could be chanted without understanding; stories were remembered without their meaning. Similarly, the *Winnipeg Free Press* pointed out that whatever went before, Sumerian acts and beliefs did not carry over into Judaism and Christianity: "We must not replace the mists of piety with equally unscholarly and unobjective contempt."

John was exasperated at being called unscholarly, but he did welcome discussion, critical or supportive, about the status of religion and how far it depended on historical authenticity. He wrote personally and at length to anyone who entered the debate on these terms; in fact, he wrote to almost anyone who bothered to read the book instead of the reviews and wrote to him or about him with rational questions or opinions. He conceded that in

---

7. *Chicago Sun-Times*, August 30, 1970.

practical terms it could well be true, for some, that the origin of a belief was less important than the meaning that had accrued to it — that if people behaved themselves because they feared God or admired Jesus, the question of how they visualized God or Jesus mattered only to themselves. But to him, the thought that the church was founded on deception was monstrous.

The most substantive criticisms were of the philology, the academic basis of the work. *The Observer* of May 17, 1970, wrote, "Can one assume that to use a word or phoneme as a metaphor turns it into the real thing? Did they actually worship the mushroom because it represented the essence of fertility?" The *Chicago Sunday Times* of August 30, 1970, added, "The premise that terms that sound alike must always be related is not proven, and would be difficult to prove in a long-dead language." And *The Humanist* of February 1971 questioned John's basic assumption that the root of a word provided a guide to its meaning over the whole of its history. Words can persist while the ideas associated with them change, for ideas *are* affected by circumstance and time. Words of the liturgy preserve archaisms that may once have come from ancient rites, "but it is precisely because the archaisms of these liturgies can no longer be understood by the worshippers that the old words can be reinterpreted and associated with new ideas." So with rites — once their old fertility purpose was lost, they became merely an expression of devotion.

Several critics pointed out that many of John's Sumerian word-combinations were speculative and not yet attested by archeological evidence; combining phonemes in the ways he suggested might seem logical, but without evidence they were too speculative to rest a theory on. The *Jewish Chronicle* of June 12, 1970, called *The Sacred Mushroom* "a few hundred pages of verbal juggling" and found it wholly unconvincing. Dialects as yet unattested could lie behind inexplicable nicknames such as Boanerges just as reasonably as John's twisted Sumerian. This type of argument frustrated John, who felt that if only people studied the section containing the notes, where he set out his academic reasoning, they would be as convinced as he was by the weight of evidence.

Many years later, with the aim of making a fair academic assessment of *The Sacred Mushroom* on its own terms, that is, as a work of philology rather than as an outrage to theology, Anna Partington published a review that pointed out both the weaknesses and strengths of John's approach:

> Many of the Sumerian expressions brought into the comparative analysis have been constructed by the author from known Sumerian word elements. They are marked as such, and no evidence is presented that they exist in actual Sumerian texts.

While the technical notes and indexes (which account for 143 pages) include a tremendous amount of information, the exposition of the reasoning behind statements based on this information is incomplete.

Even though in conventional academic terms the mushroom theory stands as unsubstantiated hypothesis, *The Sacred Mushroom and the Cross* is a work of substantial intellectual value, for its philological data offers stimulating new insights into the languages of the ancient Mediterranean Basin and Near East to those who can examine it with an open mind.[8]

Philology is a difficult science to pin down: You can pull apart long words and analyze the syllables to suit almost any purpose. It allows too much speculation and imprecise chronology. John saw mushroom references everywhere; he may have been right, but the very weight of evidence that he thought conclusive made the theory suspect, because it left readers breathlessly struggling for something they could understand.

Then there were serious doubts about the importance of word-play, and whether it was used for deliberate cryptography. The scribes of Qumran had used word-play in their biblical commentaries; study classes on the Old Testament would have been enriched by it; but would everyone have understood? Could you really hide cultic precepts in puns and expect cult members either to understand them in the sense they were intended or to go on keeping them secret from everyone else? John thought it possible, given the persecution of sects by the Romans and by each other. But most critics thought it unlikely; they felt, with the *Morning Star* of May 21, 1970, that though the book was worth reading for its challenging ideas, it was ultimately unconvincing because it failed to show with enough cogency and clarity how the secret knowledge and rites reached the early Christians and found expression there.

Many people refused to take *The Sacred Mushroom* seriously. They called it a spoof, "the most elaborate academic hoax since Piltdown Man," "a parody of historical scholarship," and so on. In September 1971, over a year after publication, the *New York Times* was still decrying "the incredible thesis that Greek and Hebrew are derived from Sumerian. . . . That way lies madness." To the person who sent him this clipping, John wrote:

> I think I must be a little weary. I have suffered so much from the idiocies of these so-called academics who just don't want to know, and that casual writing-off of so many years' intensive study by yet another of them made me just want to sit down and weep.

8. Anna Partington, *Mushroom Mystery* (Unpublished ms., 1993).

Concluding Analysis

The strength of John's argument in *The Sacred Mushroom and the Cross* was three-fold. He seemed to have found an all-embracing answer to what he perceived to be the many textual difficulties of the New Testament. He challenged assumptions and made people question the basis of their beliefs and behavior — a blow against hypocrisy and lazy thinking. And he tried to cast light on the development of language and thought by explaining and expanding our knowledge of how language and religious concepts developed together, each feeding the other. Leaving aside the implications for Christianity, he made a tremendous contribution to our understanding of our ancestors' language and thought, one that could still become one of the most fruitful and exciting fields for study in the quest for the origins of civilization. This ought to have been taken further, but it went virtually unrecognized amid the clamor of outrage from the church.

One main weakness was the inherent improbability of the cover-up theory. Most people recognize that the gospels, particularly the later ones, were written for largely Gentile audiences, even Roman ones, and are full of literary devices to help the story along. But the idea that they were really a cover story for instruction in drug lore on the streets of first-century Jerusalem seems wildly improbable.

Secondly, there were too many asterisks. John did not collect nearly enough evidence to back up his speculation — not solid evidence in the form of actual inscriptions from extant tablets. Maybe more recent Sumerian studies could fill the gaps; in 1970 there were simply gaps. From John's point of view, the clues he was finding linked together like a web. From the critics' point of view, the logic of this was flawed: To fasten one improbable link onto others was to compound the weaknesses of the web, not strengthen it. From a scholarly point of view, the word reconstructions were guesswork: They needed far more substantiation.

The third problem was the imprecision of philology as a guide to historical events. Though fascinating for the derivation of words, it has less bearing on their meaning for users. For example, "sin" means much more to Christians today, and probably to Christians in the first century, than "wasted semen." God comes with a different face and different words in every age.

CHAPTER 12

Following
The Sacred Mushroom and the Cross

The vituperation shook John more than he cared to admit. Dismissal as a spoof, refusal to take his work seriously, hurt him more than anything. No one who interviewed him in person, and few who actually studied the book, thought he was trying to deceive them. When interviewers allowed him to speak for himself, he did so with customary candor. He told the reporter in an interview for the *Sunday Mirror*, "I get a kick out of making people look at things afresh from the outside. . . . The Church is founded on a lie. I'll doubtless be accused by some of blasphemy. But these conclusions — like them or not — are the result of scientific enquiry." As the reporter put it, he spoke with his passion for the truth.

Asked if he had tried the mushroom, he told the reporter, "I wouldn't be so bloody stupid. I wouldn't touch it. Drug-taking is idiotic. Drinking is stupid. I am frightened of losing control of myself in any way. Drugs are like religion: with both you can convince yourself of things which may not be true. You suspend judgement. This leads to horrors, to war. Religion is divisive."

The reporter concluded, "He may be right or wrong. What matters is that he is not a fraud."[1]

The *Johannesburg Sunday Times* described him as "displaying a gloating obsession with the sexual allusions he finds everywhere . . . so intoxicated with his theme of orgiastic cults and drug-induced religion that he has neglected his critical faculties,"[2] and the *Church Times* called *The Sacred Mushroom and the Cross* "a book in execrable taste which in any earlier Christian

---

1. *Sunday Mirror*, March 22, 1970, p. 9.
2. *Johnnesburg Sunday Times*, July 12, 1970.

generation would have been roundly called blasphemous."[3] But the *Manchester Evening News* interviewed him in person:

> John Allegro does nothing to disguise the fact that he extracts great pleasure from stirring things up. But there's nothing malicious about him. More of a mischievous quality that loves to get people thinking. 'I like to challenge established beliefs', he says, 'for some of them are based on tenure of office, on tradition rather than objective truth. They have invested in them an aura of authority without being understood.' He doesn't see why anyone should accept face-value authority simply because it comes with the role of a chap with his collar on back to front.[4]

One or two of John's university colleagues spoke with guarded respect. A professor of comparative religion told the *Guardian* on February 16, 1970, "He is purely a semantic philologist, and when he leaves that field it is a matter of personal opinion. . . . He has an original mind and the courage to speak it."

Speaking his mind was John's stock in trade. He enjoyed being in the public eye. He didn't care whether he disconcerted people. Above all, he detested hypocrisy. Rightly or wrongly, he had decided that the church was founded on a lie and had no right to tell anyone what to think or what to do. "This thing of taking on the whole of the church single-handedly," he told the *Shropshire Star* in August 1970, "has a certain stimulus for an individual like me."

It was difficult to keep up the bravado. The barrage of hostility sharpened John's image of himself as a lone seeker after truth, but like other individualists he found it lonely work. Church reaction he could dismiss as predictable. He was disappointed but not surprised when Hodder and Stoughton's religious books editor told the press that he was sorry the firm had published the book. It was the total lack of support from the academic establishment, or more particularly the refusal to discuss the book in terms of serious scholarship, that hurt most. John knew the depth of study that had gone into it and the pains he had taken to verify or substantiate his ideas every step of the way. If his colleagues had followed the same steps and were still not convinced, he would have loved to argue it out with them, point by point; he wanted to be known as an arguing partner by people whose minds he respected. But whether none thought it worth bothering about, or none was willing to risk his reputation by consorting with Allegro, they did not take it up. At least in

3. *Church Times*, May 22, 1970.
4. *Manchester Evening News*, February 18, 1970.

public, most people wrote off *The Sacred Mushroom,* with *The Times* of December 11, 1971, as "a sensationalist lunatic theory."

John replied wearily to this charge that, even in 1971, no one else seemed willing and able to look at religion dispassionately:

> Your clerical correspondent's emotional vilification of my recent study in Near Eastern fertility philosophies and their relationship with New Testament myth . . . belies his attempt to portray modern ecclesiastical biblical criticism as a rational and objective literary exercise.
>
> It is precisely this inability on the part of the theologian to assess unemotionally the work of scholars who are prepared to treat the biblical writings as stringently as any other writings that makes their own findings so suspect. Had they really been prepared to probe deeper into their source material, completely unrestrained from the necessity to find in this extraordinarily heterogeneous body of literature 'a product of a living and developing faith' and to stamp it piously as 'the Word of God', they might have solved some of its most basic problems centuries ago. Unhappily, until their study is opened up to a wider, more disinterested range of students, even the most promising lines of research such as those I have initiated must remain unexplored.[5]

Even John's sister Cynthia said that she could not take him seriously. This news was of little consequence to John, who had hardly spoken to her since she had become a Baptist minister several years earlier. His other relations thought resignedly that he had probably gone too far for his own good this time, and Joan's family looked with concern to her.

Just before *The Sacred Mushroom and the Cross* came out, the family moved from Derbyshire to the Isle of Man. It was partly to take John away from Manchester University. He resigned of his own choice. There was no pressure to leave, and his professor told him he was sorry to see him go. John realized that reaction to *The Sacred Mushroom* might mean an end to a university career, but after sixteen years of teaching and more than his share of enmity and jealousy, he was glad to shut the door on it.

Joan took all the controversy without flinching and got on with the job of moving the household and getting the children through end-of-term exams. Having heard John expound his theories day by day, she knew they would raise hell. She knew John believed absolutely that the research was valid and essential, that he would take on all comers with relish and never back down from a fight. For her part, she hated to be in the public eye; for

---

5. J. M. Allegro to *The Times,* December 11, 1971.

John it was inevitable. She refused to do more than tell reporters when they telephoned that he was not available.

John wanted to strike out as an independent writer and broadcaster. To finance this, he was well aware that he would need to hold onto whatever money he made from the book. The publishers expected to sell a great many copies very quickly, and under the current English tax rules John stood to lose 90 percent just as quickly in tax. The Isle of Man, however, set its own and very much lower tax rates for the express purpose of attracting "come-overs" such as writers and artists, whose income was liable to fluctuate widely from one year to the next.

Besides this, the island was — and is — an entrancing place of contrasts and a thousand beauties. It is rock and gorse, moorland and pasture, hills cloven by wooded glens, the whole ringed by the unchanging, ever-changing sea. It has lawyers and financial managers as adroit as they come; marine research; a seaside-holiday industry that in 1970 looked boarded-up but was soon to start reviving; farmers prospering inside the island's import restrictions; trawlers battling as ever with the Irish Sea. First-time visitors to the Isle of Man see the quaintness, sugar-frosted; older ones get ladlings of nostalgia from the horse trams and steamships; but beneath these layers, a thousand years of island history speak to anyone who looks for it.

The Allegros bought an old and rather dilapidated parsonage, whose solid walls held in the damp and smelled of ancient hymn books. While the rest of the family stayed to pack up the house in England and finish the school term, John went across with a camp bed and a car full of tools and set about stripping, rewiring, and painting the parsonage. And waiting for the flak to fly when the book came out.

The old parsonage stood in a spinney of ash and sycamore down a stony track. Its tangled acre included a mossy lawn; a riot of blackcurrant, bramble and gooseberry bushes; scabby fruit trees that still produced baskets of apples, quinces, and plums; a nettle patch that looked promising for hens or vegetables; outbuildings for spiders, tools, or dens. At night the trees swayed under a tide of wind; on calmer days the salty mist rolled inland. Joan hoped that here they might find some shelter from the clamor and vituperation.

Nevertheless, the phone kept ringing and reporters kept arriving. John met them at the airport, whisked them home for a meal, and if they asked intelligent questions, whisked them around spectacular parts of the island as well. He talked and talked and delivered them breathless and bemused back to their plane; promises of lecture tours and public debates fluttered around after these visits but seldom came to anything.

Striding across the wide, windblown sweep of Castletown Bay day after day, John fell in with a weather-tanned, bushy-bearded figure out jogging, also day after day. Chatting turned into a friendly sparring partnership. This was the writer Bill Naughton, author of *Spring and Port Wine, Alfie,* and dozens of other stories and plays, which John now sought out with renewed respect. Bill took up new ideas and new acquaintances with delight. He bounced John's outspoken opinions up and down the beach and cannily cut his polemics down to size. They spent hours arguing happily wherever they met.

Then there were a few university people — marine biologists, retired professors, antiquarians from the Manx Museum — with whom John would discuss things more soberly over long evenings at home. He could be affable enough with anyone he met, but he did not form many other close friendships on the island. He found nothing at all in common with the ex-colonial set, starched and blue-rinsed and extremely proper, a few of whom made the mistake of inviting him for cocktails at their mansions. When he could not avoid the party, he generally arrived late, spent a maximum of forty minutes repeating, "Really? How interesting" over a glass of orange juice, told his hostess he was going home for an early night, and did so. An event that was posted as a debate on the issues of the day turned out to be what he called the Society for the Smug and Self-righteous congratulating one another on their unanimous stand against corporal punishment of children. John, who never smacked his own children — one shriveling word was enough — leaped in with some forceful if imaginative counter-arguments in the hope of stirring up a real discussion. The result — a mass creaking of corsets and popping of eyeballs — meant a welcome end to society invitations on the Isle of Man.

The End of a Road

John wrote and wrote. *The End of a Road* came out in 1970 in the slipstream of *The Sacred Mushroom and the Cross.* John saw it as a companion volume. On the premise that *The Sacred Mushroom* had demolished the church's pretensions to moral authority, he asked: Why should twentieth-century people owe any allegiance to a fertility myth? What gave a fictional first-century rabbi the right to tell people how to run their lives, then or now — apart from a set of generalized "thou shalt nots" wrested from their context and impracticably vague by comparison with real contemporary law codes? It was time for people to stand on their own feet, to close the gate at the end of the church's road, and step out on the road of compassion, responsibility, and common sense.

> This book is not a post-mortem examination of a moribund Church. In it
> I am not primarily concerned with the cult of the sacred fungus, which

fully deserved all the abusive epithets heaped upon its perversions by the Romans when they tried to suppress the 'Christians'. It deals with the end of one road, and more particularly the opening up of a new, wider highway for all men to travel. We shall look to some of the problems now facing mankind and bearing down on us with the dramatic advances in modern technology in a shrinking world, and see how old and inadequate moral sanctions can be revised or replaced by new ones. We shall discuss how the present catastrophe of a discredited Christianity can be turned to good account through seizing the opportunity for fresh, creative thinking in a society freed from the inhibitions of religious dogma. Let the dead bury their dead.[6]

He could not bear the hypocrisy that went on in the name of religion, the lazy thinking of otherwise intelligent people who did lip-service to Christianity merely for the sake of convention and, worse, pretended to call it morality. "Let our babies be presented to the community," he wrote, "our young people to each other in marriage, and the achievements of our dead to those who survive them, in solemn thanksgiving but without marring the occasion with the insincerity of meaningless religious ritual."[7]

It was a call for the world to grow up:

Now at last we can stand on our own feet. The props of religion can be thrown aside, the bishops banished from the legislature to their cathedrals and palaces to superintend their fabric funds and tea parties, and we can tackle the problems that confront twentieth-century society in the light of what we want that world to be.[8]

The church press, naturally, did not like to be called moribund and labeled *The End of a Road* an evil book. However, a few Christian writers recognized the challenge that John was presenting, not so much to the Christian past as to the post-Christian present. For example, an interviewer for *The British Weekly* of October 16, 1970, spoke out:

It is the challenge of the humanist who frankly says 'Where are we to find the sources of morality now that we no longer believe the faith which for centuries supplied it?'

Allegro says 'Undoubtedly the Bible will remain an epic of world liter-

6. J. M. Allegro, *The End of a Road* (London: McGibbon & Kee, 1970); (London: Panther Books, 1972), p. 18.
7. Allegro, *The End of a Road*, p. 166.
8. Allegro, *The End of a Road*, p. 171.

ature, and you can get spiritual value from the Psalms for instance, but we get that comfort from what we ourselves read into the Psalms and not from what we know about their background. I question whether we can get any moral teaching from the Bible without bringing to it many pre-conceptions. We can no longer rely on any sacred book or ecclesiastical authority. Man must grow up and stand on his own feet'.

At least we should thank Allegro, the humanist scholar, for being so honest. That is precisely what an enormous number of people outside the Church think, but rarely say, and we inside the Church must frankly accept this. We cannot expect people these days to accept the Bible as a kind of source-book of mankind's moral experience.

The fresh-air outlook of *The End of a Road* went down well with humanists. It is readable and thought-provoking rather than provocative; to people not brought up in a Christian tradition it presents a clear, common-sensical outlook on life and human relationships. A Canadian reviewer wrote:

His clear-cut conviction — that Christianity is not based on history — clears the ground for a completely objective look at where man is, how he got there, and where he is going. Christian and Judaic myths take their natural places among the Hindu, Babylonian, Greek, Scandinavian myths, as an integral part of man's cultural evolution.[9]

Some still found the idea that Christianity could be a cover-story for a drug cult too weird to take seriously and were reluctant to look beyond this idea to the bigger questions of godless morality that the book raised. Of course, John was not the first or last to question the historical accuracy of the gospels, though he was the only one to link them so explicitly with ancient fertility religions. But for many, Christianity meant far more than the story of a rabbi in a dubiously authentic setting. They had taken or interpreted words like *love, forgiveness, peace, understanding,* words that speak to the best in the human condition, and invested them with the weight of ecclesiastical history and influence, so that the human qualities fused with religious authority and it was hard to think of one without the other. People no longer needed to think of a god primarily as bringer of rain or grain, who only in times of war needed to bring victory in battle. Social and moral issues were the main problems for urban people, and they needed to construct a god who would sort them out. Seeking comfort, wanting to be told what to do, wanting to clarify unclear issues, people thought of their god as

9. *Humanist in Canada,* 4.1 (January 16, 1971), pp. 29-31.

a father or mother who would always look after them and show them what was right.

Wasn't it time people recognized their own responsibilities? Couldn't they do without the spurious authority of history and the infantile craving for dependency? And not dependency on their real family and friends and other human beings but on an imaginary construct idealized in as many forms as there were people to imagine it? The power of imagination is mighty and wonderful and enables us to think and love and understand and create things we perceive as of utmost beauty — but we don't need to worship it. Worshipping something makes it an object outside ourselves; therefore, it is brittle and destructible. The creations of our imagination — love and understanding and so on — live inside our imagination, not brittle but alight with life; they are all the more real to us for living inside us and being as children to us, while in our flesh-and-blood children we light a further flame of imagination to feed on and feed our own.

If you knock away the historical foundations, need the whole edifice fall? True morality is a living flame, the living and growing and changing relationship between people, so it has nothing to do with the historical foundations of religion, nor its institutional authority. Scripture can enslave us; imagination sets us free — free within the living bonds of human morality, which we create to uphold all that we value. Human quality — the nature of love, the depth of understanding, natural justice — is attained through imagination and the interplay of our imagination with that of other people. It is inside us, and it is what we must always seek. It is far more valuable than anything imposed by priests. We do not need to call it God-given, for it comes from within us. It has nothing to do with the church, except that the church can supply examples of good men and women, and for some people a channel to discover quality within themselves through sharing with others.

For John, the road to the future lay in clear thinking and responsible behavior, unencumbered by religion. Thinking for yourself was seldom comfortable or easy, but in his eyes it was worse to be patronized by having the church tell you what to do on the strength of a hollow tradition.

The Chosen People

The Chosen People: A Study of Jewish History from the Exile until the Revolt of Bar Kocheba was published by Hodder and Stoughton in 1971 in hardback and as a paperback by Panther Books in 1973. It tells the history of the Jews from the conquest of Jerusalem by Nebuchadnezzar of Babylon in 587 B.C. to the

Second Jewish Revolt of A.D. 132. John bases his account on traditional texts — books of the Old Testament, Josephus, Philo Judaeus, Dio Cassius, and others — and sets out the complicated parade of plots, counter-plots, betrayals, and insurrections in a brisk and highly readable sequence. His main theme is how the conception of the Jewish nation as a divinely chosen race was planted as a political ambition among the exiled Jews. Bringing together old customs and stories, the idea was fired by the longing of the Babylonian Jews for their traditional homeland. Many of them grew prosperous outside Palestine, and their wealthy communities manipulated the wish for identity into the idea of an exclusive Judaism embodied as a political state and fighting for autonomy against local and imperial neighbors — more dream than fact. John wrote:

> When the 'new Judaism' came to be hammered out after the return from captivity, it was around these ancient customs and a historicized mythology that it was fashioned. And the mainspring for this romantic movement came not from the bleak, desolated Jerusalem of reality, but from the emotions of Babylonian Jews feeding their imaginations on unhistorical traditions about their origins and paying fervent homage to an exclusive religious cult very largely of their own devising.[10]

John went on to explain that they had devised it not, as popularly presented, by gift of the desert god Yahweh who had manifested himself in opposition to the Canaanite fertility god Baal but by reinterpreting the Sumerian idea of a life-giving god over many generations. For there was no fundamental opposition — the god-names originally meant the same.

Critics questioned whether John had shown all sides of the story. For example, while he held that the Jews in general struggled to preserve their national identity against Hellenism, many Jews embraced the opportunity to enrich their culture with Greek and Roman traditions. But John wanted to make people think about their old assumptions, and he won some respect for doing so in his lucid presentation of "an argument against believing in the divine election of any nation or race. As such it has a serious note of warning."[11]

John saw the terrible dangers of a "Holy War" in any time or place. His warning is as valid now as it was in Old Testament times, or the Middle Ages, or 1967. Religious fervor is no excuse for atrocity: When will the nations grow out of fanaticism and revenge?

10. J. M. Allegro, *The Chosen People* (London: Hodder and Stoughton, 1971), p. 39.
11. *The Times Higher Education Supplement,* November 19, 1971.

Religious emotionalism, however stimulated and for whatever motives, is an extremely dangerous and unpredictable force. Moral and patriotic idealism that springs from a racialist religion is a perilous philosophy that can soon burst through the bounds of rational control. Modern heralds of the New Era, from whatever gods they claim their authority and wherever they raise their prophetic voices — the Jerusalem Knesset, the Meccan kiblah, or the platforms of Carnegie Hall or Wembley Stadium — should appreciate the power of the spoken word to unleash the mighty forces of religious fanaticism. Modern facilities for mass communication and hypnosis make the stimulatory drugs used by Zealotism, early Christianity and medieval Islam unnecessary. Their calls to a Holy War against supposed moral, political, or racial enemies can now be more terrifyingly effective than ever before, and more fearful in their consequences. Let the reformer and the patriot seek the infinitely more difficult and painstaking way to the Promised Land through reason and rationality.[12]

Reason, rationality, and a godless interpretation of the Jewish myth were not exciting enough to make *The Chosen People* a bestseller. John hoped it would stimulate interviews and debates, but few people took up the offer. To some extent they may have been afraid of stirring up anti-Semitism. John would have said his approach was not in the least anti-Semitic; rather the opposite, since he was trying to establish the historical reasons why the Jews felt themselves special, aside from the emotional ones that fostered their pride and inflamed others' jealousy. Perhaps these reasons can never be separated; historians must take an objective stand on all of them.

Freelancing

John's head was teeming with ideas, and now that he could call himself a full-time writer, he wanted to let them out. Branching out from academic work, he sent off articles and stories, plus synopses for books, plays, documentaries, and serials to publishers and broadcasters all over the country.

He had already taken one play as far as the New Theatre in Huddersfield. *The Living Oracle*, written with Roy Plomley, had first been staged in April 1966. It tells the story of a lecturer searching for scrolls who discovers evidence to undermine the basis of Christianity. Establishment figures try to persuade the lecturer to withdraw; persuasion turns to threat; pressures mount from

---

12. Allegro, *The Chosen People,* p. 12.

outside, from the university, and from his family. The theme, as stated in the *Yorkshire Post* on April 6, 1966, asked, "Should a discovered truth which totally undermines the foundation of a religious belief on which millions base their lives be published, and so condemn that belief as a myth, or should it be suppressed to appease sectional interests and preserve the status quo?"

John admitted at the time it was largely autobiographical, and with hindsight it looked almost prophetic. The pressures on the hero were familiar, as he described in an interview for the *Daily Mail* a few weeks before the play opened:

> Many scholars and religious leaders want to keep the significance of the Scrolls quiet and restrict it to academic common-rooms and seminars. The purpose of the play is to crystallize the significance of the Scrolls, and present this in a popular form which everyone can appreciate.[13]

From John's perspective, the clamor over *The Sacred Mushroom* sharpened the theme of the play, and in 1970 he cast around for a way to revive it. But the same clamor ruined his chances, because nobody wanted to embroil themselves in such a lurid controversy, at least to the extent of making a public demonstration about it. Besides, though the play had a strong storyline and a startling climax, the plot lost power with some rather "wooden and shallow" marital complications; it had lasted a week and been labeled "a brave and worthy failure."[14]

During the 1970s, John sent many scripts for plays, talks, and stories to the BBC and synopses to agents and publishers. There was to be a historical novel set in Herodian Jerusalem, a dramatic modern novel about genetic research, a series of articles on the nature of religion.

John began to plan a book about Josephus, who was not only a compulsive gleaner of information but a survivor who slipped from one allegiance to another with the wiliness of a modern politician. He also began compiling a collection to be known as *Folk Tales from the Bible*, intended for the bedside table of his anti-religious acquaintances. The tales featured John's own translations of various Old Testament episodes; they were more or less scurrilous and fortunately came to nothing.

Letters from agents crackled with promises, on the lines of, "Trust me, John, I will make you internationally famous and rich," "It has all the makings of a superb multi-part TV documentary," and so on. Similarly, offers from upstart film companies with grandiose ideas and not enough money all fell

13. *Daily Mail,* March 12, 1966.
14. *Daily Mail,* April 16, 1966.

flat. When it came to the point, the publishers drew back, the lecture tour arrangements fell through, the scripts would have needed too much revision . . . disillusion encroached, slow and sour. Even John realized eventually that he should get excited about nothing until a check was in the bank.

He got as far as writing *Sharing God,* a set of five-minute talks from a humanist angle for Radio 4's *Thought for the Day* — and might have got further with them if he had used a pen name. The talks were never broadcast, but they showed the arguments were moving on.

John's discussion points in *Sharing God* were a series of questions. Without presuming to supply the answers, the purpose was to make people think for themselves about what they meant by their religion. The points included these:

- **Pilgrimage** — This is the idea that for the non-committed, as for Chaucer, the journey through question and self-evaluation is more valuable than the arrival.
- **Submission** — Why accept the over-simple and self-negating idea of total submission to a beneficent deity? Happiness should mean fulfillment of one's own potential, and submission should be to one's own concept of truth, not the dictate of a priest or guru.
- **Power within** — Some people find that religion releases inner reserves of strength and self-confidence. But why focus on the self or a god? Others achieve the same — "finding themselves" — through concern for other people.
- **Sacrifice** — The original cultic meaning was restitution — restoring to nature part of its bounty in an act of thanksgiving. Why then make a virtue of self-sacrifice, self-flagellation, self-deprivation — an off-putting and guilt-laden concept that mainly serves to make us more submissive before an all-powerful god and his representatives on Earth?
- **Religious conformity** — Why? Why suppress individuality, the precious faculty of self-determination?
- **Exorcism** — Releasing bad spirits can take gruesome manifestations. But some people seem to need religious activity to relieve stress in whatever image: "The relief religion can afford may be irrational, the philosophical assumptions it demands illogical, but the subsequent peace of mind it affords is no less real, and apparently indispensable," said John.
- **Who needs priests?** — Revived with every new sect, a fundamental schism appears between personal belief and institutional religion. In something as personal as one's relationship with God, why should "nanny church" know best?

- **Sharing God** — We should acknowledge that forms of religious expression, to be true to their source in the individual mind, are as varied as ways of making love, for God has as many different faces as there are believers.

Questions kept rising, indefatigably rising. *The Sacred Mushroom* had rocked Christianity, but scarcely to its foundations; however much the church was mocked, it remained an institution of state and of every parish in the land. Older people clung to its familiar props and incantations; younger people joined this or that sect, and if they turned away from the local vicar they turned towards gurus from the east. What were they seeking? What was it in the human condition, in all places and all ages, that made people turn to religion?

Lost Gods

Sharing God sought only to sketch out a few lines of inquiry that listeners might have wanted to follow up for themselves. *Lost Gods,* published in 1977 by Michael Joseph, Ltd., looks more deeply into the need for religion.

> God is Man's response to a legacy of evolutionary discontent. The faculty of conceptual thought that has raised Man above all other forms of animal life was achieved only at the cost of a divided and tormented mind. . . . Man's response to that awful burden of self-determination was to create for himself a god and to still his self-doubts in the solace of religion.[15]

So God, John explained, was the answer to humanity's insufficiency, and humans created God to set in stone their human explanations, lend conviction to their judgments, and reassure themselves that there must be a reason for everything that happened.

Lost Gods looks at the ideas and cults of the ancient gods through age-old myths and the work of archeologists and anthropologists. It shows how primeval beliefs have persisted into modern theological thought and recur as common elements in widely disparate cults and philosophies, though the differences between them can lead to destructive enmity. John wrote:

> Gods disappear from history because they are no longer required. Man created them for specific purposes in particular circumstances; when conditions change, social or ecological, gods become outdated and are su-

15. J. M. Allegro, *Lost Gods* (London: Michael Joseph, 1977), p. 1.

John in 1977, from a print by Foley Vereker

perseded by more effective deities. . . . But human nature is more deeply rooted, and man's emotional needs are fundamentally similar whatever the time or place. The new gods must therefore speak to the same inadequacies of man in his unequal struggle against the environment, and their worship must somehow satisfy that deep longing in the human heart for peace of mind and assurance for the future. In this sense the deist is right to argue that there is but one God with many faces.

The divisiveness in religious loyalties has been disastrous for humanity, as we know too well. Wars fought to assert the claims to supremacy of rival theological systems, or even of differing ways of serving the same deity, have been among the most ruthless and bitter. In so individual a matter as that of a man's relationship with his god, it is not surprising that there should be great differences among the creeds and rituals of people living in widely different environments. . . . Regional and ethnic variations of common religious themes assume an importance in the eyes of their adherents that tend to obscure more basic concepts shared with alien faiths.[16]

One of the common elements in religion, John explained, is the way it builds dominance and submission into a moral code, where everyone is ultimately dependent on the god's mercy and has to earn it. Another is the relief that religion can afford from inbuilt anxieties, in its release rituals and the way it can formalize and therefore parcel away all sorts of emotions, sometimes through hypnotic trance. Then there is the sense of the soul's immortality: Funeral rites from Neanderthal times show the belief that the soul continues its journey without the body or is reborn, a belief that probably arises from the sense of kinship with Mother Earth and the cycle of vegetation.

The importance of fertility to people whose fortunes depend on their own fecundity and that of the earth is fundamental to religions everywhere and in all ages. Nearer our own time, some ancient fertility rites resurfaced in elements of witchcraft. The medieval church saw witchcraft as a threat to its authority, for its hold on people had roots far older and stronger than Christianity. The church treated witches along with other rival groups such as Jews or Templars as scapegoats for the sins of the world outside its domain.

John tries to bring religion out of the realms of anthropology and into our own time:

It may be, then, that despite our rightly prized rationality, religion still offers Man his best chance of survival, or at least of buying himself a little

16. Allegro, *Lost Gods*, p. 8.

more time in which to devise some more reasoned way out of his dilemma [the dilemma of how to avoid plundering the Earth's natural resources beyond the point where they are capable of regeneration]. If so, it
must be a faith that offers something more than a formal assent to a set of
highly speculative dogma about the nature of God and His divine purpose in creation; it must promise its adherents a living relationship that
answers Man's individual needs within a formal structure of communal
worship. It has to satisfy the emotions without violating the believer's intellectual integrity, and it must avoid the tragic divisiveness of ethnic or
social affiliations by finding a common reference in our biological heritage. We all travelled the same evolutionary road to manhood and so
share the same deep sensibilities about such matters as the good earth,
sexual and family relationships, and a due regard for the balance of nature. Racial, climatic, and geographical differences have imposed local
variations on Man's responses to those fundamental perceptions, but in
the depths of his consciousness there is a common awareness of basic
needs and responsibilities. Upon such conceptions it should be possible
to found some universal and cohesive faith. Historically, the cult of the
Earth-mother has probably come nearest to fulfilling this role, and, being
sexually orientated, it has been especially concerned with this most disturbing and potentially disruptive element in Man's biological constitution. Perhaps in our present concern for ecological conservation, with its
constant cry for preserving this or that species of wildlife, we are moving
towards a revival of the old Nature religion, and re-discovering in the terrestrial womb that gave us birth the allegiance we owe to our lost gods.[17]

Coming from John, who thought religion irrelevant, a mass return to
faith in Mother Earth sounds a somewhat questionable prescription. But it
was meant as observation, and to provoke discussion, and to connect with
what he saw as the free-and-easy youth culture of the 1970s.

Though a free-and-easy youth culture was not the scene in the Isle of
Man. John began to feel out of touch with the world. At home, the old house
needed constant repair. He had no interest whatsoever in the garden, which
Joan loved. She had begun to worry about her father, who was in his 80s and
living alone in Dorset. She talked of building an extension for him or convert-
ing part of the house. Having soon found demand for her accountancy skills,
she was steadily becoming the main breadwinner again and more deeply embedded in island life as the months went by. John felt a cage was closing
around him.

17. Allegro, *Lost Gods*, pp. 185-86.

He said he needed Manchester's libraries for research. He felt he needed people with ideas, go-ahead people who worked in marketing, publishing, and the media. Initially he went across for a week at a time and stayed with a family friend. Then he went for three weeks and came to an understanding with someone he met at a concert that he could rent her spare room whenever he wanted. When she moved into a new flat near the university, he moved into one nearby.

John had to spend a certain amount of time on the Isle of Man each year to qualify as a Manx resident for tax purposes. He spent the minimum. He was there to help Joan through a difficult patch with her current employers, and he was there to help her decide to move nearer the town to a house that had an annex suitable for her father. However, the house was tall and rather drafty, and its kitchen range spewed smoke back into the kitchen. Grandfather duly arrived, and it was clear that he disapproved of John's comings and goings. It was not John's scene anymore.

In Manchester there were parties with people who talked about issues and lifestyles and having a good time and relationships. Whatever job they were doing, however much they earned or didn't earn, it was affairs and relationships and self-discovery that swung their lives from one day to another. Superficial maybe, but they were always colorful, always on the go, in and out of each other's apartments, experimenting with feelings and sensations — artists of pleasure, shallow but sensual. They had money; they had contraceptives — why not enjoy themselves? Older in years but denying it, shrugging off responsibility, on the run from convention, John joined in. He was welcomed by the bright young set: He had charm, he had ideas, and some of the ideas were delightfully outrageous.

The relationship with the flat-owner persisted. She was not the first and by no means the last. There were passing liaisons relevant only to the people concerned; they did not outlast a few letters nor encroach on each other. He went abroad, though he could not afford to travel as much as he'd have liked. Holidays had to be cheap winter sunshine packages, or tacked onto lecture tours. Looking for interest, color, and, above all, sunshine, he tried the Canaries and various Mediterranean resorts. John hated the cold and hated it more and more as he grew older, especially the cold wet gloom of Manchester and the cold wet winds of the Isle of Man. He was curious about everything — landscapes, people, histories — and scurried over the surface of it all like a pond-skating insect. And the best thing about winter holidays was avoiding the family Christmas.

The most interesting specimens from the trips were the acquaintances he collected. Mostly young, female, and unattached, they were waiting to talk, and found John a ready listener. He always did like the company of women, and he could charm anyone he chose by taking an interest in their lives and problems. Somehow it was much easier to do this for strangers than for his own family. He was generous with his time, for after all he had plenty to spare, and he showed such a ready appreciation of their stories that it was easy for them to open their hearts to him. So he became, rather surprisingly, a father confessor to several. Exploring the reasons that brought them to these out-of-season resorts took them into labyrinths of amateur psychology. Naturally the young women found themselves fascinating. There were long discussions, followed by long letters about life, love, and other tribulations. Much later — after his death — the family found and destroyed boxes full of letters from this period, mostly to and from women he had met in his travels. Some sought advice on marital problems, some told him their dreams, all were young and warm and sure of his interest. He had no one to pass their secrets to and nothing to gain if he had wanted to do so; he made an ideal personal tutor.

In Joan's eyes, John spent these years wasting his talents. Looking back much later, he admitted that in many ways she was right. He dabbled in anthropology and social psychology, chased whims, and made gestures towards a lifestyle he could not afford. It was all very shallow. Yet an incubus of an idea was taking shape that would emerge in 1979 as one of his most worthwhile projects, the one he himself valued most among all the books that he wrote.

John was unfair to Joan. Nobody could condone the hurt he did her. She had given steadfast support throughout the *Sacred Mushroom* troubles. Leaving the island he took as license to dally with other women. He would take up with people of a questioning mind, people he could talk to, and before long talking would lead to flirting. The casual attitudes of the day appealed to him. He would have called it being true to his nature. Joan saw it as self-indulgence. He evidently thought that self-denial — forbearing other relationships — would be a betrayal of his own nature. Yet he went on wanting and needing her support, and she went on giving it. He behaved and probably felt like a teenager, and in some ways it felt to her more like seeing an adolescent leave home than ending a marriage.

Unfortunately, it hurt. Joan never showed the unhappiness she felt, and she claimed that in the long run it strengthened her. She got on with the job in hand, earning a living and running the family home, because she had to. She always supported John and the memory of John without a waver.

Maybe he left partly in tacit admission that she was stronger than he was, and he did not want to think he was the junior partner. Despite the jaunty defiance, the reaction to *The Sacred Mushroom* undermined his confidence as well as his credibility. He needed to rebuild both on his own terms, and he supposed it would be simpler somewhere else without a family to encumber him.

John chose to formally separate from Joan and to leave her, the family, and the island. He told Joan he had changed: He wanted his freedom. He did not want domestic responsibilities. He felt she no longer needed him for money or moral support. He thought he had nothing to share with Mark or Judith and was not inclined to look for anything. He belonged to no university, was obliged to follow no conventions, and had a small income but no debts. He thought he was a free man.

CHAPTER 13

The Dead Sea Scrolls and the Christian Myth

The Sacred Mushroom and the Cross had placed Christianity in the context of the age-old mythology that surrounded fertility religions and was sustained by a drug cult. John contended that the priests of this cult had passed on its tenets through sacred names and incantations over thousands of years. He reckoned that in the first century A.D. the messages must still be there for those who had the secret knowledge to decipher and interpret them. However, they were embedded in tales of such popular appeal that the stories, not the secrets, were what people remembered.

The church, according to John Allegro, was founded on a lie. But now in 1979, nine years after he had published his revelatory theory, the church remained apparently unshaken. So what else was it founded on? What gave it such extraordinary tenacity?

People had said, Allegro cannot be right. Christianity speaks to the human condition. It is the word of God given a human face. Jesus has never had anything to do with drug cults, then or now. Nor had his Old Testament desert forefathers, the founders of Judaism. Jesus, brought up a Jew, was a Jew with a difference, and the difference came from God.

John agreed that he was certainly different. In John's view, his story was not only different, but incoherent, inconsistent, unhistorical, and, in first-century Palestine, simply improbable. It seemed to be an amalgam of folktales and contorted Old Testament prophecy, squeezed into a spurious historical setting and ending not in glory but in ignominy on the gallows. How had this flimsy sapling of a cult grown into a mighty world religion? What roots gave it strength? Was there some undying source of human need and aspiration that fed them? Why did they grow into the shape of the Great Church?

230

God changes shape according to the needs of the worshippers. As John perceived it, the first gods of life and fertility, based on the sun and the rain, had long since merged with Yahweh, the political god of the chosen race. The chosen race looked to a messiah who would lead them to victory in a cataclysmic, flesh-and-blood war against Satan — the personification of evil in all its forms — and against Satan's human minions. But this vision of war was not Christianity. How did political messianism metamorphose into what is meant to be a religion of universal tolerance and personal redemption? And then how have people's attempts to save their own souls built up into the wealth and might of the institutional church?

The Dead Sea Scrolls and the Christian Myth is a world away from the raw and somewhat gladiatorial approach of *The Sacred Mushroom and the Cross*, which set out to shock people into a new look at religion. Yet it springs from a similar conviction that all is not as it seems in the New Testament, and it argues that to understand where our own ideas come from we need to go back into the minds of our ancestors. Their inner light may clarify our own vision.

Since first beginning to study the Dead Sea Scrolls, John had felt that the doctrines of the Essenes, in many ways so close to Christianity, in others so distant, held the keys to the early development of the church. Had the people of the scrolls given up their messianic vision? Were they all dead, routed from Qumran after the First Revolt? Or did the Essene network that proliferated among the towns and villages enable them to keep their religion alive as the secret teachings of a secret society?

The Dead Sea Scrolls and the Christian Myth shows how and why the Essenes' vision evolved into Christian concepts, and how the early church fathers spun these into a web of temporal and moral authority that often seems to have little to do with its philosophical source. It was a web of extraordinary strength, supple and elastic enough to encompass a range of ideas and adapt to historical circumstance. In John's view its strength did not come from an accident of history — the brief career of a traveling preacher in first-century Palestine — but from its source in myth and prophecy, which shaped the way people thought. In this thought-system, history is not a succession of events in the linear form that we see it, but it is like a globe lit by divine light, where past, present, and future roll around and around.

The Essene Legacy

The new book starts where *The Dead Sea Scrolls: A Reappraisal* (a revision of *The Dead Sea Scrolls*) left off in 1964. Here John had suggested "the scrolls give added ground for believing that many incidents [in the gospels] are merely projections into Jesus' own history of what was expected of the Messiah."[1] In the new book he states, "What gave the Essenes their peculiar interest to religious historians was the possibility that their kind of Judaism might have served as the matrix for that even more unorthodox Jewish faith we call Christianity."[2] This matrix, in terms of Essene thought and belief, was a philosophy of light and hope amid the darkness and terror of the community's last days. It filled the holy men of the scrolls with a mystical faith in the salvation to come, a faith that shines through their Teacher's hymns.

It also shines through the earliest Christian writings: St. Paul's letters and the fourth gospel. For example, in his letter to the Ephesians Paul refers to "the cornerstone" (2:20), "children of light" (5:8), "the Spirit, which is the word of God" (6:17), and several times to grace and predestination; and in 1 Thessalonians he states, "You are all the children of light and the children of the day; we are not of the night or of darkness" (5:5) — the language of the Essene *Thanksgiving Hymns* and the *Community Rule*. The fourth gospel similarly shares the worldview and even the phraseology of the scrolls: light and dark, the spring of living waters, and so on. In the gospel these images focus on the figure of Jesus: Jesus as the Word, Wisdom personified, and also as the lamb, the sacrifice of the firstborn.

In comparing Essene and Christian doctrine, we recognize that although the many similarities are indisputable the scrolls do not account for the stories in the gospels of Matthew, Mark, and Luke of the traveling faith-healer, stories that seem so full of local interest and human appeal that they have held people's imagination ever since. As John put it, nothing in the scrolls anticipates a messiah who kept a low life among rogues and whores. If Jesus saw himself as the Lord's Anointed, then he kept a remarkably low public profile.

But the picture in the writings of Paul and in the fourth gospel is different from that in the synoptic gospels. St. Paul and St. John are less interested in Jesus' mortal life than in the significance of his death, and in his nature as the embodiment of God's word, *logos,* on Earth. Paul seems to be writing around A.D. 50, and even by then the political vision of a messiah who would liberate Israel and establish a theocratic kingdom on Earth had given way to the idea of Christ the redeemer of individual souls, who builds "a holy temple in the Lord; in whom you also are built together spiritually into a dwelling-

---

1. J. M. Allegro, *The Dead Sea Scrolls: A Reappraisal* (Harmondsworth: Penguin Books, 1964), p. 175.

2. J. M. Allegro, *The Dead Sea Scrolls and the Christian Myth* (Newton Abbot: Westbridge Books, 1979), p. 12.

place for God" (Eph. 2:20-22). The fourth gospel, which echoes the thought and language of the scrolls so clearly that some now think it is the earliest, not the latest, of the gospels, has Jesus declare, "My kingdom is not from this world" (John 19:36). By contrast, the gospels of Mark, Matthew, and Luke are more concerned with Jesus' mortal adventures. These gospels are speaking to a different audience and in a different style. Of the New Testament writers, in John's view it is St. Paul and St. John who carry the tradition of Essene thought into Christian theology.

The ascetic Essenism of Qumran was an inward-looking faith that excluded Gentiles and other sinners. In itself it had no mass appeal; the particular grace that was born with the chosen few would die with them. But its goal was personal salvation, and in this sense, anyone inside or outside the order could attain the kingdom of God. Turned into Christianity, it held out hope to everyone and spread like fire.

How did it spread? Rumor, gossip, and open-air rallies cannot account for such swift coverage.

> The extraordinarily rapid spread of the nascent Church, if we are to believe the traditional chronology, complete with a well-developed system of inter-communicating cells around the Mediterranean area, highly organised funding arrangements, and an accepted structure of authority, demands a longer period of growth than can be accounted for between the supposed date of the crucifixion, around A.D. 30, and the earliest of the Pauline letters. The Essene order possessed such an organisation, centred on its monastic community by the Dead Sea but extending far out to the towns and villages of Judaea and very possibly beyond, into Egypt, Asia Minor, and to Rome.[3]

This "underground" network worried the Romans because it could have facilitated any sort of insurrection against their military control, and it worried other factions of Jews because it could have undermined their hierarchy of orthodox religious control. It may partly explain the spread of Christianity, but it may also partly explain why the Romans — usually content to absorb other religions into their own panoply — persecuted Christians, and why some other Jews detested them.

Which aspects of Essenism particularly influenced Christianity? The most obvious links have already been pointed out, for example the Last Supper/Messianic Banquet, the Council of Twelve, and the imagery of the cornerstone and the fount of living waters.

3. Allegro, *The Dead Sea Scrolls and the Christian Myth*, p. 16.

Then there are the strange names or titles of some New Testament characters, which John traces to Essene terms. For example, as explained in chapter 9, when Jesus calls Peter *Cephas* (John 1:42), the double pun portrays him as both the rock — the cornerstone or foundation of the community — and the *caiaphas*, "overseer," "scrutinizer," the official who examined applicants wishing to join the community and also, in both a medical and religious sense, diagnosed the evil spirits within them that warped their minds or made them sick.

The Essene connection throws more light on gospel chronology; for the timing of the story has been made to fit the rule of the community. To place the crucifixion around A.D. 30 is no historical accident; in fact, it is not necessarily historical at all. The Essenes held that the death of their leader had been foretold to take place forty years before the final confrontation with the men of war. It could have seemed to their successors, who had survived the uprising of A.D. 68-70, that this confrontation must mean the destruction of the Temple in A.D. 70. The hero had to be at least thirty years old, for this was the youngest age that the scrolls allow for a leader of the community. Luke tells us Jesus was thirty when he began his ministry (3:23). So in John's view, the gospel writers transplanted the story of the Essene Teacher to first-century Palestine and embedded it there by adding names and figures from real-life Roman and Jewish history.

These connections with the Essenes are comparatively easy to spot. Deeper than these links run their conviction of grace, their perception of human history held in the hand of God, and the central need to make atonement by redemptive sacrifice. Through it all flows the concept of divine light.

The Fulfillment of Prophecy

The Essenes, like the New Testament writers, believed that everything that happened or was yet to happen had been foretold and foreordained. Essene writings continually refer back to the prophets and, as we can see with hindsight, seem to refer forward to the gospels and book of Revelation. For the Essenes, history rolled along in waves of apostasy and restoration, which had begun with Moses and soon would culminate in a last battle and the dawn of a new millennium. Again and again, the Jews had elected a charismatic leader — Abraham, Moses, Joshua — and gone through a cycle of rebellion, chastisement, repentance, and salvation before their god. Chosen by divine favor, they had to dedicate themselves to purity and lawfulness to keep favor on their side, and each time they failed they faced exile and punishment until they had proved their repentance. Moses had wandered the wilderness for forty years; his successor, Joshua son of Nun, made the desert his own; the Essenes' Teacher of Righteousness fled there with his followers. The Teacher had come to the Jericho area in re-enactment of the scene in which Joshua had crossed the River Jordan dry-shod, which itself echoed Moses' crossing of the Red Sea. Then in his turn, Jesus (whose name is the Greek equivalent of Joshua) was said to spend forty days in the Judean desert purifying mind and body — to meet his god alone where sand met sky.

The apocryphal *Assumption of Moses* says that Moses entrusted his words (i.e. the Pentateuch) to Joshua son of Nun and told him to store them in earthen vessels to await the Last Days. Isaiah also says, "Bind up the testimony, seal the teaching among my disciples" (8:16) — so the Qumran community did exactly that with their scrolls.

The Teacher's psalms are full of the imagery of living waters, shoots of holiness, trees of life — recalling the prophecies in Isaiah 41 about bringing water to the desert and fertility to the barren lands and in Isaiah 61 about oaks of righteousness and the planting of the Lord. They also recall the Tree of Life in Genesis, and they seem to look ahead to the tree of crucifixion. The Teacher of Righteousness sees himself as a second Joshua, who in his suffering was "chosen of grace to atone for the earth," as the *Community Rule* has it.[4] The Teacher's *Thanksgiving Hymn* tells how he was persecuted, mocked, and betrayed by the "seekers after smooth things," and how he was afflicted by disease and suffering as a symbol of how God redeemed the world through suffering. And of course he was not the first or last.

From Messiah to Bringer of Light

Pious Jews of the first century B.C. felt sure the last days were upon them. Portents and prophecies foretold the ruin of the old order; current events from earth tremors to insurrection seemed to run to meet the predictions. When Pompey marched into Jerusalem in 63 B.C., some thought it signaled not the end of their hopes but the beginning: For another hundred years the Zealots were to go on preparing to fight. Only when the revolt of A.D. 68-70 fell apart in slaughter was it clear that they would have to look elsewhere for help.

The *War Scroll* had laid out the order for the apocalyptic battle. The Romans did bring fire and sword, but no angelic host came to the rescue. The survivors or their successors needed to draw a different source of strength out

---

4. *Community Rule,* VIII.7.

of their faith. They found it in the concept of grace. Provided they sought it with wholehearted resolve, this gave them the assurance they needed. For the Essenes believed themselves preordained to grace. Born to be children of light, their task was to fulfill this destiny. Having less need than others of earthly comfort or the trappings of religion, they dedicated their hearts to God and their minds to the quest for enlightenment, the true knowledge of God. This knowledge had been spelled out in the Torah revealed to Moses. To understand it lay within the gift of God, brought to them first by their law-giver Joshua son of Nun and in his turn by the Teacher of Righteousness. It was preserved as a form of words in the *Community Rule,* but to realize it in full and know it in their hearts demanded total dedication, mysticism, medi-tation, and an asceticism that denied the distractions of the flesh. The Teacher had attained this state; his poems brim with light and love, the knowledge of God that filled him body and soul. He had found assurance that God had known him since before his birth and planned all his days: "As a foster-father supporting a child in his lap, so carest Thou for all Thy creatures."[5]

God who had planned their life had also planned their death. Death was only a stage on the way to heaven. The assurance that led thousands of Chris-tian martyrs to the cross or stake is here in the scrolls. All that the community did and all the signs of the times had been foreordained and, as they worked out by some or other contortion of exegesis, had been foretold in prophecy.

For both St. Paul and St. John, the central event of the New Testament is the crucifixion, which signifies redemption. "Here is the Lamb of God who takes away the sin of the world" (John 1:29), proclaims John the Baptist, voic-ing the fundamental belief that God's firstborn, the incarnation of his word, is also God's sacrifice to save the world. The lamb dies in atonement for the people's sins and, as firstborn, in propitiation of God's mercy. Similarly, atonement through suffering had been a central theme in the hymns of the Teacher of Righteousness, who, echoing Isaiah's suffering servant who "has borne our infirmities and carried our afflictions" (53:4), sees that through his own afflictions his faith shines out to glorify God and redeem his wrongdo-ing. Suffering afflicts the old man to the point of despair: "My sore breaks out in bitter pains and in incurable sickness impossible to stay . . . my soul lan-guishes day and night without rest."[6] Yet he believes, "Thy rebuke shall be-come my joy and gladness, and my scourges shall turn to healing. . . . For as a light from out of the darkness, so wilt Thou enlighten me."[7]

5. *Thanksgiving Hymn* XVII (formerly IX).36.
6. *Thanksgiving Hymn* XVI (formerly VIII).28-29.
7. *Thanksgiving Hymn* XVII (formerly IX).25.

He seems to look ahead to martyrdom. John — as he had first suggested in 1956 — had no doubt that the fate that comes to the Teacher is crucifixion at the hands of Jannaeus, the Lion of Wrath who "hangs men up alive, [a thing never done] in Israel before."[8]

In the scrolls, the Bible, and the legends, redemptive sacrifice is timeless. When it comes to the New Testament, the gospel writers have woven into the story of Jesus' redemptive sacrifice, unlike that of other heroes, apparently realistic details of time and place. In many cases they have done this through exegesis from the Old Testament and other old texts, to enrich and deepen the story.

Wisdom Made Manifest

In John's perception, the Essene scrolls held the key to the theology of the incarnate Redeemer. For divine knowledge is wisdom. To the writers of the scrolls, all creation pre-exists in the mind of God, and all that happens on Earth is the result of this plan: a projection of the mind of God.

> In the wisdom of Thy knowledge
> Thou didst establish their destiny before ever they existed.[9]

In the scrolls, as in the biblical Proverbs, wisdom is the firstborn of God. In the Proverbs, it is personified as his companion and helpmeet:

> The Lord created me at the beginning of his work, the first of his acts of old. . . .
>   Then I was beside him, like a master workman; and I was daily his delight, rejoicing before him always, rejoicing in his inhabited world and delighting in the sons of men. (Prov. 8:22-31)[10]

The concept of wisdom comes in a range of interlinked imagery throughout the scrolls and the Bible, and also in the Gnostic apocrypha, where the world is born out of wisdom's suffering. The breath of God, the firstborn, the companion of God, the bride, and the mother of Earth are five manifestations, but wisdom is also associated with the symbolism of pillars, torches, the morning star, and ultimately, as we shall see, the lamb unified

---

8. *Nahum Commentary* I.6; Allegro, *The Dead Sea Scrolls and the Christian Myth*, p. 36.
9. *Thanksgiving Hymn IX* (formerly I).19.
10. Allegro, *The Dead Sea Scrolls and the Christian Myth*, pp. 104-5.

with the Word in an incarnation that carries God's message straight to humankind. All these manifestations are "forms," "phantoms," Greek *eidola*, Semitic *tsir* or *tsorah*, of an ideal essence or divine substance that remains in heaven. So Ezekiel describes the form, *tsurah*, of the ideal temple he dreams of, and the New Testament apocalyptist sees a vision of "the holy city, the new Jerusalem, coming down out of heaven from God, prepared as a bride adorned for her husband" (Rev. 21:2, 10). The New Jerusalem is the form or projection of the mind of God, as wisdom is the first thought.

Elsewhere the writer sees a vision of white-robed men — like Essene monks — who had passed through tribulation to the temple of God, "For the Lamb at the center of the throne will be their shepherd, and he will guide them to springs of the water of life" (Rev. 7:13-17). This directly recalls the Teacher's "fountain of running waters in a waterless land . . . a spring of living waters" from the scrolls.[11]

The wisdom of God would light up the city: ". . . Its lamp is the Lamb. The nations will walk by its light . . ." (Rev. 21:23-24). This brings us to the imagery of blazing torches and pillars of fire that parade through the books of the Bible and beyond. For example, God appears in pillars of fire and smoke in Exodus 13; there are the seven pillars of wisdom in Proverbs 9. The morning star, Luke's "dawn from on high" (1:78), is also entitled in Hebrew "Pillar of the Dawn"; and Peter's second epistle brings together the concepts of the dawn, the morning star, and the light of wisdom, "as . . . a lamp shining in a dark place, until the day dawns and the morning star rises in your hearts" (1:19).

Among the scrolls, *Thanksgiving Hymn* XII presents knowledge of God as enlightenment:

> I thank Thee, O Lord,
> for Thou hast illumined my face by Thy Covenant. . . .
> I seek Thee,
> And sure as the dawn
> Thou appearest as [perfect Light] to me.

The morning star Venus, the day-spring from on high, brought dew, and dew was thought to be the most powerful conceptual fluid of Nature. According to Pliny, "Its influence is the cause of the birth of all things upon earth; at its rising it scatters a genital dew with which it not only fills the conceptual organs of the earth, but also stimulates those of all animals."[12]

11. *Thanksgiving Hymn* XVI (formerly VIII).5.
12. Pliny, *Natural History*, II.38.

Dew brought healing and could even revive the dead, and the Psalms bear testimony to the belief that God had begotten Christ through the genital dew scattered by the morning star: "From the womb of the morning, like dew, your youth will come to you" (110:3). Dew is a manifestation of the power of God that reaches back to the ancient propitiation of fertility, and, as John perceived it, by the time the scrolls were written it had been subsumed into the doctrine of divine light.

The Word Becoming Flesh

In the incarnation, the Word takes the form of flesh. For St. Paul, the incarnation shows humans the way to regain the "image" of sonship: "For those whom he foreknew he also predestined to be conformed to the image of his Son, in order that he might be the firstborn within a large family" (Rom. 8:29). And for the writer of the fourth gospel:

> In the beginning was the Word, and the Word was with God, and the Word was God. He was in the beginning with God. All things came into being through him, and without him not one thing came into being. In him was life, and the life was the light of all people. . . . And the Word became flesh and lived among us, and we have beheld his glory, the glory as of a father's only son, full of grace and truth. . . . From his fullness we have all received, grace upon grace. . . . (John 1:1-16)

The Word became flesh in Jesus. In John's view, the Jesus stories express this doctrine of light in human terms. Jesus is of the light; like other heroes he embodies divine wisdom. He seeks to rejoin God, the source of light, and to take others with him. By becoming mortal he can share mortal troubles and by being sacrificed he atones for mortal sin: themes of mythology all over the world. In these terms the figure of Jesus carries the authority of ancient myth.

The Word also becomes the lamb. To a non-religious westerner, it seems an improbable connection, especially when the lamb goes on to appear in bizarre guise in Revelation 5:6, standing by the throne of God "as though he had been slain, with seven horns and seven eyes." But in a Semitic context, the whole idea pivots on simple word-play: the correspondence between Hebrew *'imerah*, word, and Aramaic *'imera*, lamb. At one stroke it combines the image of Christ as the Passover lamb, sacrificed for the sins of the people, with his nature as the creative principle, *Logos*, the Word. The lamb is sacrificed in atonement for sins, and so the Word becomes the redeemer of the world: "Here is the Lamb of God who takes away the sin of the world!" (John 1:29).[13]

In philological terms, John had earlier identified the Word with the seed of the old storm god, which gave fertility to the earth.[14] So if the gospel writer was aware of the connotations, the pun on *'imerah* brought the weight of a three-thousand-year-old principle of divine progeniture behind the concept of atonement through sacrifice, a concept that was a cornerstone of Pauline Christianity.

13. Allegro, *The Dead Sea Scrolls and the Christian Myth*, p. 174.
14. J. M. Allegro, *The Sacred Mushroom and the Cross*, p. 20.

CHAPTER 14

Interpreting Gnosticism
in Light of the Scrolls

St. Paul and St. John were not alone in spreading the message of the scrolls. Outside the New Testament canon, Gnostic texts supply further evidence of the link between the scrolls and Christianity.

Other documents similar in age to the scrolls had come to light around the same time, and by the 1970s (unlike most of the scrolls) were being published. They included the Gnostic writings from Nag Hammadi. The Gnostics were groups of religious thinkers in various parts of Palestine and Egypt, and though their writings included diverse ideas that often seemed contradictory — and were all condemned by the church — they showed some strong correspondences with Essenism. They also showed that the gospels were not the only stories current in first-century Palestine about the healer Jesus and similar figures. In discussing the development of Christianity, John draws on Gnostic texts such as the gospels of Thomas and Philip, and on reports about them from their opponents, as well as on the scrolls, the Old and New Testaments, and contemporary writings such as those of Josephus, Pliny, and Philo.

Gnosis was the Greek word for divine knowledge, wisdom. John held that Essene gnosis, knowledge of the inner light, developed along an unbroken line into Christian Gnosticism. The Gnostics were Christians in that they believed that God had appeared on Earth in the form of Jesus Christ, the Word incarnate, but not all believed that he had undergone a mortal death or bodily resurrection, nor, if he had, that this would be enough to save anyone but Jesus himself from perdition. For the Gnostics, the most important thing was spiritual vision, a gift of God that gave each person a conviction of truth and filled each one with the light of divine knowledge. This individualism soon brought them into conflict with church leaders. Meanwhile they kept alive the gift of Essenism — the concept of inner light that was the voice of God speaking to humans.

For the Gnostic Valentinus, wisdom was the mother of all things. The world was born out of wisdom's suffering in the shape of the four elements: earth, air, water, and fire. Yet the Valentinians held that a preoccupation with these elements spelled ignorance. A believer's quest should be to transcend the trappings of material things to reach true wisdom, the light of inner knowledge.

Gnosticism took many variant forms, but its hallmark was the redemption of the individual soul to attain inner light. God showed people the way to salvation through sending an incarnate messiah as redeemer to share their suffering. The suffering may or may not involve martyrdom; its purpose was to burn off the dross of mortality to attain the light within, the true kingdom of God.

However, this was not the outlook of the orthodox church, which emphasized the need to share the pain and passion of the Lord in mortal terms through bodily suffering. With this went a belief in the bodily resurrection of Jesus. Paradoxically, it seemed easier for people to accept the miracle of bodily resurrection than to grapple with the metaphysics of the inner light, at least for people brought up to accept miracle stories and not to question what they were told. Gnostics committed the heresy of questioning both what the bishops told them and their authority to do so.

Like other Christians, they adopted the idea of a redeemer who took human form. Shared human suffering lent itself to myth-making at any level. The redeemer could show them by example how to overcome difficulties. Or he could teach rites or incantations. For example, the apocryphal book of Enoch, several incomplete copies of which were found among the scrolls, says that to pass through the seven heavens the Children of Light needed to know the names of the guardian angels, and the passwords, and to prepare themselves by secret rites.

Different groups of Gnostics had different and sometimes conflicting beliefs and practices. Some preserved rituals that seemed to go back to the old fertility cults — for example the Therapeutae of Egypt, according to Philo, danced all night once every fifty days until joining at daybreak in homage to the rising sun.[1]

Some of the rites cast light on the way Christianity developed, for they show the range of stories and traditions once associated with Jesus that the in-

---

1. J. M. Allegro, *The Dead Sea Scrolls and the Christian Myth* (Newton Abbot: Westbridge Books, 1979), pp. 110-11.

stitutional church edited out. For example, at the monastery of Mar Saba the scholar Morton Smith found a letter from the second-century church father Clement of Alexandria. Some doubted whether the letter was authentic, but John thought it was likely to be. Clement calls his own sect "the Children of Light, illumined by the dayspring of the Lord from on high" — pure Essene terminology. The letter attacks the Carpocratian Gnostics and refers to a "secret gospel" of Mark, a version known only to certain sects. It tells of a youth whom Jesus rescued and who came to Jesus at night, "wearing a linen robe over his naked body" to be initiated into "the mystery of the Kingdom of God." Whatever the details of the ritual, Clement warns his reader "never to concede that the secret gospel is by Mark, but deny it on oath. For not everything that is true needs necessarily to be divulged to all men."[2]

Clement also throws light on the way the gospels were written: "During Peter's stay in Rome he wrote [an account of] the Lord's doings, not however declaring all, nor yet hinting at the secret ones, but selecting those he thought most useful for increasing the faith of those who were being instructed." (This early model of being economical with the truth was still in force in 1979, when Westbridge Books, the first publishers of *The Dead Sea Scrolls and the Christian Myth*, refused to include the passage about Clement's letter for fear of reaction from the church. It appeared in the subsequent paperback edition by Abacus.)

Some Gnostic sects, such as the Manicheans, were condemned for practices that involved sexual rituals. Others upheld the ideal of celibacy, but not from allegiance to the church's superstructure of morality. The Gnostic gospels of Thomas and Philip refer to an ideal androgynous unity, making male and female into one so that all could go naked and unashamed. Gnostics saw one of the difficulties facing men and women as the dissipation of light, or soul, between the different sexes and among offspring, and they saw the separation of the sexes as an original cause of death. Androgyny would mean the light remained undivided; celibacy was the nearest they could come to this.

The basic idea is of the divine light, or life-giving force, inside each human being. In John's terms, this concept stems from where religion had its roots: in fertility and procreation, the most fundamental forces of life. In nature these depend on sunshine and rain, so the god of procreation is the god of sun and storm. Therefore, sunlight is an emanation of divine light. To share this light, people could consume substances they believed contained it. The most potent human life-giving elements were semen and menses, which together were thought to create the fetus and distill the essence of light. To collect and consume these was to partake of the divine light. Orthodox bish-

---

2. Morton Smith, *The Secret Gospel* (New York: Harper & Row, 1973).

ops of the third and fourth centuries, such as Epiphanius and Augustine, described such practices with horror, and to a modern view the idea would be equally revolting. But at a deep and ancient level of faith, they may be understood not as symbols, nor as raw meat, but as essences of divine power. Anointing the body with either semen or the juice of special plants, or both, is a long and well-attested tradition with a similar purpose — to partake of divine essence. The sects who practiced these rites were invoking powers of belief thousands of years old. They certainly seem to reach beyond the Essenism of the scrolls, where it is chiefly knowledge of the law of Moses that brings the light-filled and life-giving blessing of God.

But the law is not the whole story. Earthly light comes from the sun; the sun holds the power of God to quicken all things to life. As the Manichean Gnostics saw it, the Children of Light must capture and refine divine life-giving light within themselves by taking it in through mind and body. In spiritual terms this involves prayer and contemplation. In bodily terms it means separating out the material dross through digestion, and for the celibate it means not wasting their divine seed on begetting children. Although sustaining this attitude over the generations might appear problematical, their main aim was to return the divine substance to God by way of the sun and moon.

St. Augustine explains the Manichean idea: "Everything of Light, refined from matter wherever it exists, is restored to the Kingdom of God as the ultimate source of its emanation, by the sun and moon. These vessels are similarly made of pure divine Substance." The Gnostics, says Augustine, honor the sun and moon "not as deities, rather as channels through which one may attain to God."[3] The Essenes too had recognized the power of the sun in regulating their lives "in accordance with the laws of the Great Light in heaven."[4] Its rays reflected the true light, the pleroma, and through them God sent his power to Earth.

Gnostic Parallels to the New Testament

The Simon Magus cycle of legends runs parallel in Gnostic literature to the story of Jesus. It relates through imagery of fire and light to the concepts of divine light and wisdom. In the New Testament, Acts 8:9-24, Simon gets a brief reference when Peter rebukes him for wanting to buy the secret of the

3. Augustine, *De haeresibus,* 46,2; Allegro, *The Dead Sea Scrolls and the Christian Myth,* p. 134.

4. *Thanksgiving Hymn* XX.5 (formerly XII).

laying-on of hands. In Gnostic literature the Simon stories were much more popular — which is why the church sought to discredit him. For the Gnostics, Simon was as much a symbol of divine light made flesh as was Jesus. Bishop Irenaeus tells how he is portrayed as the Son of God to the Jews, the Father to the Samaritans, and the Holy Spirit to the Gentiles.[5] The third-century writer Origen says the Simonians hold Simon, not Jesus, to be "the Power of God"; indeed, he is so entitled in Acts 8:10.

In Simon, God takes mortal guise. He shares mortal tribulations and performs many miracles. He often appears flying, a theme that is probably echoed in one of the temptations of Jesus and certainly in countless tales of hallucination and witchcraft in myth and folklore the world over. Simon's task is to teach any who would listen the secret of knowing their own souls and freeing them to merge with the light. For when they have attained this blessed state they have no further need of law or social convention: They belong in the pleroma, the full knowledge of God.

The cycle of Simon stories reported by Justin Martyr about A.D. 150[6] associates him with Helen of Tyre. Helen is variously a prostitute, a mother goddess, the bride of Simon or God, and the incarnation of Wisdom. Like her Greek namesake Helen of Troy, she symbolizes the light of divine knowledge through her name *helene*, "torch," and through her significance as the torch of wisdom that guides people through the darkness of the world back to God — as the blaze above the Trojan bedchamber guided Agamemnon. This imagery of torches or pillars of fire flickers throughout the Bible, from the pillar of fire that Moses saw to the tongues of fire at Pentecost (Acts 2:1-4) and the "seven flaming torches, which are the seven spirits of God" in Revelation 4:5. In the transfiguration of Jesus according to Matthew, "his face shone like the sun and his garments became as white as light" (17:2), an image that recalls Moses on Sinai in Exodus 34:29 whose "face shone because he had been talking with God."

Related to the pillar image is the story of the Gnostic teacher Dositheus who, like the Baptist, was said to receive the Holy Spirit from God and suffer persecution on Earth. He led a band of thirty "pillars" or disciples, and then, according to Origen, ascended to heaven. With leaping (but reasoned) speculation, John links Dositheus with Jesus: "Dositheus ('Gift-of-God') was but a representation in gnostic mythology of the Essene 'Joshua/Jesus', the Teacher of Righteousness, the real-life personality behind the New Testament Jesus of Nazareth."[7]

---

5. Irenaeus, *Against Heresies*, 1.23.1.
6. Justin Martyr, *1 Apol.*, 26-56; *Dial.*, 120.
7. Allegro, *The Dead Sea Scrolls and the Christian Myth*, p. 189.

Meanwhile, the name of Helen's city, Tyre or *tsor*, is close enough to *tsir*, form or phantom, to set the exegetes spinning stories out of it, as was their wont. Tyre is Ezekiel's "once-proud city," laid low by vainglory. Helen herself is exiled, humiliated, and rescued by Simon in a story that parallels one of the most ancient and widespread myths of humankind. This is the descent of the fertility goddess to the underworld in search of her lost lover or son. On the way she faces step-by-step humiliation and is finally rescued by a god or his messenger. It is the story of Babylonian Ishtar, Sumerian Inanna, Mesopotamian Astarte, Greek Persephone, Egyptian Isis — and Isis was a patron of the Gnostic sect of the Therapeutae. Isis cured the sick, revived the dead, and generally represented the maternal principle in the days before the exaltation of the Virgin Mary in Christian mythology.

In Gnostic myth, Helen is credited with creation. In this way she personifies the word or wisdom. Wisdom is the bride whom Solomon seeks from God "who madest all things by Thy Word, and by Thy Wisdom hast formed man."[8] In the book of Revelation, at one time, wisdom takes the form of the bride of the Apocalypse and also "the holy city Jerusalem coming down out of heaven from God" (21:10), but at another she is attired like Helen, "clothed with fine linen, bright and pure" (19:8).

It seems that in the interlinked mythology of pre-Christian, Christian, and Gnostic literature a fundamental worldview is given expression in various stories and various names. It is a vision of light, the substance of divine knowledge. It is the wisdom of God, a creative force shining as light, shared by God among all his creatures in some degree and ultimately to be reunited with God in the full light, the pleroma, the great light in heaven. Some people capture it by grace, others by study or contemplation. They express it through stories, prophecy, and interpretation of prophecy; it lights up the way they think and everything they aspire to. The goal of their lives is to reunite the spark of light inside them with the divine light from which it came.

Wisdom is the breath of God. It comes to Earth and takes many forms, as the light of lamps, of fire, of stars and the dew they scatter. Above all, it is the Word, a distillation of God's knowledge of all things that have been and are to come. It knows how all things past, present, and future are held in the hand of God. Taking human form, it can lead people to this assurance; and it can bring them redemption by showing what lies beyond sin and suffering — if they have enough faith to accept its message.

8. *Wisdom of Solomon*, 9

The Christian Myth — Telling the People

But that is a view for a philosopher or visionary. For ordinary people, religion is about their own relationship with their god or gods; it springs from their own human needs and fears and must use terms they understand. Time and again throughout history, we find the mythologies of succeeding religions intertwining with one another. It is not so surprising, for they arise from perennial questions, perennial answers, and human needs that are universal and timeless. As John put it:

> However much prophetic movements in Israel sought to purge the religion of Jehovah/Yahweh of these agricultural cult practices . . . the day-to-day needs of ordinary people were too closely tied to the fertility of their fields and livestock to separate them from the old loyalties. And the strongest of these was, and still is in the Mediterranean lands, to the Mother Goddess, protector of the womb and of the growing seed, whether she be called Isis, Astarte, Helen, Venus, or the Virgin Mary. We may analyse their myths, detect their various strands, identify their characters portrayed under a host of names and guises, but when all is done, religion is an exercise of the emotions, and the few basic needs that fuel their fires are common to all men.[9]

We should understand that these myths, whether of Simon, Jesus, or other folk heroes from Jason to Santa Claus, were not just children's fairytales, nor spun out of a single image, a phrase or a pun for the sake of playing with words. We must look on the past through our ancestors' eyes, not to impose our modern obsession with linear cause and effect but to see time held rolling like a marble in the hand of God: themes recurring, truths reiterated, proving and proving again their one source — biblical law. The message and much of the power of the stories lay in their reference to scripture. "To be able to tie a myth into Scripture," wrote John, "gave that story authority, since every word of the Bible was reckoned inspired and capable of illustrating divine truth."[10]

Word-play was one way to tie it into scripture. We have seen how word-play, including metaphor and punning, was a potent form of exegesis for the writers of the scrolls. It lent their teaching the centuries-old power of prophecy and the weight of history. Unraveling puns may seem to us a far-fetched method of interpreting the Bible, but it seemed to be how the teach-

9. Allegro, *The Dead Sea Scrolls and the Christian Myth,* p. 158.
10. Allegro, *The Dead Sea Scrolls and the Christian Myth,* p. 150.

ers of the time went about their job, extending and strengthening each passage of biblical text with layers of allusion. Any lesson based on scripture, whether fiction or fact, was equally valid, and all the more memorable for including dramatic effects. To appreciate why a story was told, said John, "we have first to look at the messianist factions which produced the story-cycles in a realistic cultural and religious perspective, and then try to find the biblical texts from which the various stories are almost certainly derived. . . . To understand Christian origins we have to put ourselves back in the time and place of the Essenes and their immediate gnostic successors, and try to look at their traditions and expectations through their eyes. Above all, they were a People of the Book, and the clues to the origins of their mythology lie in the Book itself."[11]

The Gnostic myths of Helen and Simon were not locked into any one period of history, John explained.

> Helen appeared in many forms, Simon came as all things to all people. He was not supposed to represent the life-history of the Essene Teacher. The one important theme underlying the stories was that God had communicated with His Chosen People through a succession of witnesses — prophets, priests and preachers — and in the fullness of time He had sent His own self to dwell among men and suffer the humiliation of mortality.[12]

Why such a range of stories? If Essene exegesis often seemed imaginative, the Gnostic approach seems even wilder. Gnostics came from many different cultures, could draw on a rich store of legends, and felt no constraint in embroidering others. Their themes can be difficult to follow, for the same character can embody different ideas on different occasions.

To Bishop Irenaeus, this proliferation of myths spelt chaos. Irenaeus liked order. He wanted to shape the new religion back into a uniform Judaistic mold, with one God, creator of all, redeeming a wayward humankind through his fatherly love. The Gnostics found this far too simple. They went on asking — as thinkers have asked before and since — if God created everything, where did evil come from? Either God himself must be evil, or he was incompetent. So some of them posited two gods, good and evil, with a series of heroic redeemers working in mortal guise on behalf of the better deity to guide people to light and knowledge. In the process the heroes had all sorts of earthly adventures. One of these characters was called Simon, another was called Jesus.

11. Allegro, *The Dead Sea Scrolls and the Christian Myth*, p. 151.
12. Allegro, *The Dead Sea Scrolls and the Christian Myth*, p. 159.

Choosing Jesus

Gnostic mythologizing made the church difficult to organize — it was too many things to too many people to serve the needs of a state bureaucracy. Irenaeus decided to make one cycle of myths a canon of authority in matters of teaching and practice for his church. The cycle he chose was the one about the latter-day Joshua/Jesus and his fishermen disciples.

There may or may not have been a traveling healer called Jesus, but it seems probable. In the days before the burden of a world-wide theology was placed upon his shoulders, with the label "Son of God" and all that entailed, such a man may have learned his trade from the Essenes, perhaps as some scholars suggest at Qumran. John's point is that, whatever his history, the original significance of this figure among the Gnostic successors to the Essenes was mythological: the embodiment of divine light, a mortal form of the immortal word of God. Unlike Simon or Helen, the character was given a quasi-historical setting that would anchor people's faith in what they took to be reality.

Through the political skill and determination of the early church this figure of myth, presented as a figure of history, gained enough credibility to catch and hold the allegiance of the nations, even though their outlook on God and the world may have been utterly different from the one that prevailed where the idea originated. Jesus — man, myth, or both — became not only a teacher, messiah, or intermediary with God, but essential to people's relationship with God. The church gave him this role so that, by focusing on one mortal hero that everyone could relate to, it could win a cohesive, universal authority.

The Scrolls, said John, had shown the umbilical connection between Essenism and the early Christian messianic theology of St. Paul and St. John.

> Because we now have in our hands the literary record of that Way, thanks to the discoveries by the Dead Sea, we can see how that revelation became further adapted under the pressure of socio-political events of the first century to serve people on the fringes of Judaism, or completely outside that dispensation, as an expression of an intensely personal faith.[13]

The New Testament shows how elements in the original Essenist religion — the forces of light and dark, personal salvation through grace, the salvation of the world through redemptive sacrifice — were broadened out to

---

13. Allegro, *The Dead Sea Scrolls and the Christian Myth,* p. 191.

appeal to all people. The messiah was no longer expected to liberate the chosen race but to show people how to find the kingdom of God in their own heart. Thanks to the Dead Sea Scrolls, we can now see that in the intertestamental period (Daniel to Paul) the Essene movement provided just the right mix of tradition and philosophy to produce Gnostic Christianity. What it did not produce was the improbably naïve and very much westernized conjuror-prophet of the gospels.

The Growth of the Church

Up to this point, the Old Testament, Essenism, Gnosticism, and the New Testament had formed a continuum of religious thought.

Church and Gnostics diverged. The Gnostics never fell into the trap of taking the Jesus stories seriously; their main concern was to save souls. As John put it, "They insisted on the primacy of the message, not the man; the nativity was not allowed to outshine the crucifixion."[14] This is Paul's message too: no sordid stable, no walking on water; just Christ, crucified.

The Gnostics also questioned the bodily resurrection of Jesus, which was a central tenet of orthodox faith, and they questioned the authority of bishops to dictate what people believed. The church used the disciples' claims to have met Jesus in the flesh after his crucifixion to justify apostolic succession. Gnostics, on the other hand, found this literalism crude and unspiritual. The *Apocalypse of Peter* calls bishops and deacons appointed on such claims "waterless canals." As for the idea of martyrdom, the church found it a force for cohesion, since it united anyone who had ever been hurt in sympathy with each other and Jesus. The Gnostics agreed martyrdom was a tragic waste, but they also thought it a distraction from worship of the Word. At best, bodily suffering purified the sufferer's soul. Each must realize his or her own redemption; Jesus on his cross was a symbol showing the way, but he could not do it for them.

Far more important to the Gnostics was spiritual enlightenment, a matter of personal conviction and the true, living faith. They pursued this inner light with devotion but in factions. Some understood redemption as release from all social conventions, offering complete freedom of thought. Others escaped through extreme asceticism to an intense but unworldly spiritualism. Neither could compete with the social and political authority of the orthodox church.

14. Allegro, *The Dead Sea Scrolls and the Christian Myth*, p. 161.

From the second century, Irenaeus's party gained dominance. What became the Great Church won the ear of kings and emperors. It shouted down rival sects and burned their books; it seized on one cycle of myths, the Jesus stories, and made the central figure appear historical while disparaging the rest. This Jesus cycle became dominant, exclusively so, wrote John:

> Those elements that had been excluded, including the more occult teachings such as appear in Clement's recently discovered 'secret gospel', were locked away for the use of the Church's inner circle, and the remainder either consigned to the Apocrypha or destroyed during the anti-gnostic purges which marked the Great Church's rise to power.[15]

So the Jesus cycle became central to the early church, not because of a unique God-given truth revealed in first-century Palestine, nor even because of a unique God-given truth revealed in a vision or a poem or one universal myth, but because the second-century church fathers chose to make this cycle the canon of authority. Through the power of the Great Church, the New Testament was invested with supreme and incontrovertible authority as a source of doctrine and history.

One consequence of this exclusivity is a distorted view of the origins of the movement and of the religious and political circumstances of the time. To lend the Jesus stories weight, it became essential to peg them to a historical background.

Helen and Simon were myths, no more and no less, stories that interpreted the concept of humanity's redemption into the fullness of light. The Jesus cycle was myth, too. But its stories were of a different order from most of the Gnostic legends. It was meant to be credible, to deflect Roman suspicion. As John wrote, "It brought the Essene 'Joshua/Jesus' more or less up to date, and placed him in the historical circumstances of the first century, naming names, citing places and authorities, and, above all, giving this Jewish prophet such an improbable pro-Roman stance as might warm the hearts of those gentile agents into whose hands the Gospels might quite easily fall."[16] It also preserved mystic passwords, cultic titles, and other teachings.

The Jesus cycle failed on both counts. The Romans continued to persecute the Christians, who they feared would incite trouble, and the secret messages were quite lost when everyone took the code-names at face value.

This admission represents the nearest John came to recognizing that much of the original cultic significance of the names and code-words was

---

15. Allegro, *The Dead Sea Scrolls and the Christian Myth,* p. 139.
16. Allegro, *The Dead Sea Scrolls and the Christian Myth,* p. 160.

gone. Although he continued to maintain that the language of Christianity had originated in that of the ancient fertility cults, the heat had gone out of the claim: Mushroom-worship was dead and buried. He realized that by the first century, myth-making focused on the interpretation of Essene ideas such as divine light, wisdom, and redemption through a suffering god — though the old Mother Goddess principle persisted strongly in the name of Helen or Mary. Only some of the Gnostic sects, as we have seen, kept traditions of the old cults alive in practices such as anointing with semen, which they believed to be the most potent, tangible form of divine light.

John believed that by the twentieth century people should no longer need the church to write their history books for them. He saw his task as to break through the screen of infallibility that the church had thrown up around itself and to reconstruct both the world of conflicting ideas from early times and the spring of faith that fed them. It is not easy to discard centuries of sentimental imagery and second-hand morality, but we should examine the evidence of the gospels objectively. The gospel story, in his terms, looks more and more like a highly contrived literary compilation and less like a simple narrative. In John's view, the Jesus stories were historically absurd, yet they "contained such elements of truth and reflections of deep religious sentiment, combined with a fluency of style and an illusory simplicity of content, as to procure a sympathetic and ready audience in the gentile world."[17]

The more you look at the gospels, the more you realize their many-layered construction. On the surface we have appealing folktales and pro-Roman propaganda that cannot be taken seriously:

> Had a first-century rabbi dared to shrug off a burning political issue of the day with a gentle 'render unto Caesar . . .' kind of response, he would have earned himself a Zealot dagger in the back within three minutes, let alone three years of open ministry.[18]

On deeper levels we have religious precepts, moral precepts, Old Testament prophecy come to fruition, myth disguised as history, myth concealed in imagery, many allusions to law and scripture, and the doctrines of grace and wisdom. Jesus the traveling faith-healer may or may not have plied his trade around the area, but by the time the story was written down his figure carried a vast burden of religious significance — moral, mythical, and philosophical.

17. Allegro, *The Dead Sea Scrolls and the Christian Myth,* p. 192.
18. Allegro, *The Dead Sea Scrolls and the Christian Myth,* p. 201.

John accepted that the high-toned moral teaching that most people equate with Christianity was probably authentic, and Essene in inspiration, for in a closed community like Qumran, loving your neighbor was essential to survival. But the monks would have considered it their duty to hate sinners. Sinners included Jews who rejected the law as they interpreted it, or those who collaborated with the enemy and, above all, with the powers of darkness that conspired to turn people from God.

A community walled in by hatred of outsiders could not last long in the real world. After A.D. 70, the old, closed Essene communities were scattered, and any grouping that looked like a secret society capable of insurrection would have been crushed. To widen its appeal, John wrote, the new movement evidently had to redefine sinners:

> It incorporated Jews and gentiles, Romans and Greeks, slaves and freemen. The salvation they all sought was a personal experience, offered by God freely through his grace, and not as a reward for obedience to the Jewish law, and it was therefore open to all men. They looked back to the incarnation of a Redeemer who taught mankind the way back to the Fullness of God, and if, as time went on, he showed less and less resemblance to the real-life Teacher of the Dead Sea community, and their ideas of salvation became far removed from the old messianic dream, the myths their storytellers spun for the faithful could present the Saviour in a variety of guises to suit every need in every time and place.[19]

John still held that the cover-up idea, which in *The Sacred Mushroom and the Cross* figured so prominently, was necessary to the survival of early Christianity, but less on account of the occult nature of the religion than of its potential political significance. There are scraps of history and a scattering of real names in the gospels, but to the compilers it was more important to disguise identities than advertise them:

> The secret police of the imperial power were actively seeking out cells of dissidents in that hot-bed of potential revolt, and Christian communities were regarded, probably rightly, with extreme suspicion. There were still close links between some factions of Essenism and the Zealots, for whom messianism was synonymous with the establishment of a Jewish state in Palestine.[20]

19. Allegro, *The Dead Sea Scrolls and the Christian Myth*, p. 202.
20. Allegro, *The Dead Sea Scrolls and the Christian Myth*, p. 193.

John admitted that the pre-Canaanite roots of early Christianity were by that time empty echoes of the ancient fertility cults, which had since been woven among many other strands of philosophy. They had merged, largely unrecognized, with the Essene doctrines of light, self-knowledge, grace, and the fullness of divine wisdom.

In *The Dead Sea Scrolls and the Christian Myth*, John brings together the elements of this concept of light that he perceived in the scrolls, in parts of the Old and New Testaments, and in the Gnostic apocrypha. Others may question his interpretation and feel his selection of evidence may not be completely balanced; for example, he identifies the Word with divine wisdom and links both with pillars of light and divine heroes in a way that is not explicit in the scrolls. However, he felt he had found a thread that linked all the material, a vision of God that inspired the holy men of Qumran and their successors but was largely distorted or misinterpreted by the institutional church.

To sum up John's conclusions:

The Gnostics were the direct successors to the Essenes of Qumran. When the orthodox church branched away, it took many Gnostic ideas with it, though it made Jesus the central figure in them. Hope for the Gnostic lay in the individual's own salvation. Through faith in the Redeemer, whether that be Helen, Simon, or Joshua/Jesus, the Gnostic believed that the divine spark that is in every human could be released to rejoin the pleroma from which it came, the fullness of divine light. This common fount of inspiration runs from the Dead Sea Scrolls through Gnostic and biblical literature. The storyline is less important than the underlying myth. Though we may feel we lose the "historical" Jesus of the gospels, we may rediscover what the Essenes and their successors believed to be a timeless revelation of the divine purpose: the quest for eternal light.

In many ways, as John claims, today's godless existentialists are successors to the Gnostics. "Man is nothing else but what he makes of himself," claimed Sartre.[21] According to the third-century church father Hippolytus, the Arabian Gnostic philosopher Monoimus said: "Look for God by taking yourself as the starting point. Learn who it is within you makes everything his own and says, 'My God, my mind, my thought, my soul, my body.' Learn the sources of sorrow, joy, love, hate. . . . If you carefully investigate these matters you will find him within yourself." Hippolytus cited this as a heresy,[22] but for many thinkers, subjectivity is the root of truth and more reliable than the ap-

21. Jean-Paul Sartre, *Existentialism and Humanism,* trans. Philip Mairet (Brooklyn: Haskell House, 1977), pp. 23-56.
22. Hippolytus, *Refutation of All Heresies,* VIII.15.1-2.

parent technical omnipotence that has given us the microchip and nuclear weapons. Existentialism — the quest for inner personal understanding — admits of compassion and allows for vagaries of interpretation among other people: It does not expect everyone always to behave in a rational or predictable way; therefore, it does not expect social harmony in the world or perfectibility in people. The light of human understanding comes not from a god, nor from politicians or scientists, but from human quality.

There is compassion. God or no god, technology or failed technology, there is the quest for understanding, and there is love. These remain, whatever politicians do to each other's nations, or the churches do to religion, or critics do to the churches. They are the best of human qualities. The Christian myth, like other myths, can point the way, but for people like John who look behind the myths, the source of inner light is inside man and woman.

CHAPTER 15

Following

The Dead Sea Scrolls and the Christian Myth

Scholars ignored *The Dead Sea Scrolls and the Christian Myth*. The opportunity to explore early Christian mythology or Gnosticism appeared to pass them by. John felt the publishers did little to promote the book, perhaps, as he thought, from fear of the consequences or from sloth, but probably because they didn't foresee much money in it. He seemed to have to fight all the way for recognition, publication, and promotion. Mainly he learned not to trust agents or publishers who dropped words such as "advance," "royalties," "lecture tours," or "air-time" into their conversation.

The humanist press found the book interesting, and a reviewer in *The Churchman* of October 1984 remarked how "Allegro's Essenic Joshua/Jesus, the Teacher of Righteousness, with his messianism, his moral code, his martyrdom, becomes increasingly real in these pages. The Joshua/Jesus of the Gospels becomes progressively myth-like." On the whole, however, the Christian press was reluctant to think of Christianity as they might think of other religions, that is, in terms of myth shaped by historical forces and mystic imagination. One publication wrote, "Christian believers have little to fear from a work whose twisted reasoning and dissociative interpretation are as bizarre as the Essene commentaries themselves."[1] Others described the book as "a historical travesty," "a fantastic historical reconstruction,"[2] and "a perversion of scholarship."[3] John thought this only to be expected.

Professor James Charlesworth of Princeton Theological Seminary

---

1. *Chronicle of Culture*, November 11, 1984.
2. *The Christian Century*, January 1985.
3. *Choice*, November 1984.

picked up on 4QTherapeia, the first published translation of the document, which formed the book's appendix. As mentioned in chapter 9, he agreed at the time — though he has since questioned this opinion — that the general gist of the piece was a medical report, but he did not share John's perspective on the significance of *caiaphas,* and he denigrated the book as a whole as "a sensational polemic against Christianity."[4]

John made contact with the publishers Prometheus Books in 1983 through correspondence with groups of freethinkers in the United States. The company director Paul Kurtz also produced the journal *Free Inquiry,* for which John had supplied an article on the scrolls. Prometheus promised to reissue *The Dead Sea Scrolls and the Christian Myth* for the American market. At first, true to form, there was a flurry of correspondence about hardback production, North American rights, a two thousand dollar advance, lecture tours, whom to approach for reviews, etc. As time went on, however, communication became increasingly one way. John wrote again and again demanding action, response, even acknowledgement. In blood-from-stone fashion, he extracted the promised advance in June 1984, eighteen months late. Prometheus's eventual production pleased him well enough, and so did the lofty tone of their promotional comment in booksellers' magazines. It called the book "a refreshingly original perspective on the place of the Dead Sea Scrolls in the development of Christianity, and the socio-political pressures that transformed a highly exclusive sect of Judaism into the broader-based religion of the Greek Church, and its priestly founder into the humanitarian, liberally minded, Nazarene Master of the Gospel myths." John's hopes rose again. But that was as far as the publicity went.

Lack of progress, lack of response, perpetually having to harry publishers — frustration wore him down. He turned back to Manchester University and applied to do a Ph.D. in the English Department. His thesis was to be on "the narrative styles and techniques of the King James (1611) version of the Old Testament, with particular reference to the Hebrew sources." It would look at the contemporary language forms — seventeenth-century English and classical Hebrew — and compare their grammatical and stylistic features, and would analyze in detail passages from Aelfric's tenth-century translation, the Tyndale Pentateuch of 1530, King James's 1611 version, and the Hebrew original.

For some weeks, John pursued these themes contentedly, back in familiar libraries. The days seemed unwontedly peaceful.

Too peaceful. John needed cash. And publicity. Before long, the English

---

4. J. H. Charlesworth, *The Discovery of a Dead Sea Scroll (4QTherapeia),* ICASALS Publication No. 85-1 (Lubbock, Tex.: Texas Tech University, 1985), p. 3.

project turned in his mind from an orderly intellectual pursuit to an opportunity to inspire, bedazzle, entertain, and make money. "It occurred to me," he wrote to the BBC, "that the subject of my thesis would make an illuminating documentary in two or more parts, bringing in art, music, literature, and professionally read passages from the various versions." The BBC politely declined to play. John abandoned the Ph.D. The need to plan lectures, write articles, and earn his living was too urgent.

He seemed to work in feverish bursts, but more in haste than in depth. In 1982 the publishers Charles Thomas of Springfield, Illinois, brought out *All Manner of Men.*

All Manner of Men looks at the differences between the human races. It asks how deep-rooted in our evolutionary history are the variations in our physical appearance and in our genetic constitution, and how far racial differences in anatomy and body chemistry extend to distinctive attitudes of mind and to the emotions.

This approach was not as divisive as it sounds. To understand racial differences, wrote John, is not to accentuate social discord but to appreciate the variability that enables humanity to retain its superiority in the natural world and the diversity of cultural traditions that enrich human experience. The current fashion for minimizing differences, he argued, leads to specious half-truths that merely feed prejudice and encourage bigotry. He suggested a polygenetic alternative to the popular assumption: that *homo erectus* became *homo sapiens* not in one regional population but in parallel developments in various areas of the world. That would imply that racial differences are older than our species.

In this book, John was dabbling in social anthropology. It was a new field for him, and as ever, his ideas were his own. They lacked any taint of social or intellectual prejudice and arose merely from his curiosity about people. Neither did they show much taint of serious scholarship. As the book's bibliography showed, he had crammed masses of preparatory reading into a few weeks in Manchester libraries, but the foundations of his study do not seem very solid. Celebrate the differences between people, he urged; don't gloss over them. Though original, this call was so extremely non-politically correct that it was no great surprise when the book ended up a couple of years later in pulp.

Physician, Heal Thyself

John's next book, *Physician, Heal Thyself,* published by Prometheus Books in 1985, looks at the significance of spiritual healing in early Christianity, specifically among the Gnostics and their forebears the Essenes, and as it is reflected in some of the miracles attributed to Jesus. The book examines the nature of the healers' power and where they believed it came from. John could not and did not try to "explain" miracles of healing in a western, scientific sense, nor did he analyze the medicinal properties of the herbs the Essenes used, but he brings to light the deep religious convictions that drove them to attempt their cures.

Healing in the Essenic tradition, he explains, was only partly a matter of the "investigations into medicinal roots and the properties of minerals" attested by Josephus.[5] It was a spiritual exercise, for all sickness was attributed to possession by demons, and the first step in the cure was to identify and utter the name of the evil spirit. So, for instance, to cast out the demon controlling the demented outcast at the Gadarene monastery, Jesus summons it by name (Mark 5:1-20).

To call on the help of guardian spirits, it was necessary to know their names. This knowledge of angels was part of Gnosis, the "knowledge of God," the special enlightenment bestowed by grace on members of the Qumran community, though attained by study and prayer.

The power to heal was a message of hope, not just for the sufferer but also for the world. In the dark and turbulent universe the community saw around them, it was a chink of light from the messianic age about to dawn. They believed crisis was imminent, a cosmic and moral cataclysm when God would shatter the forces of darkness and save the children of light. They had to believe this; it was the focus of their identity and purpose of their existence. It was theirs in particular, there in Qumran, because the rift valley of the Dead Sea was at the same time the epicenter of healing and the mouth of hell. The hot springs nearby bubbled out of hell fire but were also famous as a healing spa. The community believed that the valley of the Dead Sea was the abyss where God had cast the fallen angels. They lived on the edge, between redemption and damnation, seeing both sides of God's face, understanding how the angels held both the power to save and the power to sin. For with the fallen angels had gone their immortal knowledge of healing and medicines. The closer you could get to the angels' abyss, the more you could share their powers of healing — strong but dangerous, and very secret. Power lay in tapping into this source of divine knowledge. The messiah who would herald the end-time would be filled with it. Therefore he could use it to heal — as Jesus did.

There was a further reason why the Dead Sea was a place of hope as well

5. Josephus, *The Jewish War,* 2.136.

John at Capesthorne Hall in Cheshire, 1985

as damnation. This was the scene of Ezekiel's vision: That when the great day of the Lord dawned, a stream of life-giving water would flow from beneath the Temple Mount to the deserts of the eastern "galilee" (region), bringing new life, with trees for fruit and shrubs for medicine, and turning the sea to fresh water full of fish. John interpreted "galilee" as the word for any region, not necessarily the Galilee of gospel tradition, north of Samaria.

The springs at Ain Feshka had given the Qumran Community their fresh water, trees, and herbs. But the Dead Sea remained as dead as it had always been.

In John's view, since by A.D. 70 people must have realized that the transformation of the Dead Sea had been delayed along with the Apocalypse, the New Testament writers transferred Ezekiel's vision further north, to a lake in another Galilee where the water really was fresh and so full of fish that when Jesus told the disciples to let down their nets, the nets broke under the weight (Luke 5:6). Plucked from its Dead Sea context, the fishery idea packs at least three metaphors — the prophecy, Jesus' miraculous foresight, and the fishers-of-men motif — making it a gift to storytellers and sermon writers for centuries to come. Similarly, plucked from their context in Essenic "medicine," the faith-healing miracles of Jesus become expressions of his own personality and consequent on his nature as god-man. This type of literary manipulation did, after all, have a long pedigree in Old Testament exegesis, as the scroll commentaries had shown.

So spiritual healing was central to the church from its earliest beginnings — meaning its Essenic beginnings rather than Jesus Christ. To bring the healing idea up to date, John noted how faith healing has seemed to revive in the west through certain religious movements. The non-religious too seek harmony of mind and body, whether through yoga, aerobics, or holistic medicine. We do not need to believe in smoldering wing-tips to take the falling angels as symbols of the misuse of knowledge, and we can hope to gain strength from recognizing the misuse wisely and in time — or simply from learning to live at peace with our bodies.

Physician, Heal Thyself is slim and readable and was meant to appeal to anyone interested in faith healing either as a historical tradition or in current practice. It could have gone into past and present manifestations of healing in much greater detail to make a more solid intellectual case, but John saw it as a way to provoke popular discussion rather than as academic research. He prepared a film script based on the book, using plenty of photogenic Holy Land shots, and probably in these days of multi-channel television some historical/cultural film production company would have snapped it up — but not, unfortunately, in 1985.

In the United States

While John was trying to keep up a dialogue with Prometheus Books over *The Dead Sea Scrolls and the Christian Myth* and *Physician, Heal Thyself* in the hope of kick starting some publicity, some of his readers were busy behind the scenes. His books had indeed stimulated the discussion they were meant to — behind closed doors. People who read one wanted more and couldn't find them. Except for *The Dead Sea Scrolls: A Reappraisal* and the books that had yet to appear in the United States, such as *The Dead Sea Scrolls and the Christian Myth*, they were out of print by 1984.

Contacting each other mainly through humanist journals such as *Free Inquiry*, some readers came together in the hope of finding and reissuing John's books, meanwhile supplying synopses of them in newsletter form. In January 1986 the John Allegro Society began as "a society of freethinkers, brought together by a conviction that this author's fresh, undoctrinaire approach to religious, philosophical, and social problems has much to commend it at a time when our rationality is under attack."

At this point they approached John. His first reaction was horror: a fan club? He had no intention of becoming any kind of guru. On the other hand he was always keen on discussion. He agreed to contribute articles and audiotapes and to lecture to anybody who would pay his fare. He wrote personally to people who sent in a query or comment through the Society or its organizer, Ann Robertson. Ann worked tirelessly, passing on letters, locating and forwarding books and articles, preparing synopses, and generally keeping the debate about the scrolls and religion alive in the humanist press.

This was timely, for people were letting loose some poisonous attacks on John. Various people accused him of "stealing" the Copper Scroll from Milik, along with the publication rights to it, when he took it to Manchester in 1956 for opening. This accusation is astonishing and it is unfair. The correspondence from 1955-56 set out in chapter 3 shows how, in bringing the rolls of copper to Manchester, John acted on the instructions of Harding after scientists from the United States had failed to devise a method of opening them. John's translation was provisional and unofficial, and he made no claim otherwise. Chapters 5 and 6 show how he held back for three years from publishing his translation of the scroll to let Milik, in 1959, get his version out first. Maybe Cross's memory of the event had warped after thirty years. Or maybe, since criticism was currently running high against the team's handling of the scrolls, it was convenient to deflect the attack onto the rebel member. The sentiment behind the allegation appears to have contaminated other scholars' outlook and to have damaged John's reputation ever since. As foregoing chapters have shown, it is unfounded.

In April 1985, Paul Kurtz, as editor of *Free Inquiry,* organized an international symposium on Jesus in history and myth. John gave a paper on "Jesus and Qumran," and for a brief spell he felt himself come to life once more in the sunshine of popularity. *The Dead Sea Scrolls and the Christian Myth* had just come out in America, and he was able to sign mint copies in the sort of scene he had dreamed of for much of his writing career.

The following year he returned to the United States, this time to the convention of the American Atheists. He gave a lecture on "Jesus in History," which met worthy though puzzled applause. The American Atheists took up John with fervor, offered to reissue his books, and promised to publish any article he might contribute to their magazine. The chief organizers were a family powerhouse, whose matriarch was a one-woman tornado. She roared through the legal departments and press offices of the fundamentalist parties and single-handedly fended off their onslaught and shouted down their lawyers. But to John, not himself known for reticence, her aggression seemed as overblown as that of the evangelical fundamentalists. The atheists met assault with assault but offered no aid to their followers. They left far behind them the people who might have swelled their ranks, the doubters in a Bible-thumping society who needed persuading rather than deafening. John thought that hurling insults was no way to make fundamentalists change their mind. On the other hand, the American Atheists seemed to have the will and resources to reissue his books.

This brief dalliance with the American Atheists came to a sudden end at a hotel beside Loch Lomond. The matriarch wished to view the mother country and commissioned John to lay on a tour of the heritage sites of the British Isles. Finding it difficult to imagine the family confined to a tour company bus with others of the blue-rinse brigade, he arranged to drive them himself. After two days on the road, the holiday ended in the breakfast room of their Scottish hotel. Between the Earl Grey and the marmalade, this American lady whose voice and girth were of operatic proportions declaimed to the breakfasting public the Awful Truth: that they were nowhere near Buckingham Palace, Stratford-upon-Avon, or Oxford Street; that the hotel was neither the Ritz nor the Savoy; that John's aging Honda was not a limousine; and worst of all, "Allegro, you are POOR!" Sacked, and immensely relieved, John left them where they stood and went home.

The Campaign to Publish the Scrolls

13 December 1983

The Editor
The Guardian

Sir

THE DEAD SEA SCROLLS

It is difficult to believe that there is not a conspiracy of silence over these important documents. Some thirty years have elapsed since a few of us were called to Jerusalem to begin the editing and publication of a newly discovered cache of fragmentary scrolls from a cave near the Dead Sea. I am still the only member of that team to have published his entire section of the material entrusted to us (1968), and I had already made known in the learned journals the most important of those manuscripts as soon as possible after I had pieced the fragments together and deciphered them. We were all given to understand at the inception of our labours that this preliminary publication was expected from us since it was clear that the final, definitive editions of the texts might take some considerable time, there being some four hundred different documents involved. I have complained on a number of occasions of the delay in publication of my colleagues' sections but have received no more than the same old tired excuses that the work has proved exacting in time and effort, and that political difficulties, particularly since the Israeli occupation of East Jerusalem in 1967, have presented even more problems in terms of physical access to the manuscripts. In fact, the bulk of our work was done well before 1967 and the main documents could have been published, even if provisionally in journals, at any time in the last twenty or thirty years. Furthermore, although the then editor-in-chief forbade my return to the 'Scrollery' in the Palestine Archaeological Museum after 1967, my ecclesiastical colleagues did return to continue their work on many occasions.

Three years ago I was asked by the BBC to accompany a producer and film crew to Israel to make a documentary about the Dead Sea Scrolls, their significance, and the current situation regarding their publication. Despite some considerable religious and institutional pressures put upon our project before leaving and during the filming, we completed the work, and the film was finally edited in the summer of 1981. Since that time it has remained in the cans, and I am reliably informed that it will now never be screened. During the course of the programme another participant, a Dominican priest from the same Jerusalem-based biblical institution as the present and past editors-in-chief, and a noted Scrolls scholar in his own right, complains of the scandalous delays in publication which have seriously hindered his own and other scholars' researches in this field. I myself recall the discovery of more scrolls in 1956, one of which at least has mysteriously 'disappeared,' and make the point that any future finds should be quickly taken into care by some authority owing no religious allegiance to any particular persuasion, and who will ensure that the texts be quickly edited and published *in full* at the first opportunity.

Are we really to believe that the scandalous delay in the publication of the Dead Sea Scrolls and this suppression of the film we made three years ago are unconnected?

Yours faithfully,

John M. Allegro

The film to which John referred was a documentary that he had prepared for the BBC in 1980 about the significance of the scrolls. The script for *The Mystery of the Dead Sea Scrolls* began with the story of their discovery and worked up to their main significance: the light they cast on the origin and development of Christianity and the fluidity of the biblical textual tradition in the centuries before it was standardized. The film's chief purpose, from John's point of view, was to reawaken interest in the scrolls, because more than thirty years since their discovery most of them remained unpublished.

The film was to look at the relationship between Essenism and early Christianity. It would let the stones speak, as it were — the cisterns for baptism; the hall for the messianic banquet, or Last Supper; the orientation towards Jerusalem from where the river of healing was to flow at the dawn of the millennium.

"What a dream!" the script read. "But the reality was very different. The Romans broke into Jerusalem in A.D. 70 and burned down the Temple. The Dead Sea remained as dead as it is today. The monks of Qumran were driven from their monastery." By then Essenism was changing. Outside Palestine, it was developing into a sort of primitive Christianity that would appeal to Gentiles of the Hellenic world, based upon the faith of the individual in a crucified and risen Teacher.

The draft film-script shows how John imagined the "Essene-Christian myth-makers" stitching together tales, prophecies, and traditions into the story of Jesus:

Shortly after A.D. 70, these Essene-Christians developed a myth centred upon a Galilean Teacher called Jesus or Joshua who like their Teacher of

Righteousness was crucified at the instigation of a wicked priest and was expected to rise again in the Last Days. But their stories bring this Jesus much nearer their own time, into the days of Pontius Pilate around A.D. 30, and they make him live a far more relaxed life than was ever enjoyed by the real-life Teacher of Righteousness and his followers.

The Essene-Christian myth-makers wove into the Gospels other aspects of their beliefs and practices. For instance, thanks to the Dead Sea Scrolls we can recognize that many of the stories about Peter are just fictional illustrations of the various duties and responsibilities of the Essene Guardian. . . .

Dupont-Sommer, he went on, had first drawn attention to the parallels between the Qumran community and early Christianity and had brought down a storm of protest on his head. John wrote:

I would go further. I would identify the two. The Galilean Jesus *was* the Essene Teacher of Righteousness. The narratives of Jesus of Nazareth are imaginary re-workings of the history of the real-life Essene leader, who lived a century before and was crucified not at the instigation of a first-century Roman but of a Jewish High Priest and King, Alexander Jannaeus.

It was over-simplification, of course, and deliberate provocation. In his other works, John had been careful to emphasize the differences in role and outlook between the Teacher of Righteousness and Jesus. Indeed it was these differences that had made him feel the gospels could not be as authentic as they claimed to be. In the film script he wanted to make the points that many elements in Jesus' story were borrowed from the Teacher's and that, before the hero was made a god-man and thoroughly improbable, he was the leader of a desert monastery with a much more limited role. John called the rest literary manipulation and showed how he thought it had been done.

He set out the way the New Testament mixes real-life events, such as the execution of a Jewish preacher, with layers of exegesis. For example, St. Paul's focus on the tree of crucifixion may recall the reference to the Teacher's tree in the *Nahum Commentary,* which in turn recalls the tree of life in Genesis; Jesus' messianic role fulfills the prophecies of Isaiah and Ezekiel that underlie much of the story. The gospels also bring in the ancient myth of resurrection, examples of faith-healing that were the Essenes' stock-in-trade, and other homely tales. The figure of the Teacher was moved forward a century, doctored to appeal to Gentiles, and displaced to another Galilee.

John reckoned that this view placed the development of Christianity in a more realistic perspective. He continued:

Without the truncated chronology of the gospel narratives we are able to see Christianity developing over a much longer period, with roots deep in Judaism, and drawing ideas from further afield. Christianity was never the revelation of one man, however gifted and inspired, but an amalgam of beliefs, formulated under the pressure of political and social change over decades and even centuries.

John was anxious to be seen not as denigrating Christianity but as casting light upon its origins. To repay the support of King Hussein, he also wanted to bring attention to the part played by Jordan in the story of the scrolls' discovery, for the King had granted permission to film there despite misgivings about security.

However, the producer was worried about upsetting churchgoers. The film was made, scheduled — and rescheduled. Senior executives in the BBC came and went; decisions slipped between them. John wrote repeatedly in increasing exasperation to ask when and why. Bits of the film were taken out, seemingly irrelevant shots of synagogues and shrines put in.

The film was finally shelved in 1983. They said it wasn't good enough. John called it suppression.

The letter to the newspaper was neither published nor acknowledged. Though evidently not interesting enough for the *Guardian*, it showed how John's impatience over the continuing delay in the scrolls' publication was near to erupting and how frustration was souring his attitude. As shown in chapter 8, back in the 1950s it had taken considerable time to convince John that the Catholic members of the editing team had reason to suppress publication, but eventually the suspicion took hold and had rankled ever since. Other scholars denied that there had been any suppression — just incompetence. But in John's eyes people had dallied with or manipulated their findings on the scrolls again and again, had been unwilling to commit themselves to this or that interpretation, and had even avoided discussing it. He was convinced that the BBC had hung back from showing his film to avoid controversy. Avoiding controversy meant evading issues or papering them over, and to do so deliberately amounted to hypocrisy. And that was his lifelong target: to rip out the hypocrisy of church and state, to free people's minds from ecclesiastical dictatorship, to give them the facts, to raise the questions and let them decide for themselves. Right from the start, that had been his driving purpose; now it came to the forefront.

As he said in the letter, he had published all his share of the texts. Nearly all the rest remained a secret to the outside world. In April 1982, Volume VII of *Discoveries in the Judaean Desert* had come out. John wrote to *The Times* on April 17, 1982, paying tribute to the editor, Father Maurice Baillet, but repeating his call for openness:

> By far the greater proportion of the texts has yet to appear, and among the documents being so assiduously screened from public gaze are some of the most vital for our understanding of Essenism and its part in the evolution of Christianity. . . . There is no reason why the more important texts should not have been given preliminary publication in the learned journals at any time in the last quarter of a century. The sceptic can hardly be blamed if he voices once more the suspicions held by the late Edmund Wilson that the ecclesiastics who contrived to obtain supervision of the initial publication of the documents were more fearful of their effect on the faith than they were enthusiastic for the light they throw upon the origins of our culture. Only a determined effort by those responsible to open up the whole cache to specialist scrutiny will dispel those doubts on scholarly integrity.

In 1984 John restated his approach in *Free Inquiry,* deploring the monopolistic tendencies of the team:

> What our colleagues around the world really want are the infrared photographs, a transliteration of the script into printed form, and our suggested translations where they may be helpful. There is some evidence that not all of us see our work quite this simply; one suspects that some members of the team are reluctant to let the world see the precious texts in their charge before they have extracted every scrap of information they can from them to swell the initial presentation of their material and avoid religious controversy. Perhaps there is no way of ensuring that purposeful suppression of information from new discoveries does not ever happen in the future. At least, the public should be aware of the dangers that exist, even in this supposedly enlightened age, and by demanding the prompt publication of all newly acquired documents as soon as reasonably possible, and the free and unrestricted discussion of all matters affecting the issues involved, we might do something to ensure that truth is not made subject to the strictures of any one interested party.

Three years later, little had changed. The then editor-in-chief, Father Benoit, died in April 1987. Asked to write an obituary, John felt he had not known Benoit well enough to do him justice. Instead, he used the occasion to remind his former colleagues publicly to remember the commitment they had given de Vaux in 1953: that their findings would be published in learned journals before the definitive version came out as *Discoveries in the Judaean Desert of Jordan* from the Clarendon Press. Writing to the *Daily Telegraph*, John urged:

> Whoever has taken over Benoit's thankless task ought now to be given the full weight of public support for persuading those reluctant editors to do the job they agreed to do, or to acknowledge their unwillingness or incompetence to do so, and let their publishing 'rights' be redistributed on a truly international and ecumenical basis. The Dead Sea Scrolls are too important for the understanding of our cultural origins to be treated as the personal possessions of a few academicians or sequestrated as spoils of war to be used for political or religious propaganda.[6]

The *Daily Telegraph* took the issue further. In an interview reported on May 18, 1987, John calls the delays over publication of the scrolls "pathetic and inexcusable":

> He claims that for years his colleagues have been sitting on the material, which is not only of outstanding importance but also quite the most religiously sensitive. 'That has been the trouble with the Scrolls: They impinge so much on Judaism and Christianity, and then they became a political football when the Israelis marched in. They are in Israeli custody, but they are still, so far as I am aware, locked up in cabinets in the basement of the museum in Jerusalem, where one bomb could destroy them at any time.' . . . The answer, he insists, is the formation of an international, interdenominational, and ecumenical committee to decide on how best to complete the study and secure the required funding.

For once John's was not a lone voice. Other scholars wanted to study the scrolls independently of the original editing team who still guarded access to them for themselves and their graduate students. People who thought nearly everyone believed in open information and freedom of speech read in their Sunday papers that the scrolls situation was a scandal. Dr. Geza Vermes called a convention on the scrolls; John was not invited to the meeting, but his ideas were at last discussed. Strugnell, now editor-in-chief, attributed the delay to the complexity of the task and to Israeli occupation. Vermes concluded that it was lack of management more than anything and dismissed John's conspiracy theory. However, in suggesting an international governing body to oversee research and issue a catalog of manuscripts as yet unpublished, and in

6. J. M. Allegro to the *Daily Telegraph*, May 5, 1987.

calling for a transcription with brief commentary rather than a perfect edition of each set of fragments, he was taking up themes that John had been urging for years.

The solution came after John's death. Members of the John Allegro Society, led by Lowell Robertson as Chairman of the International Committee for the Full Publication of the Dead Sea Scrolls, joined in the campaign for open access to all the scroll texts. In part the breakthrough was due to the courage and determination of individuals such as Robert Eisenman and Philip Davies, who demanded access in defiance of the controlling editors and the Israeli authorities, and to the parallel campaign fought by Hershel Shanks, editor of the *Biblical Archaeology Review,* to publish facsimile texts collected by Robert Eisenman and James Robinson, in spite of official legal suits against publication. It was also thanks to the skill of computer experts Ben-Zion Wacholder and Martin Abegg, who were able to match up fragments and reconstruct texts from concordances. Then in September 1991, William Moffett of the Huntington Library in California revealed that he held a complete, archived edition of the scrolls and that in the cause of intellectual freedom he had decided to make the Huntington copies available on microfilm to any scholar who wanted to see them. Two months later, the Biblical Archaeology Society's folio edition came out. The stranglehold on the scrolls, which John had fought against for thirty-five years, was broken at last.

The Tyranny of the Creed

While the campaign for access to the scrolls was going on, John was pursuing themes he had opened up in *The Dead Sea Scrolls and the Christian Myth.* He wanted to look further into Gnosticism and the development of the church during the first centuries of its existence and relate this to its current strengths and weaknesses.

In 1986 he began to plan a book on issues in church history that had invigorated and at the same time imperiled the church since its earliest days. Between the inspiration at its source and the methods it used to survive as an institution there seemed a fundamental divide in the nature and philosophy of the church. On the one hand, people wanted religious guidance in their unending quest to know the meaning of God in their hearts. On the other hand, the church needed to solidify their hopes and inspiration into a recognizable creed, if it were to hold onto its authority and survive as a political entity. But inspiration is not solid; it must be an ever-welling source of understanding. John's basic premise in *The Tyranny of the Creed* is that to institutionalize belief is a contradiction in terms: "Individualism is a state's prime enemy; in organised religion it is the arch-enemy. The Church won an empire over the bodies of her heretics and the ashes of their books, but at the cost of her own integrity."

John contrasts the church's politicking with the Gnostics' passion: They sought the divinely given knowledge of God with ardent but unworldly single-mindedness. It led some of them to wild excesses that put them outside the laws of both church and state. The Gnostic Nag Hammadi documents show an evolving individualistic faith.

> When, in the cause of political power and security from persecution, the Church fathers suppressed the Gnostic 'heresies', they tried to replace the uncertainties of a passionate subjectivity with an unchangeable Creed, and a free range of mythological expression with a historical Christ and a sacred topography. The Gospel myth in its every particular was made history and unchallengeable; to doubt was to sin and to suffer the vengeance of outraged conformity. Yet heresy persisted in a succession of schisms as individuals rebelled against the constraints of organized religion and sought their own means of expression. In today's terms, the modern gnostics can be seen as the born-again individuals whose proliferation of splinter groups keeps faith alive but undermines the authority of the established Church: The end of gnostic individualism is organisational chaos.

He planned to show *how* the gospel myth was made history and unchallengeable. St. Paul's concept of Jesus the god-man gained acceptance in many parts of the Roman Empire and was eventually set in stone, as it were, at the Council of Nicea in A.D. 325. From then on, it was heresy not to believe in either Jesus' divinity or the apostolic succession. The apostolic succession put authority in the hands of the bishops, and this authority crystallized as institutional power and wealth. Institutional hypocrisy, John called it. For the church fathers knew what they were doing: They deliberately used the Jesus stories to maintain their authority.

Tyranny also looks at the issue of religious morality. The church's stance on morality appeals to everyone. Every society needs moral direction, and people assume this is what the church provides, whatever the details of the text. But humanitarian concern for the individual can lead to further disintegration of authority. It strays a long way from the church's original purpose of channeling divine revelation to the masses. Moreover, to be a loving, caring human being, you don't need religion. You don't need to chant liturgy or sit on hard pews to seek your god. "Organized religion is a contradiction in terms," wrote John, "the tyranny of the Creed an intolerable restraint on the freedom of the spirit."

This thesis got as far as a synopsis, introduction, and chapter outline. Manchester University Press sent it back at this stage for further development; their reader felt it likely to be one-sided in attacking the church — especially the Roman Catholic Church — without offering to put anything in its place. John could have worked it into a strong and, no doubt, controversial argument, for it brought together ideas he had been growling over for years. But this time he let practical considerations outweigh the desire for debate. He wanted more commitment from the publishers and was unwilling to invest weeks of effort in trailing around to other publishing houses.

Since then, some scholars of early church history have worked independently along the same lines as John. Gnosticism has been investigated in its own right and in comparison to the orthodox church that grew alongside and overtook it. Other writers have shown how the church tried to use its institutional power to squash the individual witness of the Gnostics out of existence — and largely succeeded. But not quite — some aspects of Gnosticism resurfaced with the Templars and their Masonic successors, while other strands appeared in Celtic Christianity, and later among the Lutherans and Quakers.

In earlier books, John had set out the mythological ancestry of Christianity and suggested how it pointed back to Egypt, and beyond Egypt to Sumer. The Egyptian links have been investigated in more detail. For example, the motifs of the dying and rising god, common to many of the world's mythologies, may be echoed in the king-making rituals of ancient Egypt, and aspects of sun-god worship merged into early Christianity by way of some Gnostic sects as well as the Roman cult of Mithras.

At the time when it would have mattered to John, however, few people admitted to sharing this sort of perspective on early church history. Non-Christians would have called it an objective view; churchgoers would have called it warped. John was growing rather weary of fighting for it.

For by then other lines of research were pulling at him. At last he was beginning to feel he was heading where he belonged and that there was no time to lose.

CHAPTER 16

Back to Philology

The Sacred Mushroom and the Cross had raised its storm and been swilled off the map by derision. Virtually everybody rejected outright the suggestion that Christianity could be founded on a fertility cult. John himself had stopped talking about a direct link — the idea that the gospel writers were deliberately weaving secret incantations into a trumped-up cover story designed to convey cultic messages to the brethren while fooling the Romans. However, he continued to see the gospels as a patchwork of literary devices. They combined themes and events important to the Qumran community with elements of myth and folk tradition, and they transformed the whole into a mystery religion centered, for the benefit of the Gentile audience, on one semi-divine hero. John had given up calling Jesus a mushroom and tacitly accepted that the secrets of the fertility cult belonged many centuries earlier, though he was still sure of their fundamental importance to the religions that eventually evolved into Judaism and Christianity.

Philology, his first academic passion, still called. He looked again at the Sumerian source-books and the body of scholarship that had been growing up around them. As he looked, ways began opening up, ways of looking at language and mythology that went far deeper into the past than the relatively recent myth of Christianity. The seeds of language itself, the beginnings of western thought and culture, lay almost within reach. Myth and history spun off them; these were clues leading towards the first things, the furthest origins of thought. In *The Sacred Mushroom and the Cross* he had been focusing on the development of Judaism and Christianity, and in viewing ancient languages through that lens he had spotted particular elements that seemed to fit what he was looking for. He went on finding clues that, to his mind, corroborated his theory about the fertility cult underlying these religions. But he also began to look more widely at other religions and cultures.

As with the research for *The Sacred Mushroom*, John studied the concordances that had been made from the word-lists found on tablets in Sumer. These lists matched Sumerian ideographs — the symbols that came to be stylized as cuneiform — to Assyro-Babylonian (Akkadian) words. Many of the ideographs carried two or more meanings. The lists showed which of these were carried over into neighboring languages and in what form. John then looked for traces of the words in Hebrew, Greek, and other languages, as well as echoes of their meaning in myth or legend or in compilations such as Pliny's *Natural History*. He began to gather the links into nets of allusion cast forward and back in time.

The mushroom cult had been John's starting point. He still believed that the use of hallucinogens had been an essential part of many or most ancient religions and offered a clue to understanding their mythologies. As mentioned in chapter 9, John used a fairly wide definition of mythology: the sets of stories through which people expressed or explained the doings and attributes of their gods, which in turn explained the cosmic phenomena such as sun and storm that governed life on earth.

The mythologies included those of Judeo-Christian traditions, and he continued to discover references in the Bible that linked back to ancient drug cults. He was compiling a collection of Old Testament stories retranslated in the light of his fertility cult theory. This was a revival of *Folk Tales from the Bible*, begun and shelved several years earlier. He called it *The Bedside Bible* and toyed with the idea of distributing it among friends. However, he recognized that scholars would not take it seriously without a mass of further substantiation, and even then no publisher would be likely to take it on. He also admitted that Near or Middle Eastern people in intertestamental times were unlikely to have consciously held onto these links to ancient drug lore, and he needed to take a wider perspective.

On October 30, 1987, John described what he was doing in an open letter to members of the John Allegro Society:

> My *Sacred Mushroom and the Cross* (1970) was a major breakthrough in philology, using ancient Sumerian as the key to penetrate for the first time in history to the roots of Semitic and Indo-European. We are now in a position to comprehend the underlying philosophies and the old Near Eastern and classical mythologies as never before, and for the first time to 'decipher' in the names of the gods, heroes, cosmic phenomena, personified animals and plants, etc. the world-wide and extremely ancient use of

the hallucinogenic fungus, the *Amanita Muscaria*. *The Sacred Mushroom* served as a medium for that somewhat limited study, which I am now in the process of expanding and verifying against the much wider backcloth of Sumerian understanding of natural phenomena, cosmic and terrestrial. The names and folklore attaching to the sacred mushroom are but a microcosm of this much larger world, since in its 'miraculous' conception, growth, and inherent hallucinatory power, the fungus seemed to the ancients a manifestation of the fertility god himself. What seems to have worried those very few scholars who bothered to read the book before committing themselves to public comment, was that it opens up before us a vast new field of research and a bridging of disciplines that has made out of date most of what we had believed and speculated upon in our previous studies of cultural origins. In particular, it has enabled us to set in a much truer perspective the languages and mythology of the Bible, in a way that must run counter to religious dogma, even though it offers a hitherto unimagined illumination of the transmission and evolution of religious and philosophical ideas. We can now see the development of Christianity as part of a continuum of ideas and theological speculation stretching back to the very beginnings of western culture in Mesopotamia and Asia Minor.

The "continuum of ideas" was generally well recognized. Ancient Sumer had become the subject of extensive research, and many scholars had published studies on various aspects of Sumerian life, including language, religion, economic activity, and relationships with other cultures. Working within this field, John wanted to cast further light on the origins and development of culture in general and language in particular through taking a philological route. His aim was to follow the clues in Sumerian words and images: to explore the way the people thought through exploring the way their language developed. It was a distant and still rather hazy vision that would have had to take into account the growing body of research by other scholars. Starting from the clues he was unearthing from the Bible and following them backwards in time, he intended this project to fill many years to come.

His research at this time was taking a two-horned approach: on one side, analysis of words and phrases to find evidence of drug cults in biblical tradition; and on the other, an insight through language into Sumerian culture. In places, Sumerian and biblical tradition ran in parallel, separated to John's mind by a thin layer: the interpretation or misinterpretation of Old Testament Hebrew. For example, as he explained to another John Allegro Society friend in February 1988:

The whole story of Joseph in Egypt is no more than a retelling of the ancient fertility myth of the descent of Tammuz to the underworld. The identification of Joseph with Tammuz is very old and long recognized by Talmudic commentators, and I myself gave this more substance with a paper I published when an undergraduate in Manchester, on the oracle of Jacob on Joseph in Genesis 49:22. I showed that it is in part a word-for-word rendering of an Akkadian hymn to Tammuz. Now I have been able to break through into the whole of the 'Israel in Egypt' myth, by appreciating that in the cosmological geography of the ancients of Palestine and the Fertile Crescent, 'Egypt' and the country to the south was simply a portrayal of the mythological 'underworld'. The part played by Joseph in restoring the fertility of the earth by first transforming the fortunes of the primal source of energy and fertility in the land of the 'waters under the earth', the Abyss, the Underworld, was again that of Tammuz, in an extended and enlivening series of stories. The whole 'Exodus' myth is similarly based, as is the Sinai revelation, the forty years' wandering and the (re)-entry in the 'Land of Milk and Honey', i.e. the crossing from death into life. None of this has any historical purport or basis.

This was one of the last theories John proposed. He never had time to substantiate it in print as he would have wanted.

Seeking order and purpose was a fundamental theme of Sumerian mythology. The myths narrated on tablets found among the ruined libraries of ancient Sumer tell of epic struggles between the gods to achieve order out of chaos, in heaven as on earth. As John saw it, in the thought-world of the Sumerians the power that governed life on earth came from the sun, moon, and stars. The gods of these heavenly bodies held this power and channeled it into the world through priests and sacred objects so that it should be used with order and control. John suggested that the name for this life-giving power was ZU, and he identified ZU as a vocalization of U, the principle of fecundity that was central to the thesis of *The Sacred Mushroom and the Cross*.

As he had in *The Sacred Mushroom*, he now assumed the primacy of the fertility issue in ancient religion. Other scholars would hold this in doubt, for many of the written legends are concerned with other aspects of order and control, such as the necessary but unstable union between earth and water, the all-seeing sun-god as the god of justice, and the way the sky-god and storm-god governed the fortunes of humans. Similar themes were appropriated by the Assyrians and Semites and are echoed throughout the Old Testament as clearly as the fertility themes with which John was primarily concerned. He was only just beginning to look more widely into the linguistic sources of these themes.

The more John studied Sumerian, the more firmly he was convinced that it held the key to the decipherment of names, myths, and ancient religions. Sumerian phonemes form names that carry myths and legends; the myths show how the language works as the language feeds the myths. John was exploring the very beginnings of both. He felt he was reaching to where thought began.

And then it all stopped. On February 17, 1988, John's sixty-fifth birthday, the window cleaner noticed the milk on the doorstep and the curtains still drawn. In the line of business he put up his ladder to begin on the bedroom window. He reached it and knew at once that he must call an ambulance. But the ambulance was too late. Completely unsuspected, completely without warning, an aortic aneurysm had stopped John Allegro's heart.

All the hopes and endeavors of sixty-five years simply stopped. The love and the anger, the verbal acrobatics, his delight when understanding came like morning to his own mind or his students', his ridicule of the pompous and his condemnation of hypocrisy, his fearless or foolhardy pursuit of truth . . . all stopped.

John Allegro's Legacy

For years the universal scorn aroused by *The Sacred Mushroom and the Cross* blackened John's name and the memory of nearly all his work on the scrolls. Before that, it seemed to be easy sport to criticize John for departing from the team's approach and methods and even to blame him for "pirating" the translation of the Copper Scroll. This account, however, has shown that he departed from convention for strong reasons — reasons of freedom of thought and opinion. And far from acting the pirate, he held back his work on the Copper Scroll to let the official translation come out first, never claimed official status for his version, but acted in the interests of open debate on a controversial topic. John Strugnell later called him "the stone in the soup" of the editing team; actually, he was more like the pepper.

As the first British member of the original Dead Sea Scrolls editing team, John made his initial contribution by sorting and deciphering the Cave 4 fragments. Compared to the other volumes of *Discoveries in the Judaean Desert*, *DJDJ V* is incomplete: John did not attempt the exhaustive editing that was meant to lead to a full and final edition. He preferred speed and openness at the expense of thoroughness, and certainly at the expense of scholarly caution. However, though some of his translations have been re-vised, many still stand. Recently some scholars have looked again at his other early work. For example, in his study of the Copper Scroll, J. K. Lefkovits de-cides that many of John's disputed translations are valid; at the very least the scroll is much more likely to be a genuine list of treasure, as John maintained, than a work of fiction.[1]

John's most tangible and lasting legacy from this work has consisted in the books he wrote and the photographs he took. The recent encyclopedic pro-duction, *The Complete World of the Dead Sea Scrolls* by Philip Davies, George Brooke, and Phillip Callaway,[2] draws on and acknowledges John's contribu-tions to the study of the scrolls, particularly his collection of photographs and his account of the discoveries in his book *The Dead Sea Scrolls: A Reappraisal.*

The complete archive of John's scroll photographs is available in *The Al-legro Qumran Collection on Microfiche.*[3] The *Allegro Qumran Collection* com-prises about fifteen hundred images, with a 51-page companion volume con-taining the Introduction and Catalog. The pictures fall into four groups. The archeological group includes black-and-white and color photographs of Qumran, Ain Feshka, and Mird, and artifacts from Murabba'at. Some of the pictures add information not apparent from the official photographs, for ex-ample, details of the cisterns, plasterwork, and cracked stairway at Qumran. Another group contains pictures of people — the editorial team, Kando, and other characters. The Copper Scroll group documents the process of cutting the scroll and includes close-ups of the sections after cutting, each section taken several times from slightly different angles to show the letter forms. Finally, the documents group contains pictures of the manuscripts and linen wrappings from Qumran, Murabba'at, and Nahal Hever. Some of these show tiny details of lettering that might possibly alter the accepted reading taken from the official photographs. In a few cases, John's pictures appear to be the only extant record of certain small fragments. In others, they show details of the line ruling and the vertical strands of papyrus that are not visible in the official version. Sometimes John's notes on the cardboard slide frames sug-gest that the fragments were originally sorted differently and possibly more accurately than in their eventual published form.

1. Judah K. Lefkovits, *The Copper Scroll (3Q15): A Re-evaluation* (Leiden: Brill, 2000).

2. P. R. Davies, G. J. Brooke, and P. R. Callaway, *The Complete World of the Dead Sea Scrolls* (London: Thames & Hudson, 2002).

3. G. J. Brooke with H. K. Bond, eds., *The Allegro Qumran Collection on Microfiche* (Leiden: Brill/IDC, 1996), published as a supplement to E. Tov with S. J. Pfann, eds., *The Dead Sea Scrolls on Microfiche: A Comprehensive Facsimile Edition of the Texts from the Judean Desert* (Leiden: Brill/IDC, 1993).

Apart from the microfiche edition, the Archeology Department of the Manchester Museum also houses the Allegro Photograph Collection. This contains more color transparencies of Qumran, some large prints taken from negatives during the 1950s and 1960s, seventeen photographs of the microscope analysis of leather fragments at Leeds University, some Christmas Cave pictures, and a 16mm film of the opening of the Copper Scroll.

The Allegro Qumran Collection has been put together for three main reasons. First, in line with John's own philosophy of open inquiry, it offers immediate public access to any materials that may be of interest so there can be no accusation of hiding anything. Second, it supports renewed interest in the scrolls, which has gathered pace since they were made available in 1991. Third, many of the images are of scholarly value, for they are clearer than the official photographs and present different angles. The collection is described in more detail in George J. Brooke's paper, "The Allegro Qumran Photograph Collection: Old Photos and New Information."[4]

John was an inspired linguist and an inspiring lecturer. He put words into action: His expeditions to the deserts of Jordan, and the books, films, and lectures that resulted from them, stirred up interest all round the world in the scrolls and in the history of religion in general. As Honorary Adviser on the Scrolls to the Jordanian government, he acted as an ambassador for the scrolls on behalf of Jordan, for he believed that, having been found there, they belonged there and Jordan should take both the credit and the responsibility for looking after them.

John's imagination could leap the centuries and bring to life the dusty footsteps of the past. Through imagination, he discovered insights that fired himself and his readers and listeners. Often scholars of more sober approach thought John's insights on the scroll texts far too speculative and insufficiently tested against the evidence. With hindsight, John's speculation on the parallels between Jesus and the Teacher of Righteousness seems well-founded. The horror with which his colleagues reacted says more about their conformism than his outspokenness.

John called philology a science, but the way in which he applied philology in *The Sacred Mushroom and the Cross* was more speculative than scientific, and it was speculation of a different order than before. He seemed to be pushing philology beyond the limits of reason, and it inevitably landed him in trouble. He overrode some of the conventions of linguistic analysis, for ex-

4. G. J. Brooke, "The Allegro Qumran Photograph Collection: Old Photos and New Information" in the series *Studies on the Texts of the Desert of Judah,* edited by F. G. Martinez and A. S. Van der Woude (Leiden: Brill, 1999).

ample, by breaking up the three-letter root of Hebrew words in a way other philologists did not accept. Too many of his word reconstructions were hypothetical and not borne out by any texts that had so far been discovered. But without speculation there would be fewer theories for science to test and fewer insights. At the very least, John's philological work helped to delineate the potential powers and limitations of the discipline, and his work showed where his theories would have needed much more substantiation if he were to take them further, as indeed he was just beginning to do in the last years of his life. As often happens with original ideas, the first flare can light the way. John's use of language analysis to explore the past could open up rich possibilities for future research.

John built up a whole new theory on the development of Christianity. He told how the beliefs and messianic hopes of the Qumran community passed into Gnosticism with its proliferation of myths on the mystic theme of the inner light, the Word of God made flesh, and the ultimate union of the human and divine spirit. He told how the leaders of the early church took one mythical hero as the central figure and made him both a man and a miracle worker; how they stitched together a medley of tales and traditions, prophecies and precepts with contorted scraps of history, and called it the New Testament; how they suppressed unorthodox views that have nevertheless resurfaced from time to time.

He knew that for some Christians, Jesus lives on in their hearts, for his words strike a chord of common humanity and seem to offer simple moral certitude. For other Christians, who accept Jesus without questioning as a divine being, all things are possible through God.

John accepted nothing. People have the capacity to think and question and test out the truth of his ideas; therefore, they must use it. Not to do so is a waste; to choose not to do so is hypocrisy. Institutional hypocrisy, in the shape of the church, John thought worst of all. As he saw it, the church sought to impose belief, and not only belief but behavior. It did so for the sake of maintaining its authority, its political power, and its specious glory. If it brought comfort to people who like to be told what to do, if it taught them a system of morals based on compassion for others — well and good, but this should be done on human terms, on what is good for one's fellow human beings; compassion should need no divine intermediary. In John's eyes, to insist that it does, to build an empire around the power to so insist, amounts to a tyranny over the human spirit. For John, the power to love and to reason, to create beauty, to understand, comes from human aspiration and human imagination. In varying degree, we are all capable of using these gifts; to the full degree, we are responsible for using them.

John's contribution to the study of the Dead Sea Scrolls goes deeper than the books and photographs he left. His ideas and approach may be disputed, but they cannot be ignored. He was not the first to raise questions about the significance of the scrolls for Christianity, but he brought it to worldwide attention. He found that the reaction of others placed him at the center of public attention, and once there he made the most of it. For he believed that the issues he raised affected everyone. It was not just a matter of dusty manuscripts and disputed translations. In John's hands it became a question of freedom of evidence, freedom of speech, the freedom to question the received wisdom of the church and with it the church's authority. His campaigns to gain open access to the scrolls, to tell what he believed to be the truth about the Copper Scroll, and to insist on looking at the New Testament as a literary compilation rather than history all reflected different lights from the same flame: the principle that people have the right and the responsibility to think for themselves and make up their own minds about what to believe and how to behave.

John posed questions. He shook up assumptions. He took delight in puncturing pomposity and blasting out laziness in speech or thought. He could not bear hypocrisy in anyone, especially among public figures in politics, universities, or the church. Nor could he bear the thought that institutions of state could be founded on what he considered a brittle amalgam of fables. Power founded on a lie was a travesty of justice, a specious and unworthy morality; wars fought and laws wrought in its name were criminal. For John the nature and substance of morality came from people and concerned people; men and women must take responsibility for their own actions. The sanctimony of those who claimed Christian morality behind political decisions he considered hollow, and a sign of contempt for human judgment. Universities, he thought, should be powerhouses of inquiry. He was enraged when the professors he met appeared to block or belittle original research or were reluctant to cross the boundaries between disciplines — for example to take a linguistic rather than theological approach to biblical studies.

His interests in this matter went beyond theology, biblical studies, or even linguistics: He wanted to know how people's ideas developed on a personal and collective level — ideas about religion, the world, each other. In academic terms this took him into an exploration of anthropology, and in personal terms it made him a most challenging and enlivening man to talk to, for he was interested in everyone with new ideas or novel experiences and was forever guessing where these might lead. Friendships were full of hope and imagination: talking to John was fun.

He had nothing against Christianity as a personal religion, that is, as a means of relating to one's god, except that he thought its premise mistaken.

Nor would he criticize the holy men and women who sought through the medium of Christianity to find their own inner light, to commune with their god. After all, as a young man he had taken up Methodism, with characteristic fervor, as a path towards deeper thought and understanding. Though for himself he later came to find that a religion based on one central god-man was insufficient and irrelevant, he realized it was a matter of opinion. He respected the community of Qumran, striving for the light of divine knowledge, as he respected modern humanists striving to understand people's relationships. He saw these as pure-hearted endeavors that had nothing to do with the trappings of institutional religion.

He left lines of inquiry for others to pursue. In particular he wanted to further explore the field of Sumerian studies. Through researching the beginnings of language, he wanted to bring to light the way the first writers looked out on their world, in the days when men and women first set about meeting their gods. Delving through words and the history of words, he was beginning to open up the thought-world of our ancestors hundreds of generations past and to bring to life a way of understanding that we have lost.

For many people, questioning the past may not matter at all. Having cultivated a thicket of customs, conventions, material necessities, and the trappings of incoherent religions, it is perfectly possible to spend life comfortably tending this thicket without peering very far inside it. For John, asking questions did matter. In matters of intellect, clarity was more important than comfort. He needed to know where ideas grew from and was not afraid to ask.

John believed that everyone had the right to get information, ask questions, discuss freely, make up their own minds. The Dead Sea Scrolls shook up people's assumptions about their cultural and religious heritage, and John's lifelong work was to bring to light the questions they raised and the ideas they put forward. He tried to do it plainly and clearly, so that people could decide their own understanding of the truth. He asked questions and made people think. Maybe some of the questions had no answer, but for John the quest was the fine thing, the grand adventure.

As a father, teacher, friend, this was his challenge: to follow ideas as far as one could go into the deepest and clearest reaches of understanding. Although even his family doubted some of his conclusions and were saddened when he left them behind, they were proud of him for standing out for what he believed in and for speaking his mind. Fearless to reject hypocrisy, lazy thinking, second-hand opinions, he stood up against the establishment time and again, and that was where he delighted to be. Scorning conformity and reckless of convention, John Allegro believed in original thought and had the courage to speak his belief.

Bibliography

Works by John Marco Allegro

Articles

"A Newly Discovered Fragment of a Commentary on Psalm 37 from Qumran," *Palestinian Exploration Quarterly* 86 (1954): 69-75.

"Further Light on the History of the Qumran Sect," *Journal of Biblical Literature* 75 (1956): 93.

"Further Messianic References in Qumran Literature," *Journal of Biblical Literature* 75 (1956): 174-76.

"More Isaiah Commentaries from Qumran's Fourth Cave," *Journal of Biblical Literature* 77 (September 1958): 215-21.

"Fragments of a Qumran Scroll of Eschatological *Midrashim*," *Journal of Biblical Literature* 75 (December 1956): 82-87 and 77 (December 1958): 350-54.

"A Recently Discovered Fragment of a Commentary on Hosea from Qumran's Fourth Cave," *Journal of Biblical Literature* 78 (June 1959): 142-47.

"An Unpublished Fragment of Essene Halakhah (4Q Ordinances)," *Journal of Semitic Studies* 6 (1961): 71-73.

"More Unpublished Pieces of a Qumran Commentary on Nahum (4QpNah)," *Journal of Semitic Studies* 7 (1962): 304-8.

"'The Wiles of the Wicked Woman,' a Sapiential Work from Qumran's Fourth Cave," *Palestine Exploration Quarterly* 96 (1964): 53-55.

"An Astrological Cryptic Document from Qumran," *Journal of Semitic Studies* 9 (1964): 291-94.

"Some Unpublished Fragments of Pseudepigraphical Literature from Qumran's Fourth Cave," *Annual of Leeds University Oriental Society* IV (1962-63) (Leiden: Brill, 1964): 3-4.

Books

The Dead Sea Scrolls. London: Penguin Books, 1956. Revised as *The Dead Sea Scrolls: A Reappraisal,* 2nd edition. London: Penguin Books, 1964. Reissued as *The Mystery of the Dead Sea Scrolls Revealed.* New York: Gramercy, 1981.

The People of the Dead Sea Scrolls. London: Routledge & Kegan Paul and New York: Doubleday, 1958.

The Treasure of the Copper Scroll. New York: Doubleday, 1960.

Search in the Desert. New York: Doubleday, 1964.

The Treasure of the Copper Scroll, 2nd, revised edition. New York: Anchor/Doubleday, 1964.

The Shapira Affair. New York: Doubleday, 1965.

Discoveries in the Judaean Desert of Jordan V (Qumran Cave 4: 4Q158-4Q186). Oxford: Clarendon Press, 1968.

The Sacred Mushroom and the Cross: A Study of the Nature and Origins of Christianity within the Fertility Cults of the Ancient Near East. London: Hodder and Stoughton, 1970.

The End of a Road. London: MacGibbon & Kee, 1970 and London: Granada/Panther Books, 1972.

The Chosen People: A Study of Jewish History from the Exile until the Revolt of Bar Kocheba. London: Hodder and Stoughton, 1971.

Lost Gods. London: Michael Joseph, 1977.

The Dead Sea Scrolls and the Christian Myth. Newton Abbot: Westbridge Books, 1979 and New York: Abacus, 1985.

All Manner of Men. Springfield, Ill.: Charles C. Thomas, 1982.

Physician, Heal Thyself. Buffalo, N.Y.: Prometheus Books, 1985.

Further Reading

Brooke, G. J., and P. R. Davies, eds. *Copper Scroll Studies*. London: Sheffield Academic Press, 2002.

Davies, P. R., G. J. Brooke, and P. R. Callaway. *The Complete World of the Dead Sea Scrolls*. London: Thames & Hudson, 2002.

Eisenman, R., and M. Wise. *The Dead Sea Scrolls Uncovered*. Shaftesbury: Element Books, 1992.

Feather, R. *The Copper Scroll Decoded*. London: Thorsons, 1999.

Flint, P. W., and J. C. Vander Kam, eds. *The Dead Sea Scrolls after Fifty Years*, 2 vols. Leiden: Brill, 1998, 1999.

Frazer, J. G. *The Golden Bough*. London: Macmillan, 1922.

Garcia Martinez, F. *The Dead Sea Scrolls Translated*, 2nd edition. Leiden: Brill, 1996.

Graves, R. *The Greek Myths*. London: Penguin, 1955.

Knight, C., and R. Lomas. *The Hiram Key*. London: Century, 1996.

Lefkovits, J. K. *The Copper Scroll (3Q15): A Re-evaluation*. Leiden: Brill, 2000.

The Orion website: http://orion.mscc.huji.ac.il/resources/bib/bib.shtml

Pagels, E. *The Gnostic Gospels*. London: Penguin, 1979.

Procter, S. *A Quiet Little Boy Goes to War*, 2nd ed. Bordon, U.K.: RiteTime Publishing, 2004.

Shanks, H. *The Mystery and Meaning of the Dead Sea Scrolls*. New York: Random House, 1998.

Vander Kam, J. C. *The Dead Sea Scrolls Today*. Grand Rapids, Mich.: Eerdmans, 1994.

Vermes, G. *The Complete Dead Sea Scrolls in English*. London: Penguin, 1962.

Wasson, R. G. *Soma, Divine Mushroom of Immortality*. New York: Harcourt, Brace & World, 1968.

Index

Ain Feshka, 106, 111, 127, 136, 138, 140-45, 261, 278
Allegro Qumran Collection, The, 278, 279
Anderson, Arnold, 152, 156, 162, 171
ASOR (American School of Oriental Research), 22, 32, 157

Baal, 191, 193, 206, 219
Baillet, Maurice, 26, 162, 268
Barthélemy, D., 26, 102
Brooke, George J., 156, 278, 279

Caiaphas, 178, 194, 234, 257
Charlesworth, James, 256, 257n.
Chosen People, The, 218-20
Clement of Alexandria, 243, 251
Community Rule, 53, 232, 235, 236
Constantine, 182
Copper Scroll: content, 72, 73, 80, 89, 102, 104, 113-17, 133, 160, 278; expedition, 122-31; John's disclosure, 98, 115, 262, 277, 279, 281; Milik's official translation, 100, 101, 110, 113, 114, 116; opening, 36, 41, 60-71, 86, 278, 279; press release, 98, 99, 114. *See also* 'Treasure of the Copper Scroll'
Cross, Frank Moore: at the Scrollery, 26, 28, 34, 36, 38, 43, 48, 101; in correspon-

dence with John, 102, 108, 156, 157; on the Copper Scroll, 72, 85, 89; on rights to publication, 164

Dajani, Awni, 70, 108, 113, 120; in correspondence with John, 158-64, 168, 169
Damascus Document, 25, 53
Dead Sea Scrolls and the Christian Myth, The, 230-40, 262, 263, 270
Dead Sea Scrolls Exhibition, 174-84
de Vaux, Roland: and archeological exploration, 24, 27, 59, 106; and the Copper Scroll, 62, 71, 72, 89-104, 113, 114; and *DJD,* 152, 155, 161-64, 171-83; and publication, 34, 153, 154, 157-60; as team leader, 22, 26, 30, 32, 36, 40, 49, 88, 107-10, 156, 162, 268
Discoveries in the Judaean Desert of Jordan (DJDJ), 63, 115, 152, 155, 161, 170, 173
Dupont-Sommer, André, 73, 75, 82, 84, 203, 204, 266
Driver, Godfrey, 21, 26, 29, 87, 204

Essenism: and healing, 56, 189, 194, 200, 259-61, 266; the sect, 25, 51-56, 71, 92, 94, 111, 175-84, 189, 194, 197, 200, 206, 231-54, 265-68

286

JMA, 71, 73, 77, 101, 106, 107, 114; and
DJD, 155, 162; on JMA's radio talks, 75,
80-83, 92, 96; at the Scrollery, 26, 36,
45 (picture), 48, 58, 108, 109, 120, 154,
156, 158
Sumer, 186-88, 272, 274-76
Sumerian, 186-96, 199-209, 219, 246, 273-
77, 282

Teacher of Righteousness: 176, 180, 181,
200, 232-38, 245, 253, 266, 279; and Jesus, 84, 89, 92-96, 176, 180, 203, 204

University of Leeds, Department of
Leather Technology, 104, 105, 106, 174,
279

Wasson, R. G., 194, 206
Wilson, Edmund, 91, 103, 268
Wright Baker, 64, 65 (pictures), 66-70,
86-87, 88, 90, 95, 96

Yadin, Yigael, 25, 84, 112, 115, 116, 133

Zealots, 117, 118, 133, 235, 252, 253

CPSIA information can be obtained at www.ICGtesting.com
Printed in the USA
LVOW01s1054250915

455726LV00013B/320/P